best hikes with

CONNECTICUT MASSACHUSETTS & RHODE ISLAND

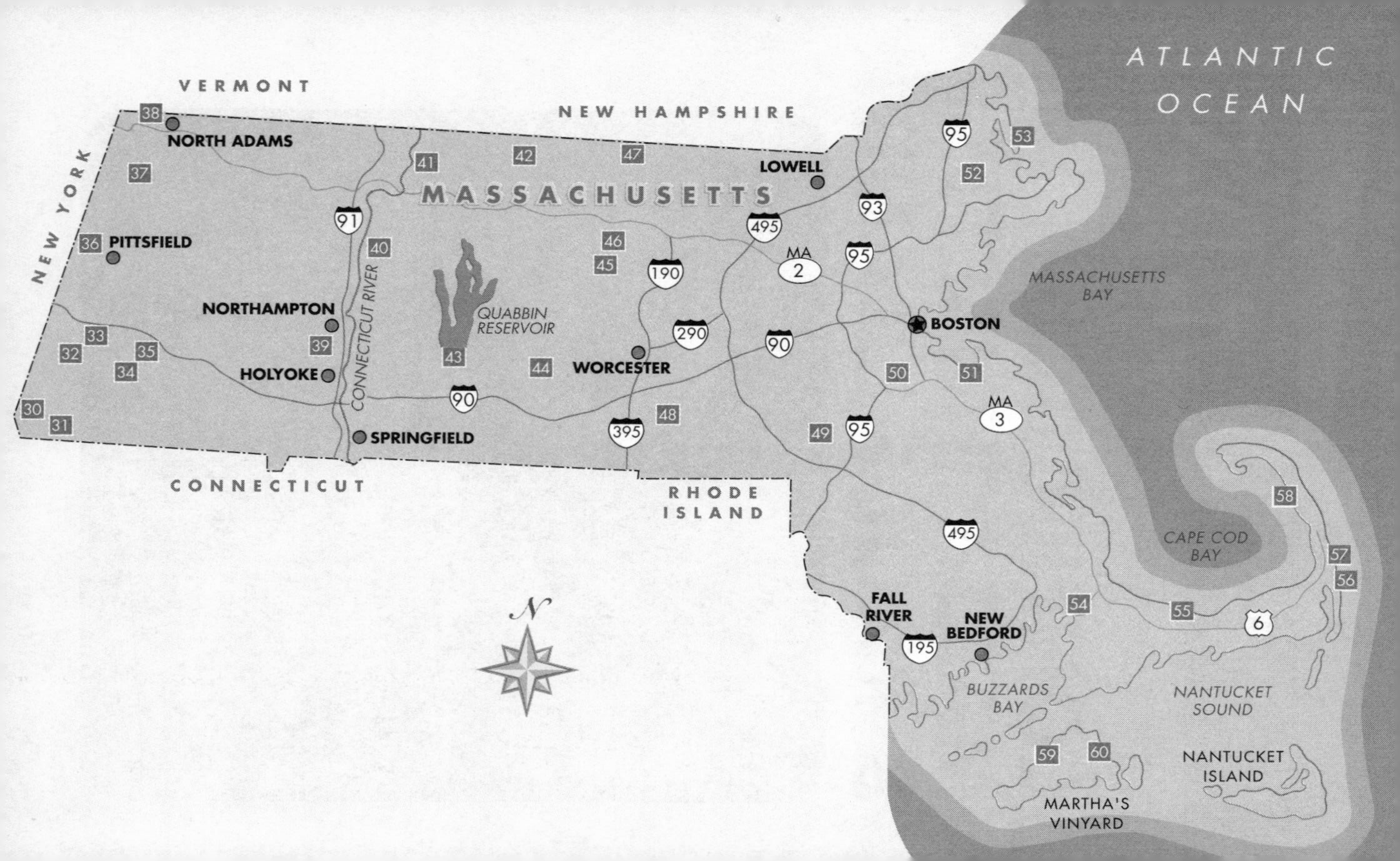
ATLANTIC OCEAN
VERMONT
NEW HAMPSHIRE
NEW YORK
CONNECTICUT
RHODE ISLAND
MASSACHUSETTS
NORTH ADAMS
PITTSFIELD
NORTHAMPTON
HOLYOKE
SPRINGFIELD
WORCESTER
LOWELL
BOSTON
FALL RIVER
NEW BEDFORD
CONNECTICUT RIVER
QUABBIN RESERVOIR
MASSACHUSETTS BAY
CAPE COD BAY
BUZZARDS BAY
NANTUCKET SOUND
NANTUCKET ISLAND
MARTHA'S VINYARD
N
30
31
32
33
34
35
36
37
38
39
40
41
42
43
44
45
46
47
48
49
50
51
52
53
54
55
56
57
58
59
60
91
90
190
290
395
495
93
95
195
MA 2
MA 3
6

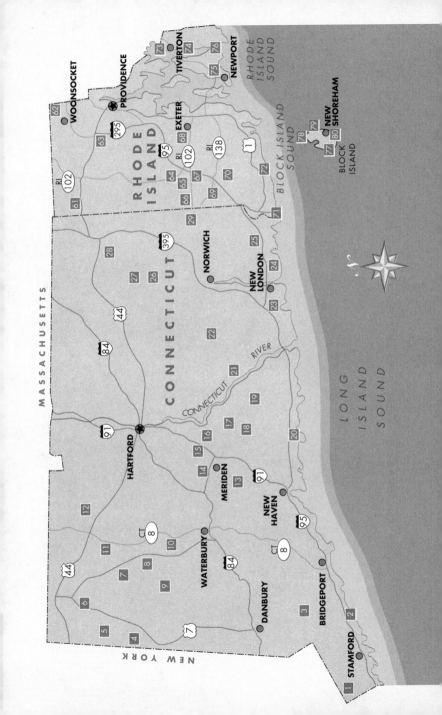

best hikes with

CONNECTICUT MASSACHUSETTS & RHODE ISLAND

Cynthia Copeland
Thomas J. Lewis
Emily Kerr

THE MOUNTAINEERS BOOKS

THE MOUNTAINEERS BOOKS
is the nonprofit publishing arm of The Mountaineers, an organization founded in 1906 and dedicated to the exploration, preservation, and enjoyment of outdoor and wilderness areas.

© 2007, 1998, 1991 by Cynthia Copeland and Thomas J. Lewis

First edition, 1991. Second edition, 1998. Third edition, revised by Emily Kerr: first printing 2007, second printing 2014

Manufactured in the United States of America

Copy Editor: Erin Moore
Cover and Book Design: Mayumi Thompson
Layout: Jennifer Shontz, Red Shoe Design
Mapmaker: Jennifer Shontz, Red Shoe Design
Cover photograph: © Photodisc/Royalty-Free
Page 1 photograph: *Having fun on the trail is what it's all about. (Photo by Emily Kerr)*
Page 4 photograph: *Sometimes the view is better from Daddy's shoulders. (Photo by Emily Kerr)*

Library of Congress Cataloging-in-Publication Data
Lewis, Cynthia Copeland, 1960–
    Best hikes with kids : Connecticut, Massachusetts, & Rhode Island / Cynthia C. Lewis & Thomas J. Lewis ; revised by Emily Kerr. — 3rd ed.
        p.   cm.
    Rev. ed. of: Best hikes with children in Connecticut, Massachusetts, and Rhode Island / by Cynthia C. Lewis & Thomas J. Lewis. 2nd ed. 1998.
    Includes index.
    ISBN 0-89886-872-6 (paperbound)
    1. Hiking—New England—Guidebooks. 2. Family recreation—New England—Guidebooks. 3. Children—Travel—New England—Guidebooks. I. Lewis, Thomas J. (Thomas Joseph), 1958- II. Kerr, Emily, 1970- III. Lewis, Cynthia Copeland, 1960- Best hikes with children in Connecticut, Massachusetts, and Rhode Island. IV. Title.
GV199.42.N38L48 2007
796.510974—dc22

                                    2006036717

ISBN (paperback): 978-0-89886-872-2
ISBN (ebook): 978-1-59485-177-3

CONTENTS

Acknowledgments 10
Preface 11
Introduction 13

CONNECTICUT

1. Audubon Center in Greenwich 32
2. Sherwood Island 35
3. Lucius Pond Ordway/Devils Den Preserve 37
4. Macedonia Brook State Park 41
5. Sharon Audubon Center 44
6. Dean Ravine and Barrack Mountain 47
7. Mohawk Mountain 49
8. The White Memorial Foundation and Conservation Center 53
9. Mount Tom Tower 55
10. Leatherman Cave 58
11. Burr Pond State Park 60
12. Jessie Gerard Trail 63
13. Sleeping Giant 66
14. Castle Craig and West Peak 69
15. Chauncey Peak and Lamentation Mountain 72
16. Wadsworth Falls State Park 75
17. Coginchaug Cave 78
18. Bluff Head on Totoket Mountain 80
19. Chatfield Hollow State Park 82
20. Westwoods 85
21. Gillette Castle State Park 88
22. Devils Hopyard State Park 91
23. Rocky Neck State Park 94
24. Bluff Point State Park and Coastal Reserve 97
25. The Denison Pequotsepos Nature Center 100
26. Rock Spring Preserve 103
27. Edwin Way Teale Memorial Sanctuary at Trail Wood 106
28. Mashamoquet Brook State Park 109
29. Rhododendron Sanctuary and Mount Misery 112

MASSACHUSETTS

30. Bash Bish Falls 116
31. Race Brook Falls and Mount Everett 119
32. Devils Pulpit and Squaw Peak 122
33. Lauras Tower and Ice Glen 125
34. Tyringham Cobble 127
35. Upper Goose Pond 130
36. Berry Pond 132
37. March Cataract Falls 135
38. Pine Cobble Trail 138
39. Goat Peak Lookout 140
40. Mount Toby 142
41. Northfield Mountain 145

42. Jacobs Hill 148
43. Quabbin Hill 150
44. Rock House Reservation 152
45. Wachusett Meadow Wildlife Sanctuary 155
46. Wachusett Mountain 158
47. Mount Watatic 160
48. Purgatory Chasm 162
49. Stony Brook Wildlife Sanctuary/Bristol Blake State Reservation 164
50. Great Blue Hill 166
51. Worlds End Reservation 169
52. Ipswich River Wildlife Sanctuary 171
53. Sandy Point State Reservation/Parker River National Wildlife Refuge 174
54. Lyman Reserve 176
55. Sandy Neck 179
56. Fort Hill Trail 181
57. Nauset Marsh Trail 183
58. Great Island Trail 185
59. Cedar Tree Neck Sanctuary 187
60. Felix Neck Wildlife Sanctuary 190

61. Walkabout Trail 194
62. Diamond Hill 196
63. Powder Mill Ledges Wildlife Refuge 198
64. Ben Utter Trail to Stepstone Falls 200
65. Escoheag and Mount Tom Trails 203
66. Pachaug Trail around Beach Pond 205
67. Arcadia Trail 207
68. Fisherville Brook Wildlife Refuge 210
69. Long Pond Woods 212
70. Francis C. Carter Memorial Preserve 215
71. East Beach, Ninigret Conservation Area 218
72. Trustom Pond National Wildlife Refuge 219
73. Fort Barton/Sin and Flesh Brook 222
74. Emilie Ruecker Wildlife Refuge 224
75. Cliff Walk 227
76. Norman Bird Sanctuary 229
77. Rodmans Hollow 232
78. Block Island National Wildlife Refuge 234
79. Clay Head Trail 236
80. Mohegan Bluffs 237

Useful Contacts 240
Index 249

LEGEND

———	paved road or highway	⁎ ⁎ ⁎	marsh
———	secondary paved road	▲	mountain summit
▪▪▪▪▪	improved road	ⵂ or ⌂	lookout (tower or on ground)
═══	unimproved road	◾	guard station
------	primitive road	▪	building
▪▪▪▪▪▪	railroad tracks	▫	restroom
••••••••	trail described	] [	bridge
············	other trail	) (	pass
┼——┼——┼	powerlines	♠	tree or forest
—·——·—	state border	✿	flowers
⑨⓪	interstate highway	▲	campground
②	US highway	⛱	picnic area
CT ⑯⑤	state highway	✕	mine
�	body of water	🚗	parking
～	river or stream	Ⓢ	hike start point
⋙	waterfall	📷	viewpoint
⁚⁚	beach	▱	boardwalk

ACKNOWLEDGMENTS

Cynthia Copeland and Thomas J. Lewis wish to thank Daniel and Cecelia Lewis and Sharlene and Clayton Copeland for the many babysitting assignments they cheerfully accepted while the authors finished the field work for this book. We appreciate the efforts of Julie and Ellie White and Gary and Carrie Copeland, who lent materials and assistance.

Emily Kerr would like to thank Janet and Margaret for encouraging me, and my whole family for supporting me. Carter and Davis, I'm proud of how rugged and determined you are. Thank you to Amy and Nancy for being great hiking partners, and special thanks to the Pangans, who gave up several Thursdays to either help with kids or participate in many of my wild goose chases.

You're sure to see dragonflies in Firefly Meadow. (Photo by Emily Kerr)

PREFACE

Best Hikes with Children in Connecticut, Massachusetts and Rhode Island has been a classic source of great hikes for kids for over fifteen years. Scout leaders, camp counselors, and parents have used this book to discover the best trails that these states have to offer, as well as to get helpful ideas when hiking with kids. The book also appeals to those hiking without kids—those possibly looking for shorter hikes or that like the detailed nature of the guide with its suggestions of good turn-around points and information on natural history and points of interest. The new edition now has interesting sidebars and more detailed contact information.

When I was researching material for the new edition, someone commented to me, "Well, they're not exactly adding new hikes in these states." It's true that land is at a premium and development is booming. As this happens, however, people and communities are also realizing the importance of protecting their natural areas. It is encouraging to learn that not only well-known groups such as the Audubon Society and the Nature Conservancy are working hard to make sure natural areas are safe from development, but many local conservation groups and land trusts have formed for this purpose. These natural spaces provide many great opportunities for hiking, and there are indeed new and rerouted trails, many of which are included in this book. The updated contact information for these conservation groups and land trusts in this guide can lead you to additional hiking opportunities in these states. Or better yet, it can serve as a starting point for you and your kids to get involved!

Emily Kerr

INTRODUCTION

It's only after we shell out a lot of money for the latest electronic game that we realize little Frank would rather spend the afternoon outside, giving a rock family a bath in a puddle. Kids and the outdoors are a natural combination. And family hiking adds an element of adventure to the outdoors: What will we find around the next bend? A cave? A boardwalk? A waterfall maybe? The feeling of accomplishment shared by everyone after the final climb to the summit is especially valuable for the youngster who may not excel in football or long division. Hiking is within the capabilities of nearly every child and it builds self-confidence and heightens self-esteem. Also, it's fun for everyone—no one has to compromise. As a final bonus, it's one of the healthiest family activities around.

To be sure, there are potential complications in family hiking. Fatigue, sore feet, and bug bites may not be serious but will make a hike less enjoyable for the little tykes. Children become bored, hungry, and just plain cranky. Injuries, serious bites, contact with poisonous plants, getting lost, or finding yourself in the midst of a spring blizzard present more serious difficulties. Planning for the obvious (hunger) as well as for the less likely (an encounter with poison ivy) will reduce if not eliminate any problems. Because children seem to have excellent memories for the less-than-terrific times, adequate preparation is critical.

HIKING TIPS

Here are a few pointers for hiking with young children.

- Bring a little buddy. A friend is a distraction from that blister on his big toe and a deterrent to whining: Nobody wants to look wimpy in front of a school chum!
- Set a realistic pace. A child's pace varies tremendously within the course of a walk, ranging from ambling along, examining every stone, leaf, and blade of grass to racing ahead like the lead runner in the Boston Marathon. By letting the child set the pace (within reason), you will convey the message that a hike's success is not measured in terms of miles covered but rather in the pleasure taken in each step along the way.
- Choose an appropriate hike. When in doubt, easier is better than harder, but an athletic twelve-year-old will be bored with the mile-long amble through the woods that is better suited for a preschooler.
- Give compliments. Nothing means more to a child than a parent patting her on the back and saying that she is the best climber around. Such praise makes sore feet suddenly feel a whole lot better.

Opposite page: Hiking among the boulders near The Rockery
(photo by Emily Kerr)

- Make frequent stops. Stop to admire a trailside boulder, a fallen tree, a breezy peninsula. Children may need more frequent rests than adults, but they tend to recover more quickly. Teach them to pace themselves; remind them as they dash out of the car that it will be a long climb to the summit.

- Offer snacks. Granola bars, bananas, cheese cubes, a mixture of nuts, chocolate chips, and dried fruits, boxes of raisins—bring along any favorite that will boost energy. Bring plenty of water, too.

- Play games on the trail. Have in mind things for children to listen and look for, such as croaking frogs, deer tracks, birds flying south for the winter. Collect acorns, autumn leaves, or pretty stones. Offer incentives and distractions—"we're halfway there," "the waterfall is just over the hill"—and talk about the day's goals. Have fun—laughter lightens the load for everyone.

- Encourage responsibility. Children, like adults, tend to meet the level of expectation. An older child who is given the responsibility of following the hike on the map, keeping an eye out for a loon through the binoculars, or charting directions with the compass will proudly fulfill his duties and will be less likely to engage in horseplay.

- Maintain a good attitude. Misery is contagious, so even if you are anxious because you think it might rain or your pack has somehow doubled its weight in the last half-mile, don't complain in front of your kids. A bad attitude will kill a good time much faster than a pair of soggy sneakers.

ENVIRONMENTAL CONCERNS

Sometimes the very qualities that make children so much fun to have along on a hike can present the most problems. Adults recognize that what our ancestors referred to as "dismal wilderness" is our most valuable and threatened resource, but to children the outdoors is a vast playground. While the seven-year-old is gleefully stripping a boulder of its moss blanket in search of worms and beetles, his younger sister is stomping among the wildflowers reciting a spontaneous ode to posies. But by springing to the defense of each cluster of ferns, parents may be concerned that they will turn what should be a relaxed family outing

BEST HIKES FOR SEEING A NATURAL WATERFALL

Dean Ravine and Barrack Mountain, Hike 6

Wadsworth Falls State Park, Hike 16

Devils Hopyard State Park, Hike 22

Bash Bish Falls, Hike 30

Race Brook Falls and Mount Everett, Hike 31

March Cataract Falls, Hike 37

Ben Utter Trail to Stepstone Falls, Hike 64

into a battle. How can parents creatively direct their children's enthusiasm toward nature-friendly pursuits?

Older children can anticipate the consequences of their own actions on the environment. They will learn respect for the wilderness and its inhabitants from their parents' examples. By recycling, buying biodegradable products, and supporting environmental concerns, parents integrate a conservation ethic into the family's daily life so that "clean hiking" and "clean camping" come naturally to their children. Youngsters so raised understand that as hikers and campers they are becoming, for a time, part of the wilderness; they are not seeking to dominate or ruin it. Willingly, they'll "take nothing but pictures, leave nothing but footprints, and kill nothing but time." Children old enough to distinguish safe garbage from potentially harmful trash can be encouraged to pick up the litter of previous hikers as well.

An observant hiker gently examines a toad. (Photo by Emily Kerr)

Younger children are more likely than older ones to act recklessly and without concern for the environment and its inhabitants. Offering desirable options rather than simply forbidding certain behavior works best with most children. Instead of picking a wildflower, your child can smell it, examine the petals under a magnifying glass, or take a photograph. Binoculars, as well, focus attention on soaring birds or far horizons. Such equipment retains its appeal when it is reserved just for special outings. One of the greatest gifts we can give our children is to instill in them a respect for the living things that share our planet and an understanding of their own importance in determining the future of our natural environment.

Here are some specific ways that hikers can leave the forest without a trace:

- Prepare to take trash out with you by bringing along appropriate bags or containers.
- Stick to the trails and, when presented with the choice of stepping on either delicate vegetation or hardy rocks, pick the rocks.
- Trails are most vulnerable during "mud season" in March and April; be especially careful during that time.
- Don't wash directly in streams or lakes.
- If restroom facilities are not provided, dig a small hole for human waste at least 200 feet from any water source and cover it with soil afterward.

■ Conform to the specific regulations of the state park, wildlife refuge, or other recreation area you are visiting.

SAFETY

While you cannot completely eliminate the risks inherent in hiking mountain or forest trails, you can minimize them by taking proper precautions and by educating yourself and your children. To help combat the most frequent problems, you should carry the Ten Essentials, including a well-equipped first-aid kit, flashlight, map, and extra food and clothing. Recognize your own limitations and those of your children: Don't attempt to climb something extremely steep and challenging on your first family outing. If you are hiking with very young children, you will probably wind up carrying them or their packs for some of the way, so choose a hike that is well within your own capabilities.

Getting Lost

Although we have described as accurately as possible the trail conditions and routes, conditions may be different when you embark on a given hike. Blazes may be painted over or seasonal changes, such as erosion or fallen trees, may cause a trail to be rerouted or bridges and boardwalks to collapse. You may want to change your plans if the trail seems too poorly marked to follow or if the condition of the trail is dangerous.

Prepare for the possibility of getting lost. Leave your itinerary with a friend or relative. Carry enough extra food and clothing so that if an overnight is necessary, you are prepared.

Teach older kids to read maps and all children to pay close attention to trail markers. On most marked trails, they should be able to see two blazes (one ahead of them and one behind them) at all times. They need to know that double blazes indicate a significant change of direction and triple blazes usually signal the end of the trail. You may want to equip everyone with a whistle and establish a whistle code or insist on the buddy system. Encourage children to stay put as soon as they realize they are lost. Above all, emphasize the importance of alertness and remaining calm. If you are unable to attempt a return to your car because you are lost or injured or both, make a smoky fire using green wood and vegetation that will help signal anyone looking.

BEST HIKES FOR OCEAN VIEWS

Worlds End Reservation, Hike 51
Nauset Marsh Trail, Hike 57
Felix Neck Wildlife Sanctuary, Hike 60
Trustom Pond National Wildlife Refuge, Hike 72
Cliff Walk, Hike 75
Norman Bird Sanctuary, Hike 76
Rodmans Hollow, Hike 77

BEST HIKES FOR BEACHWALKING

Sherwood Island, Hike 2
Bluff Point State Park and Coastal
   Reserve, Hike 18
Quabbin Hill (along reservoir),
   Hike 43
Sandy Point State Reservation,
   Hike 53
Lyman Reserve, Hike 54
Sandy Neck, Hike 55

Great Island Trail, Hike 58
Cedar Tree Neck Sanctuary,
   Hike 59
East Beach, Ninigret Conservation
   Area, Hike 71
Block Island National Wildlife
   Refuge, Hike 78
Clay Head Trail, Hike 79
Mohegan Bluffs, Hike 80

Weather

Be conscious of weather conditions and do not hesitate to rechart your course due to a potential storm. Even the least challenging trail can pose a hazard in foul weather. The only thing worse than getting caught in a severe thunderstorm or blizzard while hiking is getting caught in such a storm while hiking with your children.

If children are particularly engrossed in what they are doing, they may ignore discomfort or an injury. (Remember how they will swim in a lake for hours until they have blue lips and are covered with goose bumps, coming ashore only at your insistence?) Watch for signs of fatigue—encourage rest and food stops. Remember, too, that certain conditions, such as hypothermia, may affect children sooner than adults exposed to the same climate. If a child seems listless and cranky (early signs of hypothermia), and certainly once he complains of being cold or begins shivering, add another layer of warm clothes or offer hot chocolate or soup.

Water

Hikers need to drink frequently and the best way to ensure a safe water supply is to bring it along. It's never a good idea to drink water from an unknown source. If you must, boil it first (for at least 10 to 15 minutes, including cooking water) or use a filter designed to remove *Giardia lamblia,* a microscopic parasite. You can also use iodine tablets, which are light to carry and work extremely well. Although they may make your water taste a little funny, they are much better than nothing in a pinch.

Ticks

The ticks that spread Lyme disease are known to inhabit much of the area covered by this guide, most notably the coastal sections. In its later stages Lyme disease can lead to arthritis and heart and neurological problems, but if detected early it can be effectively treated with antibiotics. A red, ringlike rash at the site of the bite is the most common first symptom, often followed by a flulike fever, fatigue, a headache, and stiff, sore joints.

BEST HIKES FOR INVESTIGATING A POND OR LAKE

Audubon Center in Greenwich, Hike 1
Lucius Pond Ordway/Devils Den
    Preserve, Hike 3
Sharon Audubon Center, Hike 5
The White Memorial Foundation and
    Conservation Center, Hike 8
Burr Pond State Park, Hike 11
Chatfield Hollow State Park, Hike 19
The Denison Pequotsepos Nature
    Center, Hike 25
Edwin Way Teale Memorial Sanctuary
    at Trail Wood, Hike 27
Upper Goose Pond, Hike 35
Berry Pond, Hike 36
Rock House Reservation, Hike 44
Wachusett Meadow Wildlife
    Sanctuary, Hike 45
Stony Brook Wildlife Sanctuary/
    Bristol Blake State Reservation,
    Hike 49

Ipswich River Wildlife Sanctuary,
    Hike 52
Nauset Marsh Trail, Hike 57
Cedar Tree Neck Sanctuary, Hike 59
Felix Neck Wildlife Sanctuary,
    Hike 60
Walkabout Trail, Hike 61
Powder Mill Ledges Wildlife Refuge,
    Hike 63
Pachaug Trail around Beach Pond,
    Hike 66
Arcadia Trail, Hike 67
Fisherville Brook Wildlife Refuge,
    Hike 68
Long Pond Woods, Hike 69
East Beach, Ninigret Conservation
    Area, Hike 71
Trustom Pond National Wildlife
    Refuge, Hike 72

As important as recognizing early symptoms, however, is knowing how to prevent the disease. When hiking in places known to harbor ticks, wear light-colored clothing because the ticks are easier to see on light colors. Opt for a long-sleeved shirt with snug collar and cuffs, and tuck long pants into high socks. After the hike, check yourself and your children for the tiny ticks. If you remove a tick with tweezers within 24 hours, the disease is usually not transmitted, and not all ticks carry the disease.

Poison Ivy

Poison ivy, a caustic vine famous for its "leaves in threes," is common throughout the New England states. Make sure to learn to recognize the plant; and teach the kids, too. Carrying a strong soap for cleaning off the oils might also be a good idea, should anyone in your party happen to get exposed.

BEST HIKES FOR FOLLOWING A STREAM, BROOK, OR RIVER

Dean Ravine and Barrack Mountain,
    Hike 6
Devils Hopyard State Park, Hike 22
Rocky Neck State Park, Hike 23
Rock Spring Preserve, Hike 26
Race Brook Falls and Mount Everett,
    Hike 31

Jacobs Hill, Hike 42
Lyman Reserve, Hike 54
Ben Utter Trail to Stepstone Falls,
    Hike 64
Fort Barton/Sin and Flesh Brook,
    Hike 73

Dogs

Dogs can also present a danger to your kids. Locals often use trails to exercise unleashed pets. While it's rare that kids are bitten or attacked, they may get knocked over or frightened by an unexpected encounter with an unknown dog. On trails that allow dogs, you may want to stay close to small children.

Encounters with Wildlife

While one of the great benefits of hiking is the opportunity to see wildlife, there are many important safety and environmental concerns to keep in mind. You should always keep your distance from wildlife for a variety of reasons. Many animals can pose threats for you and your children. Squirrels, bats, and other animals can carry rabies and other diseases, and some species—such as moose—may charge when threatened. For the protection of the animals as well, it is best to view from afar. Getting too close may damage an animal's health—such as when birds become physiologically stressed with young children running after them—or alter natural behavior. Never feed or pet wild animals.

Hunting Season

Hunting is allowed on many of the properties in this book. Be sure to check with each state about hunting seasons (late autumn) and rules and regulations before you go. If you choose to hike during hunting season, make sure everyone is dressed in brightly colored clothing—blaze orange works the best.

Fire Towers

On hikes with fire towers, make sure you obey all posted signs regarding access. Many fire towers are no longer maintained and can be dangerous to climb, so inspect them carefully before heading up the stairs. Never use a fire tower for overnight camping.

BEST HIKES FOR VISITING A NATURE CENTER OR VISITOR CENTER

Audubon Center in Greenwich, Hike 1
Lucius Pond Ordway/Devils Den Preserve (nearby), Hike 3
Sharon Audubon Center, Hike 5
The White Memorial Foundation and Conservation Center, Hike 8
Gillette Castle State Park (castle tour), Hike 21
The Denison Pequotsepos Nature Center, Hike 25

Goat Peak Lookout, Hike 39
Sandy Point State Reservation (nearby), Hike 53
Nauset Marsh Trail, Hike 57
Felix Neck Wildlife Sanctuary, Hike 60
Trustom Pond National Wildlife Refuge, Hike 72
Northfield Mountain, Hike 41
Great Blue Hill (nearby), Hike 50
Norman Bird Sanctuary, Hike 76

BEST HIKES FOR EXPLORING A SWAMP OR MARSH

Sharon Audubon Center, Hike 5
Rhododendron Sanctuary and
   Mount Misery, Hike 29
Jacobs Hill, Hike 42
Stony Brook Wildlife Sanctuary/
   Bristol Blake State Reservation,
   Hike 49
Sandy Neck, Hike 55
Fort Hill Trail, Hike 56

Nauset Marsh Trail, Hike 57
Great Island Trail, Hike 58
Felix Neck Wildlife Sanctuary,
   Hike 60
Emilie Ruecker Wildlife Refuge,
   Hike 74
Norman Bird Sanctuary, Hike 76
Clay Head Trail, Hike 79

The Ten Essentials

The Mountaineers recommends ten items that should be taken on every hike, whether a day trip or an overnight. When children are involved and you are particularly intent on making the trip as trouble-free as possible, these Ten Essentials may help you avert disaster.

1. **Navigation (map and compass).** Don't assume you'll just "feel" your way to the summit. Teach your children how to read a compass, too.
2. **Sun protection (sunglasses and sunscreen).** Look for sunglasses that screen UV rays and sunscreen with a minimum SPF rating of 15. Children especially need protection from the sun. And remember that kids can get sunburned even in wintertime.
3. **Insulation (extra clothing).** It may shower, the temperature may drop, or wading may be too tempting to pass up. Be sure to include rain gear, extra shoes and socks (especially a pair of shoes that can be used for wading when bare feet might mean sliced toes), a warm sweater, and hat and mittens.
4. **Illumination (headlamp or flashlight).** Check the batteries before you begin your hike.
5. **First-aid supplies.** Don't forget to include moleskin for blisters, baking soda to apply to stings, and any special medication your child might need if he is allergic to bee stings or other insect bites.
6. **Fire (fire starter and matches/lighter).** If you must build a fire, these are indispensable.
7. **Repair kit and tools (including knife).** You never know when you might need to fix a boot, strap, or other piece of equipment. You'll be sorry when the occasion arises and you find you left your duct tape and knife in the drawer at home.
8. **Nutrition (extra food).** Too much food is better than not enough.
9. **Hydration (extra water).** Carry sufficient water in canteens or fanny packs in case no suitable source is available on the trail.
10. **Emergency shelter.** Chances are you won't need it, but it's a necessity if you get stuck on the trail unexpectedly.

In addition to the Ten Essentials, a few other items can come in mighty handy, especially when young children are along.

Until you've hiked or camped during black fly season, it's hard to describe how extraordinarily annoying a swarm of the little buggers can be. Insect repellent doesn't deter them all, but it helps. (Be sure the repellent you have is appropriate for children.) In addition to this protection, dress children in lightweight, long-sleeved shirts and pants. A cap may come in handy as well. A head cover made of mosquito netting (with elastic to gather it at the neck or waist) may be a hike-saver, especially during spring hikes.

Binoculars, a camera, a magnifying glass, and a small field guide are fun to have along and might keep children from trying to push each other into the brook.

Out of respect for others, leave your portable radio and noisy toys at home.

EQUIPMENT
Footgear

In selecting footgear, make comfort the number one priority. You do not want to find out two miles from the car that Mikey's boots (which were a tad small in the store but were half-price) have turned his toes purple. Buying shoes that are too small, in fact, is probably the most common mistake that new hikers make. Many stores specializing in outdoor equipment have steep ramps that your child can stand on to simulate a downhill hike. If her toes press against the tip of the boot when she is standing on the ramp, try a larger size. When buying boots, be sure to bring the liners and socks that the kids plan to wear on hikes for a more accurate fit. (In most cases, the salespeople in sporting goods stores are very helpful and will be able to guide you to an appropriate pair of boots.) For yourself and for the children you'll probably want lightweight, ankle-high, leather—or fabric and leather—boots. In a few cases, sneakers or running shoes will be adequate but, on most trails, hiking boots are preferable. If you will be doing a lot of hiking, invest in a good pair that will hold up to rugged terrain. (Be sure to wear new boots at home for several days before hitting the trails.)

BEST HIKES FOR EXPLORING A CAVE OR OTHER ROCK FORMATIONS

Lucius Pond Ordway/Devils Den Preserve, Hike 3
Leatherman Cave, Hike 10
Coginchaug Cave, Hike 17
Westwoods, Hike 20
Devils Hopyard State Park, Hike 22
Mashamoquet Brook State Park, Hike 28
Lauras Tower and Ice Glen, Hike 33

Rock House Reservation, Hike 44
Purgatory Chasm, Hike 48
Ipswich River Wildlife Sanctuary, Hike 52
Escoheag and Mount Tom Trails, Hike 65
Pachaug Trail around Beach Pond, Hike 66
Norman Bird Sanctuary, Hike 76

In the wintertime, insulated boots are a must, and in the spring or after a rainstorm, opt for waterproof boots. Snowshoes or cross-country skis can also be used for winter hikes on fairly level terrain.

Clothing

As with footgear, comfort is top priority. Think layers—they can be added or taken off as the temperature allows. Often, if you will be visiting a ravine or heading to a summit, factors such as wind and temperature will change noticeably. With layers, the moment you begin to feel warm you can remove an article of clothing to avoid becoming wet with sweat. In bug season, long sleeves paired with long pants are best. Jeans, a perennial favorite among kids, aren't necessarily the most comfortable walking pants. When wet they are heavy and cold, seem to take forever to dry, and unless well worn can chafe and be stiff as cardboard. A better bet might be sweatpants, cotton slacks, or tights. Nylon pants are fashionable these days for kids and dry quickly if gotten wet.

For hiking in cool weather, consider synthetic thermal long underwear. Cotton tends to retain moisture, whereas polypropylene keeps it away from your skin. You don't want to perspire on your climb and then become chilled once you stop for a rest or head back to the car. Socks should be wool or smart wool; try the rag-knit type found in most shoe or sporting goods stores. Wear a thin, silken liner under the socks. (Thick over thin will usually prevent blisters.) Hats will help keep the sun out of your eyes and the black flies out of your hair, and protect your head should a rain shower take you by surprise.

A light rain poncho with a hood that can be folded up into a small pack is essential for every member of the family.

Packs

Older children will probably want to carry their own packs while the little ones will want to move unencumbered. Child-sized packs can be purchased at stores carrying hiking and camping supplies; be aware, though, that they may quickly become too small as your child grows. Unless you have a number of other little hikers who will be using a small pack, you

Mother Nature supplies a cozy resting spot. (Photo by Cynthia Copeland and Thomas J. Lewis)

may want to just fill an adult pack with a light load. Kids like to carry their own drinks and snacks.

Adults should carry as light a load as possible because inevitably there will be times when a child needs or wants to be carried. Backpacks should have a lightweight but sturdy frame, fit comfortably, and have a waist belt to distribute the load.

Child-Related Equipment

Infants can be carried easily in front packs. We took our oldest daughter for a hike up Blue Hill in Massachusetts when she was just three weeks old. The walking rhythm and closeness to a parent is comforting to the littlest tykes. Older babies and toddlers do well in backpacks; they enjoy gazing around from a high vantage point and are easily carried by an adult. Look for a backpack that also has a large pouch for carrying other hiking essentials. We have also used a carrier resembling a hip sling that will accommodate children up to four years old. Ours folds into a wallet-sized pouch and can be put on when younger kids have had enough walking for the day. Look for ideas in outdoor stores, toy stores, and stores specializing in baby furniture and supplies. Ask hiking friends what they have found useful and, whenever possible, try before you buy.

Some of our hikes include sections with paved or hard-packed surfaces. For these hikes, a young child can be pushed in a stroller (bigger wheels make for easier pushing). However, none of our hikes are entirely on pavement, so you are probably better off finding some way of packing them.

Kids are never too young to enjoy hiking. (Photo by Emily Kerr)

Additional Equipment for Overnights

You will need additional equipment if you plan to spend the night on the trail. Sleeping bags, foam pads, a small stove, and cooking utensils as well as a tent are obvious necessities. Generally, folks who work at stores stocking outdoor supplies are more than willing to help you outfit your family for an overnighter. In some cases, trailside shelters, tent platforms, or lean-tos will be available. Learn everything about the accommodations (including whether you need to reserve space) *before* your trip.

Food

If you are staying overnight, you may want to buy freeze-dried food, although the kids might prefer more familiar nourishment. While a food's nutritional value, weight, and ease of preparation should take precedence over taste, kids—even hungry ones—may turn up their noses at something that just doesn't taste right. You can try one-pot meals such as chili or beef stew, or bring foods that require no cooking at all. Cooking equipment is cumbersome and it usually takes more time than you expect to prepare and cook the meal.

Day hikers need easy-to-carry, high-energy snack foods. Forget about three filling meals and eat light snacks as often as you and the kids are hungry. The time of year will affect your choices: Kids won't want to be peeling an orange with fingers frozen by the cold—they'd be better off with meatballs. Fruit that is not soft or easily squished is good: try dried fruit, raisins, papaya sticks, and banana chips. Fig bars, cheese cubes, granola, and nuts are other hiking favorites. Let the kids help you mix chocolate chips, peanuts, raisins, and other gorp ingredients, because it's fun to do, and cheaper than buying the ready-made trail mix. My kids like granola bars—store-bought or homemade. Often, we buy a loaf of our favorite bakery bread and a hunk of mild cheese that will appeal to the kids and then hard-boil some eggs to take with us. Let your family's tastes and your good judgment determine what you take along.

BEST HIKES FOR OVERNIGHT CAMPING

Macedonia Brook State Park, Hike 4

The White Memorial Foundation and Conservation Center, Hike 8

Devils Hopyard State Park, Hike 22

Rocky Neck State Park, Hike 23

Mashamoquet Brook State Park, Hike 28

Rhododendron Sanctuary and Mount Misery, Hike 29

Race Brook Falls and Mount Everett, Hike 31

Upper Goose Pond, Hike 35

Berry Pond, Hike 36

March Cataract Falls, Hike 37

Walkabout Trail, Hike 61

Ben Utter Trail to Stepstone Falls, Hike 64

East Beach, Ninigret Conservation Area, Hike 71

BEST HIKES FOR BIRDWATCHING OR VIEWING WILDLIFE

Audubon Center in Greenwich, Hike 1

Sherwood Island, Hike 2

Sharon Audubon Center, Hike 5

The White Memorial Foundation and Conservation Center, Hike 8

Bluff Point State Park and Coastal Reserve, Hike 18

The Denison Pequotsepos Nature Center, Hike 25

Edwin Way Teale Memorial Sanctuary at Trail Wood, Hike 27

Tyringham Cobble, Hike 34

Goat Peak Lookout, Hike 39

Wachusett Meadow Wildlife Sanctuary, Hike 45

Wachusett Mountain, Hike 46

Stony Brook Wildlife Sanctuary/ Bristol Blake State Reservation, Hike 49

Worlds End Reservation, Hike 51

Ipswich River Wildlife Sanctuary, Hike 52

Sandy Point State Reservation, Hike 53

Sandy Neck, Hike 55

Cedar Tree Neck Sanctuary, Hike 59

Felix Neck Wildlife Sanctuary, Hike 60

Powder Mill Ledges Wildlife Refuge, Hike 63

Francis C. Carter Memorial Preserve, Hike 70

Trustom Pond National Wildlife Refuge, Hike 72

Emilie Ruecker Wildlife Refuge, Hike 74

Norman Bird Sanctuary, Hike 76

Rodmans Hollow, Hike 77

Block Island National Wildlife Refuge, Hike 78

Clay Head Trail, Hike 79

Mohegan Bluffs, Hike 80

My kids love these homemade energy bars (let yours help you make them):

¾ cup firmly packed brown sugar
½ cup honey
1½ cups chunky peanut butter
5 cups raisin bran cereal
6 ounces mixed dried fruit pieces

Grease a medium-sized baking pan and set aside. Stir the brown sugar and honey together in a saucepan. Bring the mixture to a boil, stirring continuously. Remove the brown sugar and honey from the heat and add the peanut butter. Stir until smooth. Add the cereal; mix well. Set aside ⅓ cup of the dried fruit pieces and add the rest to the peanut butter mixture. Spread the peanut butter mixture evenly in the prepared pan and top with the remaining fruit bits, pressing down firmly. After the mixture has cooled, cut it into bars and wrap each individually. (You can experiment by adding peanuts, chocolate chips, or any family favorite.)

HOW TO USE THIS BOOK

This book covers southern New England: Connecticut, Massachusetts, and Rhode Island. (A companion volume covers Vermont, New Hampshire, and Maine.) The guide is divided into three sections by state, with a map for each that shows the locations of the hikes.

Selecting a Hike

Read the trip description thoroughly before selecting a hike. Each entry includes enough information for you to make a good choice.

Number: Use this to locate the hike on the state maps.

Name: This is the name of the mountain, lake, or park as it will appear on most road maps.

The following information is contained in the "Before You Go" box:

Maps: For each hike the name of the topographic map published by the U.S. Geological Survey (USGS) is included for your reference. The contour lines indicate terrain features and are a good supplement to the maps in this guide. Be aware, however, that the trails may have changed since the map was printed, so don't follow USGS maps exclusively. Many of the hikes have maps available on site. You can also find maps online before you go.

Current conditions: The name and phone number for the appropriate land management agency is listed, so you can call for current trail information such as closures, late-season snow, and the like.

Fees: In some cases, a fee is charged for entry or parking. These fees are generally minimal (between $1 and $10) and some fees, such as those for Audubon properties, do not apply to members. Be aware that fees can increase, and some places that only charged in-season or didn't charge at all when we did our research may now have changed their policies. It's best to come prepared with some cash. Many of the hikes in this book are maintained by conservation organizations that may or may not charge a fee. Donations are always appreciated and new members always welcome. Think about joining!

The following information is contained in the "About the Hike" box:

Type: There are two possible choices for each entry. A "day hike" means that this hike can easily be completed in a day or part of a day for most families. Camping overnight on the trail is prohibited. "Day hike or overnight" refers to trails on which there are camping spots, lean-tos, shelters, or some place for you to stay overnight. Or, it may mean that a campground located within the recreation area that you are visiting is within reasonable walking distance of the hiking route. In either case, the overnight location is evident on the trail map. This indication does not mean that the hike is too long or difficult to be completed in an afternoon, but that overnighting is optional for the hike.

Difficulty: Hikes are rated easy, moderate, or challenging for children. Ratings are approximate, taking into consideration the length of the trip, elevation gains, and trail conditions. Don't reject a hike based on a challenging rating before noting the turnaround point or reading about an optional shortcut—the first section of trail might be perfect for little guys.

Hikable: Based on such varied criteria as crowds, mosquito season, mud season, preferred hiking conditions, extra features along the trail (a swimming hole or view of the hawk migration), and hunting season (when applicable), we have recommended the months and season best for hiking the trails.

Distance: This is the route length. If a side trip to a waterfall or view is included in the text and on the map as the main hiking route, it is also included in the total distance. A part of the hike shown on the map as "other trail" is not factored into the total distance.

Elevation gain: Elevation gain indicates the total number of vertical feet gained during the course of the hike. When analyzing a hike, this notation will be more significant than the high point in determining difficulty.

High point: This number reflects the height above sea level of the highest point on the trail.

Hiking time: Again, this is an estimate based on hiking length, elevation gains, and trail conditions and the actual hiking times will vary somewhat from family to family. Short rest stops are factored into hiking times given; longer lunch stops are not.

Accessibility: Some hikes or portions of hikes are suitable for wheelchairs or strollers. If so, that information is indicated here. Many places are striving to become more accessible, so check ahead of time for possible improvements.

Hiking with buddies (photo by Emily Kerr)

BEST HIKES FOR SWIMMING AT A PUBLIC BEACH

Mount Tom Tower, Hike 9
Burr Pond State Park, Hike 11
Wadsworth Falls State Park, Hike 16
Chatfield Hollow State Park,
    Hike 19
Rocky Neck State Park, Hike 23

Great Blue Hill, Hike 50
Sandy Neck, Hike 55
Walkabout Trail, Hike 61
Arcadia Trail, Hike 67
East Beach, Ninigret Conservation
    Area, Hike 71

Below the "Before You Go" and "About the Hike" boxes are symbols reiterating basic information you'll need to decide whether the hike is a good choice for you.

  Day hikes. These hikes can easily be completed in a day or part of a day. Camping along the trail is either not recommended or it is prohibited.

 Backpack trips. Overnight camping is permitted along the trail in designated areas (some with structures or facilities), or a public campground is within reasonable walking distance of the hiking trail. In every case, the campground or camping area appears on the accompanying map.

 Easy trails. These are relatively short, smooth, gentle trails suitable for small children or first-time hikers.

 Moderate trails. Most of these are 2 to 4 miles total distance and feature more than 500 feet of elevation gain. The trail may be rough and uneven. Hikers should wear lug-soled boots and be sure to carry the Ten Essentials.

   Challenging trails. These are often rough, with considerable elevation gain or distance to travel. They are suitable for older or experienced children. Lug-soled boots and the Ten Essentials are standard equipment.

Hikable. The best times of year to hike each trail are indicated by the following symbols: flower—spring; sun—summer; leaf—fall; snowflake—winter.

"Getting There" driving instructions, when given relative to a town, generally refer to the greater township boundaries. "On the Trail" write-ups include a summary or history of the hike and region, as well as a complete description of the hike. Maps show hike direction and special features. Symbols included in the text margins serve as visual signposts to the hikes, highlighting the following features:

 Turnarounds. These are places, mostly along moderate trails, where families can cut their hike short yet still have a satisfying outing. Turnarounds usually offer picnic opportunities, views, or special natural attractions.

 Cautions. These mark potential hazards—cliffs, stream or highway crossings, and the like—where close supervision of children is strongly recommended.

A WORD ABOUT CAMPING

Vandalism and overuse of the trails has led to some strict regulations regarding backpack camping.

Massachusetts allows wilderness camping only in those areas designated with signs as camping areas. Along the Appalachian Trail, camping is permitted in the Appalachian Trail shelters, designated campsites, and dispersed camping zones (also indicated by signs). If you would like more specific information, a copy of all Massachusetts regulations governing forests and parks is available from the Department of Environmental Management. (See Useful Contacts at the back of this book for the mailing address.)

In Connecticut, camping along the trails in undesignated spots is prohibited. Some backpack camping sites have been created in association with the Connecticut Blue Trail system and the Appalachian Trail. These offer rustic or limited (if any) facilities. In some spots, shelters have been erected; here, the stay is limited to one night.

In Rhode Island, overnight camping is prohibited in rest or picnic areas, in noncamping state or municipal parks, or on beaches. Check with local police or conservation officers if there is a question about the legality of an overnight stay. Camping areas are mentioned within a hike entry when they are operated by the same group that maintains the trail.

HIKING WITH DOGS

It is fun to bring your canine companion along, but not very fun to show up at the trailhead only to find a big "No dogs allowed" sign. Call or go online beforehand to make sure dogs are permitted. As a rule, most wildlife refuges, wildlife sanctuaries, and preserves do not allow pets, nor are they allowed on most beaches. You can take your dog along—on a leash, of course—on many of the trails managed by state parks and forests, but they are usually prohibited from campgrounds and on beaches on these lands. Many of the properties maintained by the

Trustees of Reservations in Massachusetts allow dogs on leashes, but a few require you to obtain a permit ahead of time. It's always best to call ahead if unsure. A sidebar in each state section lists the hikes where dogs are allowed on leash.

Hiking with dogs requires some extra equipment. Make sure you have food, water, and first-aid supplies for your pet as well as for you and the kids. Reference a dog first-aid book to find out what you may need to be prepared for bites, stings, and injuries.

Make sure you have extra bags on hand so you can always, always, always clean up after your pet.

Keeping your dog leashed will prevent it from disturbing wildlife and from getting lost, not to mention that it is respectful to other hikers.

A NOTE ABOUT SAFETY

Safety is an important concern in all outdoor activities. No guidebook can alert you to every hazard or anticipate the limitations of every reader. Therefore, the descriptions of roads, trails, routes, and natural features in this book are not representations that a particular place or excursion will be safe for your party. When you follow any of the routes described in this book, you assume responsibility for your own safety. Under normal conditions, such excursions require the usual attention to traffic, road and trail conditions, weather, terrain, the capabilities of your party, and other factors. Because many of the lands in this book are subject to development and/or change of ownership, conditions may have changed since this book was written that make your use of some of these routes unwise. Always check for current conditions, obey posted private property signs, and avoid confrontations with property owners or managers. Keeping informed on current conditions and exercising common sense are the keys to a safe, enjoyable outing.

—*The Mountaineers Books*

Opposite page: Kicking through leaves on an autumn hike
(photo by Cynthia Copeland and Thomas J. Lewis)

AUDUBON CENTER IN GREENWICH

BEFORE YOU GO
Map USGS Glenville
Current Conditions The
Audubon Center in Greenwich
(203) 869-5272
Fees Nonmembers, moderate
fee for visitor center;
members, free

ABOUT THE HIKE
Day hike
Easy for children
February–October
1.8 miles loop trip
Elevation gain 150 feet
High point 500 feet
Hiking time 1.5 hours
Accessibility Building and
nature center accessible

GETTING THERE

- From the Merritt Parkway (I-15) in Greenwich, take the Round Hill Road (exit 28).
- Turn north and follow Round Hill Road 1.5 miles uphill to John Street.
- Turn left on John Street for 1.4 miles.
- The center's entrance is on the right at the Riversville Road intersection.

ON THE TRAIL

Where else can you listen to a talking and singing worm, create your own storms and droughts, and observe bees making honeycomb all in a "green building"? This is just a small sampling of what the Kimberlin Nature Education Center at the Audubon Center in Greenwich—the National Audubon Society's first educational center in the United States—has to offer. Top this off with a hike on a portion of their ten miles of trails, and a trip here is bound to be a memorable event. Definitely start off by visiting the nature center. The promise of a return visit after the hike will be great incentive to keep tired kids going on the trail. Check in at the store for admissions, trail maps, current trail conditions or advisories, and updates of recent natural history sightings.

Begin your hike by walking through the pedestrian gate to the side of the nature center, down a gravel road, and onto the Discovery Trail on the right immediately beyond the Research Center. Soon you will come to Indian Spring Pond, where you will most likely be greeted by the croaking of frogs. Can the kids find any? How about any turtles sunning themselves? From here, turn left on Old Forest Trail. You and your children will be amazed at the size of some of the trees. Can they see

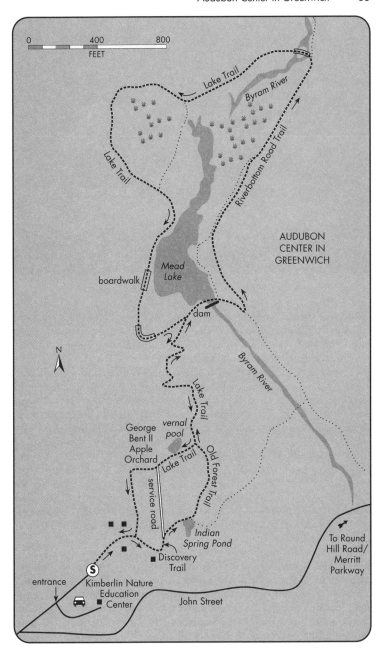

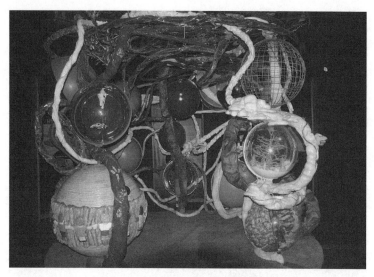

Inside the nature center—the web of life (photo by Emily Kerr)

the tops of the tallest ones? Who can find the biggest tree? This is where tree identification can be fun. If the kids noticed the display inside, they will know that the sanctuary contains maple, American beech, red oak, shagbark hickory, tulip trees, and sassafras.

Follow the Old Forest Trail to where it meets up with the Lake Trail. Bear right on the Lake Trail and descend a series of switchbacks to your next junction. Here, the trail makes a mile-long loop around Mead Lake, with plenty of stream crossings and boardwalks to keep the kids interested. Turn right and in 200 feet reach a dam. This dam, originally built in 1885 across the middle branch of the Byram River, created Mead Lake. Cross T.J.'s Bridge over the dam and turn right. A short side trail will lead you to Byram River. Return to the main trail and very quickly turn left onto Riverbottom Road Trail. This trail merges with the Lake Trail and in 0.3 miles continues straight while the Lake Trail heads left (west). Make the left turn onto the Lake Trail, cross the Byram River, and remain on the Lake Trail as it heads west, then south around Mead Lake.

You will pass by areas of shrub wetlands and over a fun series of boardwalks before once more reaching the beginning of the loop around Mead Lake, 1.4 miles from the start. Turn right on the Lake Trail and follow it to the junction with Old Forest Trail. Turn right again to remain on the Lake Trail. On your right, you will see a vernal pool, which may be teeming with life depending on the time of year. At the next junction, turn left onto the Service Road, and then immediately right (west) onto a trail (still the Lake Trail) through the serene George Bent II Apple Orchard. Follow this approximately 200 feet to the next major junction, where you will turn left. Hear the buzzing of bees? Up ahead, you can see the center's beehives. (Be sure to return to the educational display in the nature center to learn more about how they function.) Continue on the trail to a right turn onto the gravel road and back to the start.

REPTILES AND AMPHIBIANS

Do your children know the difference between these cold-blooded animals? Amphibians depend on moisture, as they have no protective scales over their skin. Most begin their lives in fresh water and hatch from gelatinous eggs. After going through metamorphosis they start their lives on land. Good places to look for amphibians—such as frogs, toads, salamanders, and newts—are Indian Spring Pond, Mead Lake, and vernal pools. Most reptiles hatch from leathery eggs on land and have scales to keep them from drying out. Look for reptiles—such as snakes and turtles—in sunny spots or swimming in the lake.

SHERWOOD ISLAND

BEFORE YOU GO
Map USGS Sherwood Point
Current Conditions
Sherwood Island State Park, Connecticut Department of Environmental Protection
(203) 226-6983
Fees Moderate fee in-season

ABOUT THE HIKE
Day hike
Easy for children
Year-round
2.7 miles round-trip
Elevation gain 10 feet
High point 10 feet
Hiking time 2 hours
Accessibility Accessible restrooms and picnic areas

GETTING THERE
- From the Connecticut Turnpike (I-95) in Westport, take exit 18 (Sherwood Island).
- Turn south onto the Sherwood Island Connector.
- Arrive at the gatehouse in 0.6 mile.
- Drive to the easternmost parking lot.

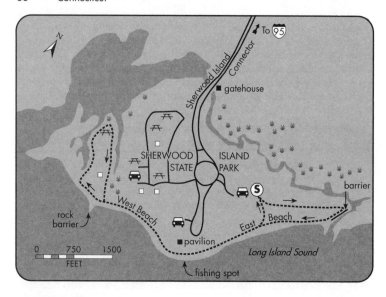

ON THE TRAIL

Sherwood Island State Park in Westport has the honor of being the first state park in Connecticut and one of the first in the United States. Sherwood Island's 234 acres include marsh areas, wooded terrain, and more than a mile of beachfront. If you visit the island in the winter, you will probably have this stretch of beach to yourself. Children can bring along

Playing games on the trail keeps the kids laughing. (Photo by Emily Kerr)

bird guidebooks and binoculars and try to identify sea birds and other feathered fellows that have decided to brave the New England winter.

Begin by walking along the grassy road heading toward the far eastern end of the park's beach (marked by a tidal stream bordered with flat boulders and a wooden barrier). The barrier makes a good balance beam for kids to test their skills. From here, travel west along the water's edge on a sandy beach. If you visit during low tide, watch for the birds that flock to the area to feed on trapped fish. Soon, the windswept beach surrenders to a rocky point that juts into Long Island Sound, a favorite spot for local fishermen. Shore fishermen are particularly numerous in autumn, when striped bass, flounder, and bluefish are active in the shallow waters near the beach. Beyond this section, the sandy beach returns. Ask the kids about ocean smells: What does seaweed smell like? Continue walking toward the westernmost end of the beach. At the rock barrier, sit and enjoy lunch or a snack. Turn right (north) at the far end of Sherwood Island and travel away from the beach onto a wooded, grassy knoll. Even when the island is crowded with sunbathers in the summer, this section of the island attracts few people. This peninsula, which extends into the inland salt marshes, is an ideal spot for bird watching. Follow along the perimeter of the peninsula into the marsh at low tide. When you are ready, return to the beach and follow it back to your car.

 LUCIUS POND ORDWAY/DEVILS DEN PRESERVE

BEFORE YOU GO
Map USGS Norwalk North
Current Conditions
The Nature Conservancy,
Connecticut Chapter Office
(860) 344-0716
Fees None

ABOUT THE HIKE
Day hike
Moderate for children
April–November
5.6 miles, loop trip
Elevation gain 300 feet
High point 510 feet
Hiking time 4 hours
Accessibility No special
access

GETTING THERE
- Take exit 42 off the Merritt Parkway (I-15).
- Travel north on CT 57 for 3 miles to Weston Center.
- At the northern junction of CT 57 and CT 53 in Weston, travel 1.6 miles north on CT 53.
- Turn left (west) on Godfrey Road.
- In 0.5 mile turn right on Pent Road at the sign for the Nature Conservancy, Devils Den Preserve.
- In 0.4 mile, the road ends at the parking area.

ON THE TRAIL
This 1756-acre property, maintained by the Nature Conservancy, is the largest nature preserve in southwestern Connecticut. The 20 miles of well-maintained and easy-to-follow trails make this a great place for a family that is physically up to a longer hike but doesn't have a

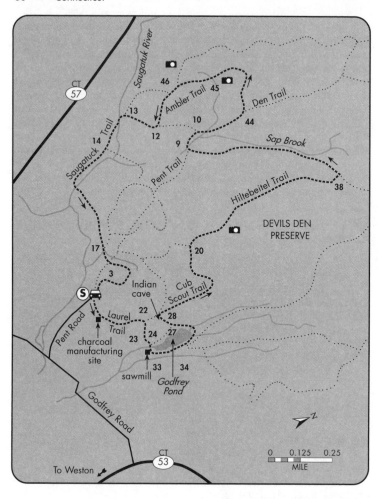

great deal of hiking experience. You will sign in and out at the map shelter; the staff will check to see that all hikers have returned before nightfall. This preserve, with its prehistoric Native American shelter cave, man-made lake and mill site, charcoal-manufacturing display, and meandering stone walls, offers kids an interesting look at how humankind has affected and been affected by the natural world.

From the right-hand (east) side of the parking lot, locate the Laurel Trail and signs to Godfrey Pond. (Register here and pick up a trail map.) The yellow-blazed Laurel Trail is wide and carpeted with wood chips. Soon, you pass a re-creation of a charcoal-manufacturing site.

*Family crossing a footbridge on the edge of Godfrey Pond
(photo by Cynthia Copeland and Thomas J. Lewis)*

Parents can explain that charcoal is partially combusted wood. In the early 1800s, charcoal production was a major industry here. Most of the land was bare because the trees were constantly being cut to make charcoal. The trail continues, wandering through quiet woods and leading through breaks in stone walls. Tell the kids about farmers long ago who built stone walls to rid planted fields of rocks and keep farm animals penned in. No bulldozers or backhoes helped these hardy souls.

When you arrive at junction 22 (the number is found on top of telephone pole stumps as the path divides), bear right, still on the manicured path.

Shortly, at junction 23, turn left and cross over a stream on a footbridge. At junction 24 (marked as junction 25 on the preserve's trail map), turn right. After a brief ascent followed by an equivalent descent you will arrive at Godfrey Pond. This man-made lake was created to provide power for a sawmill that operated in the late 1700s and early 1800s. At the southern outlet to the pond is a small waterfall and the site of the old mill. This is an interesting area for kids to explore.

Cross the dam and turn left at junction 33 to follow along the eastern edge of the pond. At first, this red-blazed jeep path travels some distance from the pond. But when you follow the yellow trail that departs from the jeep path at junction 34, you descend to pond's edge. The trail curves around the pond over rocky terrain, crossing two streams on footbridges and sweeping along the western side of the pond. At junction 27, swing right onto Harrison Trail. Soon you arrive at an impressive rock overhang. As long ago as 5,000 BC, this cave served as a shelter for Native Americans who roamed the area to hunt, fish, and gather. Can the kids imagine what life must have been like for these prehistoric wanderers?

Junction 28 marks about 1 mile of hiking. Here, you can turn left and then right at junction 22 to return to your car via the Laurel Trail for a total hike of 1.5 miles, or you can continue by turning right at junction 28 onto Cub Scout Trail. Maintained by a local scout troop, this narrow path winds through the hilly terrain, passing through a swamp over a unique log bridge. In a clearing at junction 20, 1.75 miles from the start, turn right onto the Hiltebeitel Trail. Don't be surprised if your footsteps urge a ruffed grouse out of the underbrush, startling the kids with its noisy flapping wings. Soon, you climb to a lookout at Deer Knoll A (485 feet above sea level) with westerly vistas to Long Island Sound. You may be able to catch a glimpse of migrating hawks from here.

The trail continues over rock outcroppings and through dense woodlands, arriving at junction 38 at 2.5 miles. Turn left. This trail follows along Sap Brook and jumps across the stream several times before emerging at trail intersection 9, 3.25 miles from the start. Here, turn right onto the wide Pent Trail and soon bear right at junction 10, now on the Den Trail. Cross Sap Brook and in 300 yards at marker 44, turn left onto the narrow path called Ambler Trail. At the 4-mile mark, after an ascent, you arrive at a vista looking west over Ambler Gorge. To head back to the parking area from the Ambler Trail, bear left at junctions 45 and 46 and turn right at number 12 onto a wide, cross-country ski trail. At junction 13, 4.5 miles from the start of the hike, turn left onto Saugatuck Trail and continue straight through junctions 14, 17, and 3 to the parking lot and your car.

Notes: The park is open from dawn to dusk. There are no restroom facilities, but there is a public telephone. Picnicking, camping, and swimming are prohibited.

MACEDONIA BROOK STATE PARK

BEFORE YOU GO
Map USGS Kent
Current Conditions
Macedonia Brook State Park,
Connecticut Department of
Environmental Protection
(860) 927-3238
Fees None for trails;
moderate fee for campsites

ABOUT THE HIKE
Day hike or overnight
Moderate for children
April–November
3 miles, loop trip
Elevation gain 700 feet
High point 1350 feet
Hiking time 3.5 hours
Accessibility Accessible
restrooms and picnic tables/
shelters

GETTING THERE
- From the junction of US 7 and CT 341 in Kent, travel west on CT 341.
- In 1.7 miles, turn right on Macedonia Brook Road, following a sign to Macedonia Brook State Park.
- In 1 mile, continue straight as Fuller Mountain Road heads right.
- Pass the park office 1 mile later and continue for another 0.1 mile to a parking area on the left.

ON THE TRAIL
Nothing about tranquil, undisturbed Macedonia Brook State Park discloses its eventful past. Long ago, the Schaghitcoke Indians and other local tribes traded their goods along the nearby Housatonic and Ten Mile Rivers. Many years after, in the late nineteenth century, the iron and charcoal industries flourished here. After the industries' decline, Litchfield's White Memorial Foundation donated 1500 acres of land to create a large part of this popular state park.

Families can plan to stay overnight, setting up camp in one of the rustic sites. Hiking trails abound and stream fishing is permitted (though swimming is not). The hiking route we've chosen offers a choice

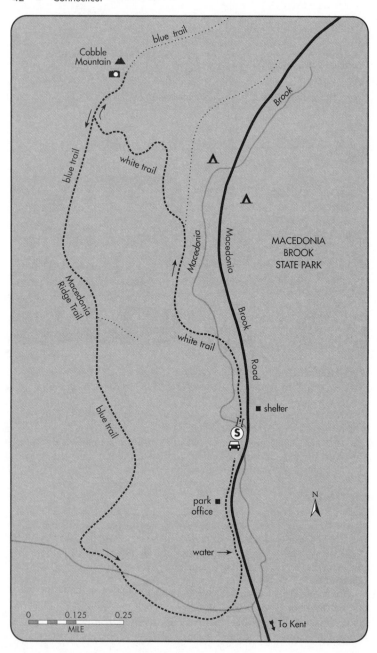

blue trail

Cobble
Mountain

blue trail

white trail

Macedonia
Ridge Trail

blue trail

white trail

Brook

Macedonia

Macedonia

MACEDONIA
BROOK
STATE PARK

Brook

Road

shelter

S

park ■
office

water →

N

0   0.125   0.25
MILE

↓ To Kent

BEST HIKES WITH LEASHED DOGS IN CONNECTICUT

Dogs are typically not allowed on beaches or in campgrounds, even if permitted on trails. Before you go, double-check regulations, as they can change.

Macedonia Brook State Park, Hike 4—dogs not allowed in campgrounds
Mohawk Mountain, Hike 7
Mount Tom Tower, Hike 9—dogs not allowed on beach
Burr Pond State Park, Hike 11—dogs not allowed on beach
Jessie Gerard Trail, Hike 12
Sleeping Giant, Hike 13
Wadsworth Falls State Park, Hike 16—dogs not allowed on beach
Chatfield Hollow State Park, Hike 19—dogs not allowed on beach
Devils Hopyard State Park, Hike 22—dogs not allowed in campgrounds
Rocky Neck State Park, Hike 23—dogs not allowed on beach or in campgrounds
Bluff Point State Park and Coastal Reserve, Hike 24
Mashamoquet Brook State Park, Hike 28—dogs not allowed on beach or in campgrounds

on the return route to accommodate younger hikers. After working up the demanding white-blazed trail to the delightful summit of Cobble Mountain, you can return the same way (although steep descents can be tricky for tired little legs), or you can meander back along the gentler, blue-blazed Macedonia Ridge Trail.

Cross the footbridge over Macedonia Brook and bear right, following a wide, grassy lane marked by white blazes. At 0.1 mile, head left and climb up a short hill to an overgrown road. Turn right onto the road, still following white blazes. In another 0.1 mile, turn left off of the road to join a well-worn path (still marked in white). Motivate the kids with encouraging words as you embark on a demanding 0.3-mile climb that climaxes with three switchbacks. Promise the little ones (and yourselves!) a reward for their efforts; as you scramble across an expanse of exposed ledge, look back for pleasing views across the Housatonic River Valley. Shortly, you'll reach the junction with the blue-blazed trail that later offers the option of an easier return route. For now, turn right onto the blue trail.

The ascent to the Cobble Mountain summit along the blue trail continues at a moderate pitch. Soon, the path crests and, less than 1 mile from the start, you arrive atop the mountain. Let the children explore the safe, open ledges that offer superb westerly views over the Catskill Mountains of New York.

When you are ready to descend, return the way you came to the blue and white trail intersection. You can elect to return the way you came along the shorter, more challenging white trail, or you can continue to follow the blue blazes of the Macedonia Ridge Trail, which descends more gradually and meanders through dense woods. If you choose the blue trail, you will begin a gentle descent into an area of dense deciduous woods about 0.2 mile from the blue/white junction. In another 0.1 mile (1.5 miles into the hike), avoid an unmarked trail heading left and continue straight along the blue trail. At 1 mile from the junction of the white and blue trails, descend through mountain laurel. Be sure not to miss the fleeting (and final) long-range views in another 0.25 mile.

Continue to descend gradually, watching for the double blue blazes that indicate a significant change in trail direction and lead to an easy stream crossing. The trail drops, at times down along the banks of the stream, and reaches the park access road, Macedonia Brook Road. Turn left onto the park road and walk the final 0.25 mile to your car.

SHARON AUDUBON CENTER

BEFORE YOU GO
Map USGS Ellsworth
Current Conditions
Sharon Audubon Center
(860) 364-0520
Fees Nonmembers,
moderate fee; members, free

ABOUT THE HIKE
Day hike
Easy for children
Year-round
1.5 miles, loop trip
Elevation gain 140 feet
High point 1050 feet
Hiking time 1 hour
Accessibility In planning
stages

GETTING THERE
- From the junction of US 7 and CT 4 in Cornwall Bridge, drive west on CT 4 for 7 miles.
- Watch for the Audubon Center signs on the left leading to the parking area.

ON THE TRAIL
Need a hiking suggestion for an overcast day? Try the Sharon Audubon Center. The captivating views along the Hendrickson Bog Meadow and Fern Trails are short range, so a few clouds won't detract from your enjoyment. And, on a dreary day, you may have the place to yourself. These paths take you past two ponds teeming with wildlife—primarily geese, ducks, and beavers (we saw a swan)—through some spacious meadows and dense woods that shelter deer, foxes, coyotes, and bobcats. All of the kids—from toddlers to teenagers—will have fun on this walk. This property comprises some 1147 acres with 11 miles of hiking

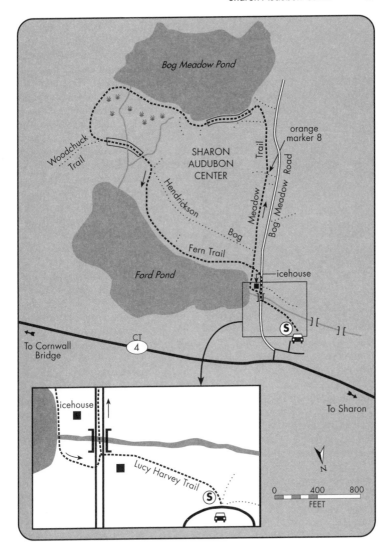

trails. The nature museum features live reptiles, birds, and amphibians and has a well-stocked gift shop.

From the large wooden trail map at the far end of the parking area, head southeast on the Lucy Harvey Trail to the Hendrickson Bog Meadow and Fern Trails. At the junction with Bog Meadow Road, turn right to cross the spillway of Ford Pond. An old icehouse perched near the spillway

Boardwalk near Bog Meadow Pond (photo by Cynthia Copeland and Thomas J. Lewis)

dates from the days when this 30-acre pond was used for ice harvesting. In fewer than 100 yards, turn left at the sign indicating the way to Hendrickson Bog Meadow and Fern Trails and then right onto Hendrickson Bog Meadow Trail. As you pass Ford Pond, the trail splits: The Fern Trail heads left, but you should follow the Hendrickson Bog Meadow Trail to the right. The path winds through a mixed hardwood and evergreen forest along a rocky path. In the fall, the kids can collect multicolored leaves along the trail.

Soon, the Hendrickson Bog Meadow Trail divides (the trail itself is a loop); follow the right-hand path as it climbs gradually and then levels off. At orange marker 8, walk through an opening in a stone wall and cross a field on a mowed path. (Keep the kids on the path because the meadow is a popular nesting spot for birds.) Less than 0.3 mile from the split in the Hendrickson Bog Meadow Trail, you will reach Bog Meadow Pond. Turn left. The kids can keep an eye out for natural dams and gnawed tree stumps—signs of beaver activity. In the spring, look into the shallow water for the eggs of frogs and toads. Frogs lay their eggs in a large, jelly-coated mass while toads lay theirs in a long, thin ribbon.

Head quietly across a boardwalk, then follow the soggy path that squeezes between the pond's edge on the right and a bog on the left. You may see a river otter if you don't make too much noise. Pause and listen to the birds and bullfrogs. In spring, smell the big-leaved, yellow-flowered skunk cabbage plants that punctuate the lush vegetation by the pond. At the intersection with the Woodchuck Trail, turn left, remaining on the Hendrickson Bog Meadow Trail. Though occasional arrows guide your way, the worn trail is obvious and easy to follow. After crossing a swamp along another boardwalk, turn right at a four-way intersection to join the Fern Trail. As you head north along the Fern Trail, you'll soon glimpse Ford Pond through the trees. Kids may stumble along this rocky and rooted trail, especially if they are watching ducks floating on the pond. Fern Trail exits onto the beginning of Hendrickson Bog Meadow

Trail. Turn right and walk along the top of the dam at the head of Ford Pond. Rest on the wrought iron bench and enjoy the pretty pond views (look for swans!) before returning to your car on the Lucy Harvey Trail.

Notes: Trails are open dawn to dusk. The buildings (including a museum and store) are open Tuesday through Saturday, 9:00 AM to 5:00 PM, and Sunday, 1:00 PM to 5:00 PM. They are closed on major holidays.

 ## DEAN RAVINE AND BARRACK MOUNTAIN

BEFORE YOU GO
Map USGS South Canaan
Current Conditions
Connecticut Forest and Park
Association (860) 346-2372
Fees None

ABOUT THE HIKE
Day hike
Challenging for children
April–November
3.8 miles round-trip
Elevation gain 750 feet
High point 1140 feet
Hiking time 3.5 hours
Accessibility No special access

GETTING THERE

- From the junction of CT 112 and US 7 near Lime Rock, drive north on US 7 across the Housatonic River.
- In 0.2 mile turn right onto Lime Rock Station Road following signs to Music Mountain.
- In 0.9 mile, turn left onto Music Mountain Road, still following signs.
- In another 0.8 mile, at a junction with Cream Hill Road, park on the left.

ON THE TRAIL

In New England, they say that if today's weather doesn't suit you, just wait a few weeks—it's sure to change. On this hike, if a particular section of trail doesn't inspire you, just walk a few tenths of a mile—it'll change. Climb from a cool ravine through a heavily wooded section across a boulder field to a steep, exposed ridge. Even the temperature changes as you hike from the "air-conditioned" ravine to the exposed summit. This hike holds something for everyone, provided "everyone" is outfitted with proper hiking gear and has had some trail experience.

The trail leads northward from the back of the parking area, immediately joining the blue-blazed Mohawk Trail. Continue north then curl west, guided by a trail sign leading hikers down into the ravine that cradles a swiftly moving stream. Under a thick canopy of hemlocks, the brook spawns numerous whirlpools on its descent. What happens to

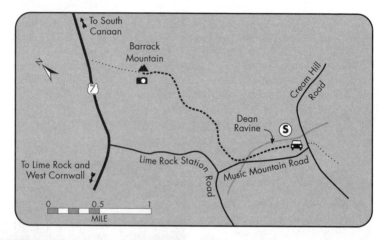

sticks and leaves tossed into the hurrying brook? The trail plunges to the depths of the ravine, temporarily departing the riverbank to skirt a drop-off with scenic falls and a cascade. The footpath rejoins the brook at the bottom of the cascade. If the day is steamy and hot, pause here to drink in the gorge's cool, damp air. Wander along the stream for 0.5 mile to where the stream opens up into a series of wading pools.

The trail now bends away from the stream and merges onto Music Mountain Road. Turn right (west) onto this paved road and in 0.15 mile, turn right again, reentering the woods (double blue blazes mark a telephone pole on the opposite side of the road).

Climb moderately on the wooded ridge heading north and east. After a short plateau, climb along a second rocky ridge. Beyond this

In Dean Ravine (photo by Cynthia Copeland and Thomas J. Lewis)

second ridge, the path threads its way through a brief, boulder-strewn section, reminiscent of the trails that wind through the White Mountains of New Hampshire. The trail then veers left and descends for 0.2 mile. If you time your hike just right, the distant roar of cars racing at Lime Rock mingles with the subtler sounds of the forest. After traveling briefly on level ground, the trail begins a moderate ascent.

Approaching the summit of Barrack Mountain, the trail traverses the top of a 30-foot rock cliff, turns right and then left, and scales a steep slope to the top of the ridge. Here, the expansive southwesterly vistas are the first unobstructed views along this route. Beyond this overlook, a ravine cuts into the mountain on the left and you'll pass by a rocky ledge that juts out to create a tunnel leading into the gorge. On the final climb to the peak, you must lean hard into the hill; scrambling on all fours may be the easiest way to scale the slope. Give younger kids a hand and older ones a word of encouragement. Nearly 2 miles from the start, from Barrack Mountain's bald face, the rolling hills of Connecticut stretch before you. Spread out the picnic lunch while the kids watch the road races at Lime Rock through the binoculars. Can anyone see Paul Newman, Lime Rock's most famous driver? With caution and patience, climb down the mountain the way you came. It's a tough descent, so take care to allow the kids the time they need to establish solid footing. When you reach the car, be sure to compliment everyone on a hike well done.

 MOHAWK MOUNTAIN

BEFORE YOU GO
Map USGS Cornwall
Current Conditions Mohawk State Forest, Connecticut Department of Environmental Protection (860) 491-3620
Fees None

ABOUT THE HIKE
Day hike
Moderate for children
April–November
5.5 miles, loop trip
Elevation gain 700 feet
High point 1683 feet
Hiking time 4 hours
Accessibility No special access

GETTING THERE
- From the junction of CT 63 and CT 4 in Goshen (at a rotary), travel west on CT 4 for 4 miles to the entrance to Mohawk State Forest on the left.

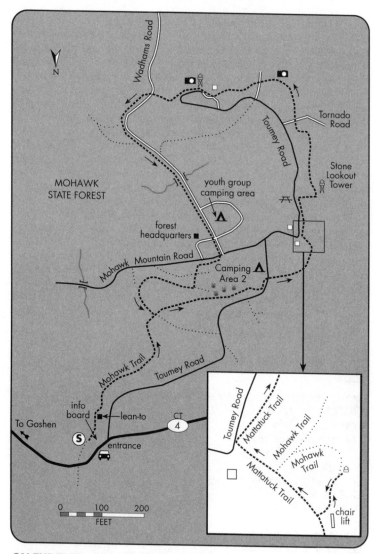

ON THE TRAIL

You likely already know that this park as a terrific place for winter sports, but did you realize that Mohawk's warmer weather trail system is also superb? The extensive views from Mohawk's 1683-foot summit not only have been admired by hikers but also put to practical use since colonial days. Centuries ago, Tunxis and Paugussett Indians sent smoke signals from the mountaintop to warn fellow tribesmen of any aggressive moves made by the enemy Mohawks (thus, the name of the mountain). In recent years, rangers have scanned the hillsides from the summit lookout tower for forest fires. The facilities here are extensive, also. So, if you've only thought to visit Mohawk Mountain after the first snowfall, think again!

Begin your hike at the information bulletin board just inside the gate and park entrance. Travel east on a dirt park road for approximately 100 yards to a light blue double blaze on the right that directs you into the woods. (This is the Mohawk Trail joining you from the north; be sure to head south along the path.) The path swerves to the left of a lean-to and dips down into a damp area. In approximately 0.1 mile, the path abruptly swerves right to skirt a rock outcrop. Notice the fissure to the left of this massive stone face. Follow the trail as it curls up and around the fissure. At 0.8 mile, after a steady descent, the footpath intersects a cross-country ski trail. Here is where you'll rejoin the initial section of trail after completing the loop. For now, continue straight, following the blue blazes. Did you bring along a book of animal tracks? The kids can look for indications of deer, bobcats, and foxes.

Soon, you skirt the right-hand side of a camping area, with a lean-to, campfire sites, and picnic table. When the trail emerges onto Toumey Road at 1.3 miles, turn left (south) and, 0.1 mile later, turn right into

Stone tower on the way to Mohawk Mountain (photo by Cynthia Copeland and Thomas J. Lewis)

the woods at double blue blazes. The path leads to the chairlifts at the top of Mohawk Mountain ski area. Near the second lift, at 1.5 miles, is a stone observation platform. From the platform you can see across the expansive ski area to the distant mountains of Connecticut, New York, and Massachusetts.

Back at the second ski-lift outlet, follow a jeep road as it branches off from the blue trail to the left (south) at the second chairlift outlet. A short descent leads to an intersection with the Mattatuck Trail, also blue blazed. Head straight (southeast) along the Mattatuck Trail, which shortly joins Toumey Road. The trail follows the road southerly for about 0.2 mile then ducks back into the woods on the right, across the road from a picnic area.

After another 0.2 mile, expect the kids to experience a resurgence in energy as they catch sight of a massive stone tower. The path curls left away from the tower and crosses a once-logged area where a ridge of Mohawk Mountain is visible to the southeast. Plunging once more beneath the canopy of the forest, the trail snakes through a swampy area to cross a stone wall and then a stream. After cutting across another section of the wall 2.2 miles from the start, the trail climbs to and crosses the Tornado Road, and begins a moderate ascent, at first on stone steps through an exposed ledge. Walk along rolling terrain with emerging views that promise even more dramatic vistas from the summit. Cross a grassy road and make your way along more exposed ledges. Turn right onto a gravel road, following the blue blazes to the summit and its lookout tower. Here, at 2.85 miles, enjoy the dramatic views and a picnic. Views to the north and northwest include the Taconic, Catskill, and Berkshire mountain ranges. It won't be hard for kids to imagine the Tunxis Indians scanning the countryside for signs of the dreaded Mohawks.

To return, walk east down the paved park road and in 100 yards, at a hairpin turn, leave the road and continue straight into the woods on a rutted trail marked with yellow triangular blazes. At the gravel Wadhams Road at 3 miles, turn left. Follow this road for a total of 1 mile, passing access to a camping area on the left and forest headquarters on the right before meeting the paved Mohawk Mountain Road. Turn right here. In 0.1 mile (just beyond another access for the headquarters buildings), a sign for a cross-country ski trail indicates a left-hand turn onto a grassy road. Follow this wide path, continuing straight across an intersection 0.1 mile later. Climb a short, steep hill to a split in the trail; follow the trail right, on a gradual incline, while the left-hand path drops to a swamp. Watch for the occasional plastic markers with a skiing figure. Climb to the height of a hill, sidestep Mohawk Mountain Road, and drop to a T intersection with another cross-country ski trail; turn left. At the 4.7-mile mark, turn right at the intersection with the Mohawk Trail. Follow this blue-blazed trail to your car, 0.8 mile away.

THE WHITE MEMORIAL FOUNDATION AND CONSERVATION CENTER

BEFORE YOU GO
Map USGS Litchfield
Current Conditions The White Memorial Conservation Center (860) 567-0857
Fees Nonmembers, moderate fee at nature museum; members, free

ABOUT THE HIKE
Day hike or overnight (with advance reservations)
Easy for children
Year-round
2.2 miles, loop trip
Elevation gain 140 feet
High point 980 feet
Hiking time 2 hours
Accessibility Nature museum accessible to the physically disabled, blind, and visually impaired

GETTING THERE
- From the junction of US 202 and CT 63 in Litchfield center, drive south on US 202 for about 2 miles.
- Turn left on Bissell Road.
- Make an immediate right onto a gravel road that leads in 0.5 mile to the White Memorial Foundation headquarters and parking area.

ON THE TRAIL
Even with 4000 acres and 35 miles of trails and woodland roads, the nature museum may be the feature that appeals most to children visiting the White Memorial Conservation Center. The exhibits are fascinating. They include live animals, interactive exhibits, and a children's corner which has books, puzzles, and games. Other features that attract families to the property are its two campgrounds, the most popular being Point Folly, a peninsula that juts into Bantam Lake and offers campsites at water's edge.

Begin on the L Trail near the Carriage House. Head south to follow the yellow rectangular blazes along the edge of a field and enter the woods through a gate on a wide, grassy path. Let the kids run ahead. At junctions with two woods roads, bear left, and ignore foot trails that branch off to the left. The easy-to-follow trail descends very gradually, and in 0.5 mile reaches Bantam Lake. Turn right to reach the observation platform. Continue west along the L Trail, now a footpath, through wetlands. Watch for swamp sparrows, yellow warblers, and red-winged blackbirds. Tell the kids to keep an eye out for signs of muskrats and beavers. Bring binoculars for close-up views of wildlife.

Three-tenths of a mile from the lake, the trail intersects a woods road.

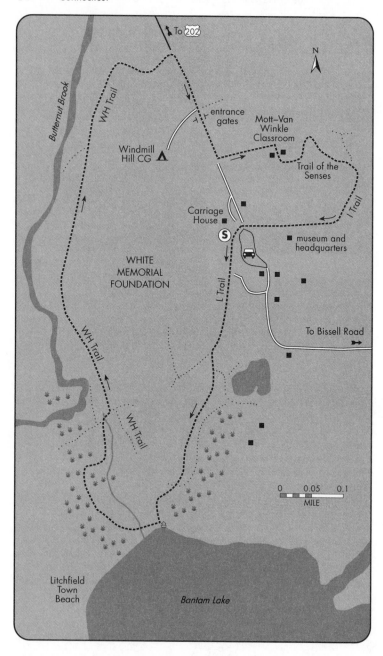

Zzzzzzzz (photo by Cynthia Copeland and Thomas J. Lewis)

Turn right and quickly left onto a green-blazed trail, the WH Trail, and follow this grassy woods road in a northerly direction for 0.7 mile until you reach the entrance road. Turn right onto the road and walk through the entrance gates. Behind the buildings of the Mott–Van Winkle Classroom (down a side road to the left) locate the trailhead for the Trail of the Senses, which shortly merges with the I (Interpretive Nature) Trail. The interpretive trail is level and easy with 17 numbered stations corresponding to descriptions in a brochure available (for a small price) in the nature museum. Turn right at this merger following both trails and in 0.3 mile you will pass the museum to return to the parking lot.

9 MOUNT TOM TOWER

BEFORE YOU GO
Map USGS New Preston
Current Conditions Mount Tom State Park, Connecticut Department of Environmental Protection (860) 868-2592
Fees Moderate fee; higher on weekends and holidays

ABOUT THE HIKE
Day hike
Moderate for children
April–November
1 mile, loop trip
Elevation gain 400 feet
High point 1325 feet
Hiking time 1.5 hours
Accessibility Accessible restrooms, and concession and picnic areas

GETTING THERE
- From the junction of US 202 and CT 63 in Litchfield center, drive 6.3 miles south on US 202.

- Pass Mount Tom Pond on the left, with Mount Tom rising over the water.
- Turn left at the sign for Mount Tom (onto Old Town Road) and in 100 yards a "Mount Tom State Park Entrance" sign indicates another left-hand turn.
- Drive past a booth, where you will pay a small fee.
- After another 0.2 mile, park near a large, wooden trail-map sign.

ON THE TRAIL

This short hike is still a challenging one for small hikers because you will gain 400 feet within 0.5 mile. The summit, at 1291 feet, stands more than 100 feet higher than the Massachusetts mountain that shares its name. The climb through dense forest culminates in a fabulous view from atop the stone tower. After the hike, the whole family can take a dive into the pristine water of Mount Tom Pond and then finish the day with a beachside picnic. Toilets, changing houses, and drinking water are available near the beach. (If you hike midwinter, bring your ice skates and explore the pond Dorothy Hamill–style at the end of your walk.)

At the trail plaque, begin your ascent on a trail marked with yellow blazes. Within 0.1 mile, you will pass an old foundation and stone fireplace on the left. This is all that is left of Camp Sepunkum, a Boy Scout camp dating from the early 1900s. The fireplace once heated the scouts' assembly hall. Avoiding unblazed side trails, continue to follow

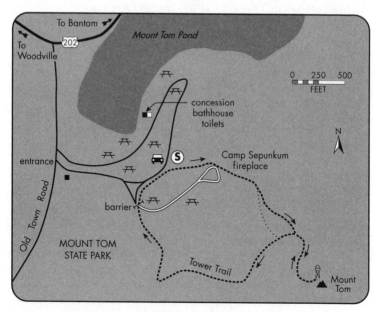

*View of Connecticut's rolling hills from the Mount Tom Tower (photo by
Cynthia Copeland and Thomas J. Lewis)*

the rocky and rugged, well-worn path to the summit. In another 0.1
mile, a second yellow-blazed trail joins the first. Bear left here and also
at the second intersection with the yellow trail, 0.1 mile later. The trail
curls roughly to the mountaintop, cutting through swampy areas and
crossing streams by way of stepping stones. Take turns leading the way,
with the group following directly in the leader's footsteps (it's more fun
that way).

In about 0.4 mile, you will reach the summit and the stone tower. The
view from the ground here is limited but side paths lead to overlooks;
the view from the top of the tower, at 1325 feet, is magnificent. (Children
will need help climbing the stairs because there are no railings; warn
taller kids to watch their heads on the final set of steps.) When this
cement and bluestone tower was being built in 1921, horses had to
pull wagons full of sand, water, stones, and cement up the side of the
mountain. Look to the northwest to see Bear Mountain (Connecticut's
highest peak) and the Mount Riga Range and nearby Mount Everett in
Massachusetts. On the descent along the Tower Trail, bear left within
the first 0.2 mile at two junctions with yellow-blazed paths and arrive at
the base of the mountain near a barrier. Head down a dirt road through
a picnic area and turn right onto a paved road; walk 100 yards to the
trailhead and parking area or go straight for the lake.

WHAT KIND OF ROCKS DO YOU SEE?

As you walk up the trail, pay attention to the different kinds of rocks that
you pass. If you look closely, you will see different colors and patterns
within the rocks, caused by mineral deposits, weathering, and type of
rock. Then, when you reach the tower, see if you recognize any of the
rocks from which it's built. It is made from the types you just walked on!

LEATHERMAN CAVE

BEFORE YOU GO
Map USGS Thomaston
Current Conditions
Connecticut Forest and Park
Association (860) 346-2372
Fees None

ABOUT THE HIKE
Day hike
Moderate for children
April–November
2 miles round-trip
Elevation gain 450 feet
High point 860 feet
Hiking time 1.5 hours
Accessibility No special
access

GETTING THERE
- From the intersection of CT 109 and US 6 in Thomaston, drive southwest on US 6.
- In 0.5 mile, you will pass Black Rock State Park.
- At 0.9 mile, look on the right-hand side of the road for a blue oval marker indicating a junction with the Mattatuck Trail.
- Park off the road near the sign.

ON THE TRAIL
Little is known about the peculiar man for whom this cave is named. He was said to be Jules Bourglay, who left his home in Lyons, France, when his poor financial judgment ruined the family leather business and his future wife left him. Dressed completely in leather clothing (which was estimated to weigh 60 pounds) and sleeping only in caves, he roamed

Exploring the legendary Leatherman Cave (photo by Cynthia Copeland and Thomas J. Lewis)

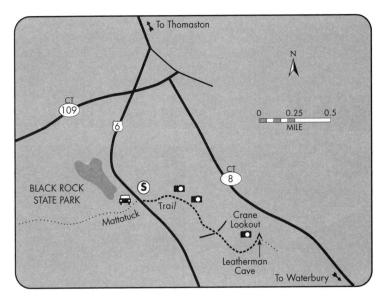

Connecticut for nearly 30 years in the late 1800s. He refused to sleep in barns or homes but did accept food handouts, expressing his thanks with grunts. His body was eventually found in a cave near Ossining, New York. The trip along the Mattatuck Trail to Leatherman Cave, one of this wanderer's favorite resting places, offers breathtaking views of the nearby rolling hills. Be warned, however, that these panoramas are from atop precipitous cliffs at trail's edge. Kids who are not "trail-wise" should postpone this hike until they have more experience.

Cross the road to begin the hike, heading southeast. The blue-blazed Mattatuck Trail leads through a pine grove and ascends on a narrow, rocky path. Often traversing large expanses of rock that sparkle with mica chips, the path curls upward, tucked into the forest between boulders and mountain laurel. Within the first 0.4 mile, you will travel along a precipitous ledge with stunning views of the nearby hills. These panoramas will convince you that a series of rolling hills (especially in autumn) can look just as awesome to a hiker as a giant ice-capped mountain. To the left of the trail is a sheer drop of at least 65 feet, so hold the hand of any child who isn't surefooted. Look southeasterly across the canyon at the hill that lies beyond; this is your destination. Continue to follow the rutted, blue-blazed trail as it winds downhill through the woods. (Side trails enter and exit, so watch for the blue blazes.) Turn left onto a jeep trail at the 0.6-mile mark; in about 100 yards, turn right onto a trail that begins a moderate climb. Nearly 1 mile into the hike, you will reach Crane Lookout with more lovely views.

Leatherman Cave is at the southern base of this overlook. This rock labyrinth with its dark tunnels and mysterious passageways will keep the kids intrigued long enough to allow the adults to set out a picnic lunch on the grassy hill nearby. When you're ready, retrace your steps through the woods and along the ridge back to your car.

 BURR POND STATE PARK

BEFORE YOU GO
Map USGS Torrington
Current Conditions Burr Pond State Park, Connecticut Department of Environmental Protection (860) 482-1817
Fees Moderate fee; higher on weekends and holidays

ABOUT THE HIKE
Day hike
Easy for children
Year-round
3 miles, loop trip
Elevation gain 170 feet
High point 1080 feet
Hiking time 2 hours
Accessibility Accessible restrooms, parking, and picnic tables

GETTING THERE
- From CT 8 in Torrington, take exit 46 to Pinewoods Road in Burrville.
- Travel west 0.3 mile to an intersection and turn left onto Winsted Road, following a sign to Burr Pond.
- In 0.9 mile, turn right at a blinking light onto Burr Mountain Road.
- In 0.5 mile, pass the entrance to Burr Pond State Park and drive 0.2 mile farther to a boat launch parking lot on the left.

ON THE TRAIL
Nestled in the hills of northwestern Connecticut, Burr Pond State Park is the site of Borden's first condensed milk factory, built in 1854. The well-worn Blue Trail encircles the 88-acre Burr Pond, passing by glacial boulders once used by Native Americans for caves, and leads through a public park with a sandy beach. Wear your bathing suit under your shorts and tee-shirt so that you will be ready for a swim here, close to the end of the hike. This is a can't-get-lost trip—just keep the shoreline in sight on your left and you'll eventually return to your starting point. Even in wintertime this is a pretty hike: the surroundings never seem barren and bleak because dense hemlock forests and colonies of mountain laurel ensure year-round color. Burr Pond State Park offers forty campsites at its Taylor Brook Campground.

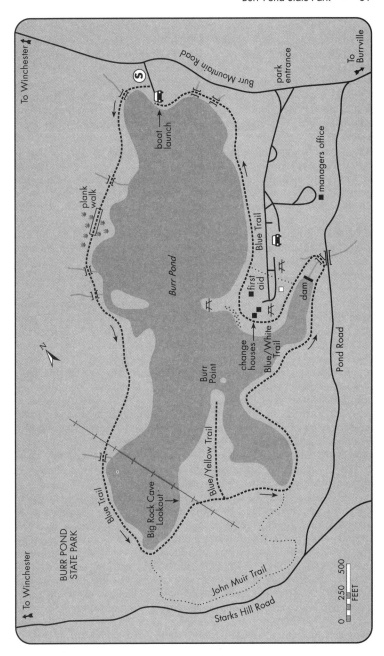

To Winchester

To Burrville

Burr Mountain Road

park entrance

managers office

boat launch

S

plank walk

Blue Trail

first aid

Blue/White Trail

change houses

dam

Burr Pond

Burr Point

Blue/Yellow Trail

Big Rock Cave Lookout

Blue Trail

To Winchester

BURR POND STATE PARK

N

Pond Road

John Muir Trail

Starks Hill Road

0   250   500

FEET

The hike begins on the west side of the parking lot, 50 yards from water's edge, on a trail blazed with blue paint. Head in a northwesterly direction with the pond on your left. Within the first 0.1 mile, the trail curls to the left (southwest) and crosses a small stream by way of a footbridge. The narrow gravel trail hugs the shoreline initially, passing through a hemlock grove and thick stands of mountain laurel. If you are hiking during the colder months, the kids may be surprised that the laurel bushes have remained green. Have them touch the leaves. The waxy coating shields the leaves from the effects of freezing temperatures. And the leaves are poisonous to many animals, so even during the winter when food is scarce, these bushes do not tempt deer or other wildlife.

Cross another stream at the 0.3-mile mark and then weave through a wetland on a plank walk. Alert the kids that the worn boards can be slippery. More footbridges cross slow-moving streams within the next 0.2 mile. At these frequent stream crossings, children may want to stop for a few minutes to examine a frog or coax a turtle out of its shell. It's a 3-mile walk around the pond, so frequent stops now will help conserve energy. As the path travels through a clearing cut for power lines, hikers are treated to a panoramic view of the pond. At the far end of the clearing, another stream meanders past.

As the path travels along the southwestern end of the pond, the trail climbs a small hill (the hike's only notable elevation gain). A mile from the start, turn left to remain on the Blue Trail as the John Muir Trail heads right, eventually leading to Sunnybrook Park. The path drops along rugged terrain, soon leveling out and passing within 100 feet of Big Rock Cave Lookout at 1.1 miles. Take a vote: Do your kids think this dramatic boulder resembles a fish head or candle flame? After traveling under the power lines once more, a side trail, the Blue and Yellow Trail, leads to Burr Point. This trail weaves through thickets of mountain laurel (spectacular in June when the plants blossom) and over exposed granite. Listen and look for signs of woodpeckers. The tip of the peninsula, at 1.4 miles, is an ideal spot for a picnic lunch. Although the nearby public beach offers picnic tables and manicured lawns, here your family will enjoy a peaceful and solitary meal.

Leave the point and return to the Blue Trail, turning left (southeast). At a second junction with the Muir Trail turn left to head northeast, then north. The trail winds along the water's edge on a rock-laden bank and arrives at a dam with water spilling over the top at 2.2 miles. As the trail sweeps past the dam, a solid footbridge carries you across the river that feeds the pond. Bending left (west), the Blue and White Trail follows the shoreline and cuts through the beach and picnic area, just 0.6 mile from your car. Here, the comforts of civilization await you: a telephone, restrooms, a concession stand, and a first-aid station. Drinking water is available at several spots near the beach. Peel off that hiking gear and dive in! (Lifeguards are on duty from 10:00 AM to 6:00 PM.)

Beyond this busy spot, the Blue Trail leads through the woods past picnic sites that are not used as much, following along the water back to the boat launch area and your car. You may wish to begin and end the hike from the parking area near the public beach. You will pay a parking fee in season, and pets and alcoholic beverages are not allowed at the beach.

 JESSIE GERARD TRAIL

BEFORE YOU GO
Map USGS New Hartford
Current Conditions Peoples State Forest, Connecticut Department of Environmental Protection (860) 379-2469
Fees Moderate fee; higher on weekends and holidays

ABOUT THE HIKE
Day hike
Moderate for children
April–October
2.6 miles round-trip
Elevation gain 400 feet
High point 1120 feet
Hiking time 3 hours
Accessibility Accessible parking, picnic tables, and shelter

GETTING THERE

- From US 44 in Barkhamsted, turn northeast onto CT 181/CT 318, following signs to Peoples State Forest.
- In 0.7 mile, after crossing the Farmington River, turn left (north) on East River Road.
- Travel 2.3 miles to a parking turnout on the left next to the river.

ON THE TRAIL

The Jessie Gerard Trail is one of many interesting paths that wander through the 3000-acre Peoples State Forest. Each trail is named for an individual who played a significant role in acquiring or developing the land for the park. The Jessie Gerard Trail begins at the site of an old Native American settlement known as Barkhamsted Lighthouse near East River Road and climbs to an overlook by way of 299 stone steps. Challenging climbs, pleasant forest surroundings, and magnificent views from two overlooks make this a great hike for families in good condition with some previous hiking experience. Although no camping is allowed at Peoples State Forest, the neighboring American Legion State Forest (just across the Farmington River) does have camping facilities.

The trail begins on the opposite side of the road at two wooden posts bearing "Trail" signs. Fifty feet along, the yellow-blazed trail splits; you should bear left. At 0.1 mile register at the sign-in box. The path

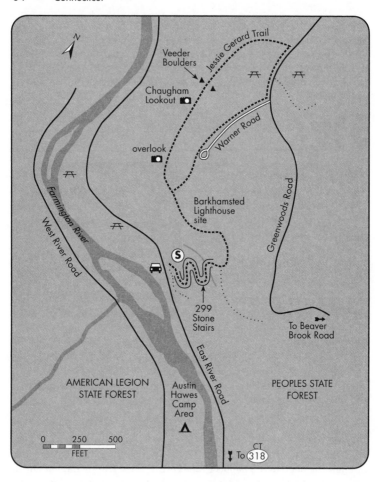

climbs moderately, then more steeply for the first 0.3 mile as it travels up a wet ravine lined with the so-called 299 Stone Stairs. (Kids can try to keep count.) Above you, to the right, are huge rock walls that dazzle winter hikers with the natural ice sculptures that form as cascading water freezes in turquoise-colored masses. At the stream crossing, you are close to the crest of this rugged section. Soon, the yellow-blazed trail intersects a trail marked with blue blazes. Turn left on this path, now dotted with both yellow and blue blazes. After a modest 0.4-mile climb, the blue-blazed trail exits right. (You will later return by this trail.) Continue straight on the yellow blazes, still encountering some steep, rocky ascents.

Shortly, you will reach a small clearing and an overlook with dizzy-ing views of the adjacent ridges. Kids can enjoy the view from a distance while more sure-footed adults can venture closer to the edge of the cliff. The trail reenters the woods and travels atop the ridge, passing through stands of majestic evergreens over level ground. With little underbrush and a thick carpet of pine needles, children may be inclined to wander off the path in search of pinecones or other forest collectibles.

Soon a second overlook, Chaugham Lookout, is reached at just un-der a mile with similar wide panoramas. As the trail crawls back into the forest, let the kids run ahead with instructions to wait for you when the trail passes between two car-sized twin boulders (called the Veeder Boulders) in another 0.1 mile.

At the 1.3-mile mark, the yellow-blazed trail joins paved Green-woods Road. Turn right and in 0.1 mile you will see a picnic area with reliable water. Stop here so the kids can take a breather and have a snack. Another 0.1 mile beyond the picnic area, you will pass by the yellow-blazed trail that turns left into the woods; continue walking straight on the paved road. As you approach the top of a short hill, turn right onto gravel Warner Road. Follow this lane for 0.5 mile to its end at a turnaround. A blue-blazed trail exits right from the beginning of the turnaround and in 0.2 mile rejoins the yellow trail. Turn left and hike the 0.4 mile back, descending to your car via the 299 Stone Stairs.

Hikers along the Jessie Gerard Trail (photo by Cynthia Copeland and Thomas J. Lewis)

SLEEPING GIANT

BEFORE YOU GO
Map USGS Mount Carmel
Current Conditions
Sleeping Giant State Park,
Connecticut Department of
Environmental Protection
(203) 789-7498
Fees Moderate fee on
weekends and holidays

ABOUT THE HIKE
Day hike
Short route easy for children;
long route challenging for
children
April–November
**3.2 miles (short route);
4.2 miles, loop trip (long
route)**
Elevation gain 600 feet (short
route); 800 feet (long route)
High point 740 feet
Hiking time 2.5 hours (short
route); 4.5 hours (long route)
Accessibility Accessible
parking and picnic tables

GETTING THERE
- From the junction of CT 70 and CT 10 in Cheshire, travel south on CT 10 for approximately 5 miles.
- Turn left onto Mount Carmel Avenue following a sign for Sleeping Giant State Park.
- In 0.2 mile, turn into the parking area for Sleeping Giant State Park.

ON THE TRAIL
To appreciate the Sleeping Giant, you must view him from a distance. If you look north from New Haven harbor, you'll see him lying on his back with his head to the west and his feet facing east. According to one Native American legend, the Sleeping Giant is the spirit Hobbamock, who, after causing the Connecticut River to change course, became the victim of a spell cast by another spirit that put him to sleep forever. Encourage your kids to make up their own versions of the legend!

Initially, you'll follow the 1.6-mile Tower Trail, a wide trail that rises gradually to reach the stone tower situated on the giant's left hip. This is a worry-free trail for those leading a group of youngsters (scout leaders or teachers, for example), because there is little chance of children getting lost or hurt. You may elect to return the way you came or you can follow the more rugged and demanding White Trail back to your car. The second option is great preparation for hiking in the White Mountains or other "serious" mountain ranges.

In addition to promoting hiking on its 1500 acres, the Sleeping Giant

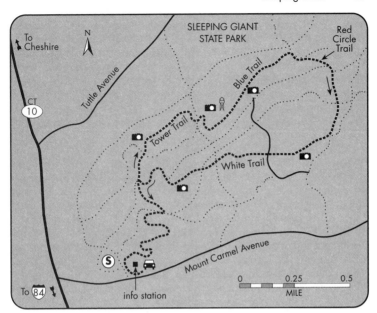

Park Association encourages horseback riding and fishing during the warmer months and snowshoeing and cross-country skiing in wintertime on the trails designated for those uses.

Walk up the paved road past the water bubbler and information station (where you can borrow a trail map). Look for the sign to the Tower Trail on the right (point out to the kids that restrooms are located on the left) and go around the metal gate that marks the beginning of the trail. You'll follow this smooth, generous (essentially unblazed) path for the entire 1.6 miles to the tower. Only sporadic patches of loose stone will present difficulty for children. (On this particular trail, no bicycles, horses, or motorized vehicles are permitted, and all visitors must leave by sunset.) The trail climbs gradually through thick deciduous forest and mountain laurel with numerous side trails splitting left and right (most of these are shortcuts that were forged by overeager hikers).

In 0.1 mile, the trail curls to the left and switches back and forth up the mountain four more times during the next 0.5 mile, seeking the easiest route. At 0.6 mile, the trail runs beside lofty cliffs and a hillside littered with hunks of stone, the remains of an old quarrying operation. Who will be the first to see the plaque on the right side of the trail that tells the story of a boy who fell while attempting to climb the rocky hillside? Many years later, he successfully fought to stop the quarrying operation and turn the area into a state park.

Make note of the white-blazed trail (the alternate return route) that crosses your path here. One mile from the start, just after the trail crests, pass a short side trail on the left that leads to an overlook with good westerly views. At 1.3 miles, the trail switches upward again. Soon, have the kids look left—who'll be the first to spot the stone tower? When you arrive, spread out your picnic lunch on the table near the tower's base, or find a room in the "castle" for your lunch. Kids will enjoy exploring the tower (bars on the openings will keep them from tumbling out). From the top floor, views extend to the New Haven skyline, Long Island Sound, and Long Island.

When you are ready to head back, you can return along the familiar Tower Trail or take on the challenging blue-blazed trail that leaves below the tower (the tower's south side) and darts quickly into thick woods. Immediately emerge high above the first of two dangerous cliffs—keep the children by your side for the next 0.1 mile. Two miles from the start, the trail drops steeply into a rock-strewn gully and meets the red-blazed Red Circle Trail. Turn right onto the Red Circle Trail, cross the rock scree, and follow the Red Circle Trail as it cuts across the mountain ridge from north to south.

At 2.3 miles, continue straight at an intersection with the green-blazed trail and scramble up a steep incline. In another 0.2 mile, stay straight again as the orange-blazed trail crosses. Soon, you will enter a deep gorge with the giant's right knee on the left. You'll have to watch closely for the camouflaged white-blazed trail that cuts across your path. Turn right onto the rugged, narrow White Trail and hike up a moderate ascent to a southerly overlook on the giant's right leg. Continue to follow the white blazes, ignoring the trails that depart to the left and right.

After enjoying the lovely views from another overlook about 3 miles from the start, descend cautiously on a rocky switchback. After a brief

Take time to view the Connecticut countryside from every side of the tower. (Photo by Cynthia Copeland and Thomas J. Lewis)

climb, pause on the giant's chest to enjoy expansive views with Quinnipiac College below you. Drop steadily along the White Trail, heading straight as the Blue Trail merges from the right. Before long you'll reach the Tower Trail (3.6 miles from the start). Turn left and descend 0.6 mile to your car.

 CASTLE CRAIG AND WEST PEAK

BEFORE YOU GO
Map USGS Meriden
Current Conditions
Connecticut Forest and Park
Association (860) 346-2372;
City of Meriden/Hubbard Park
(203) 630-4123
Fees None

ABOUT THE HIKE
Day hike
Challenging for children
April–October
6 miles round-trip
Elevation gain 850 feet
High point 1024 feet
Hiking time 4.5 hours
Accessibility No special
access

GETTING THERE
- From I-691 in Meriden, take exit 4 (West Main Street).
- Turn east onto West Main Street and travel 0.7 mile to the entrance to Hubbard Park.
- Turn left into the park and follow the park road as it winds through the recreation area.
- At the first intersection turn right and at the second, left, approaching the highway bridge.
- Travel under the bridge and through the gates onto Park Drive. (These gates are not always open—be sure to call beforehand for hours.)
- At the far end of Merimere Reservoir, 1.7 miles from West Main Street, park on the right-hand side of the road at a barricaded intersection.

ON THE TRAIL
From atop the tower at Castle Craig, you will be able to see the Sleeping Giant hills to the south, the Metacomet ridges to the north, and, far away, Mount Tom in Massachusetts and the distant hills of the Holyoke range. Pick a clear day to hike this section of the Metacomet Trail to take full advantage of the views. It's fairly tough—long, with some steep climbs—so be prepared to carry small children who may tire out. But the stone lookout tower at Castle Craig is a perfect turnaround point

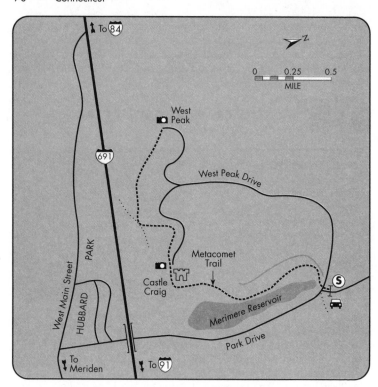

for those who choose not to follow the path all the way to West Peak. As you drive along I-691, have the kids look for the "castle" perched on the side of the hill.

From the parking area, walk across the dam on Park Drive at the head of the reservoir. Here, at the reservoir's northern tip, the blue-blazed Metacomet Trail heads left off of the paved road into a gully, then climbs an embankment and dives into the woods. The trail ascends gradually then moderately over the 1.5-mile trek to Castle Craig. Initially, the trail leads through stands of evergreens along an often dormant stream that feeds the reservoir. In 0.3 mile, the trail curls left and follows above the reservoir.

About halfway down the reservoir, the trail turns to the right, plunging deeper into the woods, and begins a series of stiffer ascents. To the right of the path, a thin stream flows through a shallow ravine. After about 0.5 mile of climbing, the trail again turns to the left, approaching the high ridge that leads to Castle Craig atop the East Peak of Meriden's Hanging Hills. Soon, the trail flirts with the edge and provides fine views to the east over the adjacent ridge and to the south past the city of Meriden. Parents should take the hands of young hikers here.

As the trail begins to level out, traveling across rock outcrops, the views and the character of the ledges become more spectacular. Who will be the first to see the castle tower? As the tower comes into view, a rock peninsula juts out from the cliffs, reaching for the panoramas. It offers a picnic spot for those who don't suffer from vertigo. Soon, the Metacomet Trail emerges onto the eastern side of a parking lot. From here, walk to the stone tower set at the edge of a sheer cliff (976 feet above sea level) with breathtaking views east and south. You

Tower at Castle Craig (photo by Cynthia Copeland and Thomas J. Lewis)

may have to vie for space in the tower with a few other folks who drove up West Peak Drive. Head back to your car the way you came for a total hike of 3 miles or continue another 1.5 miles to West Peak for a 6-mile round-trip total.

To continue to West Peak, from the parking lot, facing the tower, search for the trail on the right-hand (western) side of the paved expanse. After traveling beside the paved road, the trail splits; turn left and descend sharply for 0.2 mile. Turn right onto a tote road for a brief walk and then turn right again back onto the narrow blue-blazed trail. Here the trail ascends steeply along a rim of the hill for 0.3 mile. Soon, your feet will begin slipping on the loose, grapefruit-sized rocks lining the path. Ask kids what might make a trail slippery and hard to walk on: loose rocks, wet moss or leaves, pine needles, etc. As you look to the left, the woods open up and an impressive rock slide soon comes into view. Near the crest of West Peak, you must scramble over the upper reaches of this rock slide, which has formed a narrow ravine. Let the kids go first and challenge them to find the surest footing. The Sleeping Giant naps on a lush, green carpet in the distance. On a clear day you can see Long Island Sound sparkling on the southern horizon approximately 30 miles away. You emerge onto a gravel path at the summit after 3 miles of tough hiking. Turn right onto the path that leads to the parking lot for West Peak. Access the precipitous ledges of West Peak through a gate in the fence that borders the south side of the parking lot. Exercise caution here with the smaller ones but enjoy the dramatic 270-degree view. Return as you came.

CASTLE CRAIG

This tower, which stands at 1002 feet above sea level, was built in 1900. It was given to the people of Meriden that same year by Walter Hubbard, a generous philanthropic citizen of the time. At its dedication many people were in attendance. Can your children picture people in carriages making their way to the site? One of the legends that surrounds this tower is about the "Black Dog." It is said that whoever sees this dog roaming around will see it not once, but three times. Each sighting results in a different outcome for the viewer: The first, an increase of wealth; the second, suffering of physical ailments; and the third, death.

 CHAUNCEY PEAK AND LAMENTATION MOUNTAIN

BEFORE YOU GO
Maps USGS Middletown, Meriden
Current Conditions
Connecticut Forest and Park Association (860) 346-2372
Fees None

ABOUT THE HIKE
Day hike
Moderate for children
May–October
4.2 miles round-trip
Elevation gain 650 feet
High point 720 feet
Hiking time 4 hours
Accessibility No special access

GETTING THERE

- Take exit 20 (Country Club Road and Middle Street) off I-91 in Middletown.
- Travel west on Country Club Road, crossing the Meriden city line and passing a trap rock quarry.
- Notice blue blazes on the telephone poles 2.2 miles from the highway.
- At 2.5 miles, just before the road turns sharply left and another road splits off to the right, park on the widened shoulder on the right-hand side of the road.

ON THE TRAIL

This one will take your breath away—literally, at first, as you pick your way up a steep slope for 0.25 mile and then figuratively as you gaze from atop a rocky outcrop at the distant hills and the towns nestled in the faraway valleys. The vistas are so magnificent they seem almost unreal. It feels as if you are standing on a stage with a spectacular backdrop rather than perching on the edge of a 300-foot cliff. As you inch

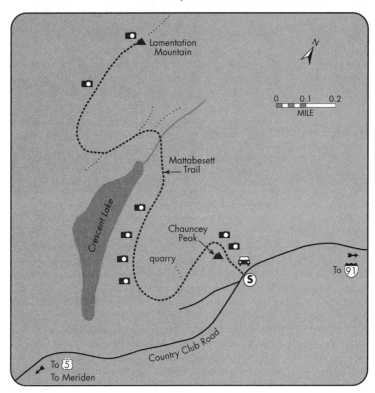

along the edge of the ridge that rises over Crescent Lake, the breathtaking panoramas continue until the path curls into the woods and heads for Lamentation Mountain. In this case, good judgment is more critical to a successful hike than physical stamina—the only significant vertical gain occurs immediately. Older children with previous hiking experience and the ability to proceed with caution will thoroughly enjoy this trip.

Light blue rectangular blazes mark the Mattabesett Trail that heads west into the woods up a moderate incline. The climb steepens as you continue, and the way becomes littered with loose stones, turning steps into backward slides. Though this will be a difficult section for kids to navigate, remind them that their efforts will take them to the crest quickly where the trail then leads along relatively level terrain. Approaching the height of the hill, natural rock steps carved in the granite face assist hikers in the final scramble.

At the top, 0.25 mile from the base, the trail turns right and follows along the southeast rim of Chauncey Peak. Here the trail reveals its daring character as it inches along exposed granite, precariously close

A fallen tree frames a curious hiker. (Photo by Cynthia Copeland and Thomas J. Lewis)

to the cliffs rising hundreds of feet over scenic central Connecticut. Children will enjoy the same delightful "top-of-the-world" sensation from their safe position well back from the drop-off. A narrow ravine cut into the cliffs on the right will beckon adventurous kids, but the walls drop steeply and parents may have to distract their Tarzans-to-be with promises of more trailside challenges to come.

Beyond this first overlook, the trail begins its western journey along the wooded ridge, heading for the cliffs that rise from Crescent Lake. To the right, a quarry mining operation has eaten into the hillside. Take a right-hand side trail to examine this operation from above. Beyond the quarry path, the Mattabesett Trail dips and then mounts a section of the ridge at 0.6 mile with impressive views over Crescent Lake to similar ridges across the water and beyond. Soon, the wide trail extends to cliff's edge. You may want to take a lunch break here, because the views are as magnificent as any you will encounter for the remainder of the hike.

Consider turning around here if the kids are getting tired—remember, you have a 0.75-mile walk back to your car. As you continue carefully picking your way along the exposed ledge to the lake's northern tip, the trail begins to curl around the head of the lake and then drops steeply through a hemlock forest. Watch for the blue blazes as side trails enter and exit the Mattabesett.

As the trail bottoms out, cross a stream that feeds the lake and follow the footpath as it swerves right and begins the gradual, rocky ascent of Lamentation Mountain. Sections of this trail may swell with water during spring runoff. Soon, the trail bears left away from this sometimes-dormant streambed, continuing on blue blazes. This ascent, though constant, is not nearly as severe as the climb to Chauncey Peak. The blue-blazed trail intersects with jeep trails and fire roads, at times joining them for a stretch and at other times cutting across them. The kids can help you watch for the frequent blue markings at these junctions to avoid turning off the Mattabesett Trail. Soon the path leaves the crisscrossing jeep trails and narrows, still on a moderate ascent. Lamentation's wooded summit, at 2.1 miles, offers good views of the tower on Castle Craig to the west and the Sleeping Giant to the south. Turn around at the USGS marker that announces the elevation to be 720 feet. Return carefully the way you came.

 ## WADSWORTH FALLS STATE PARK

BEFORE YOU GO
Map USGS Middletown
Current Conditions
Wadsworth Falls State Park,
Connecticut Department of
Environmental Protection
(860) 663-2030
Fees Moderate fee; higher on
weekends and holidays

ABOUT THE HIKE
Day hike
Easy for children
Year-round
3.2 miles round-trip
Elevation gain 240 feet
High point 210 feet
Hiking time 2 hours
Accessibility Accessible
parking, restrooms, and picnic
tables; accessible path down to
Wadsworth Falls off of Cherry
Hill Road

GETTING THERE
- From CT 66 in Middletown, take CT 157 south (Wadsworth Street), following signs to Wadsworth Falls in Middlefield.
- You'll reach the park entrance on the left in 1.5 miles; turn here.

ON THE TRAIL
Waterfalls are favorite trailside features for adults as well as kids. On this hike, you'll encounter two of them. Even better, these falls can be enjoyed by the youngest hikers because the route we've chosen is appropriate for everyone. If you visit in the spring, you'll get the full effect of swelled rivers exploding over the cliffs. In the warmer months, you can cool off after your hike with a swim at the pond located near the park's main entrance. Picnic tables and fireplaces are available for those who want to cook up a post-hike feast.

The well-marked Main Trail starts to the left of the parking area (as you face the pond) behind the picnic area and horseshoe pits. This wide clay path, blazed infrequently with orange marks, is crisscrossed by numerous other trails; be sure to stick to the orange blazes of the main trail. Shortly, a sign shows the way to Big Falls, 1.6 miles away. Can you

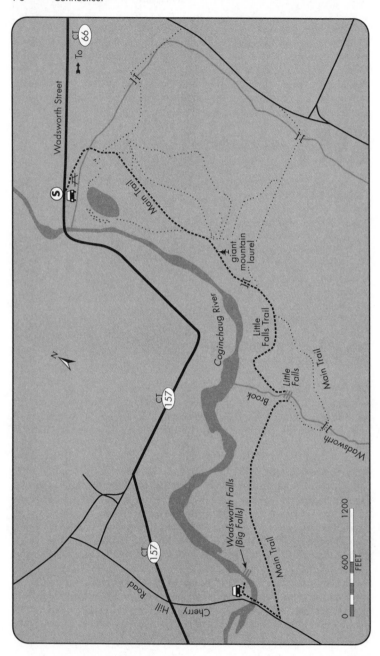

Big Falls at Wadsworth Falls State Park (photo by Cynthia Copeland and Thomas J. Lewis)

hear the chattering of the red squirrels? One-half mile from the start, a sign points out the colony of giant mountain laurel bordering the path. Stop for a rest on the bench near the park's trail map. How well can the kids read a trail map? Ask them how far it is to the falls and how far you have already come. Even a little child can trace the route with a finger. Then see if anyone wants to guess how much time it will take to reach the falls based on how long it has taken to get to this point.

Continue along the well-trodden path to a stone bridge over a frequently dry streambed. At an intersection 0.7 mile from the start, the orange-blazed trail swerves left, but take the right-hand path marked in blue to Little Falls. In 0.2 mile, this narrow, rugged path plummets into a ravine at the base of the falls. Wadsworth Brook tumbles over the rocks in a 30-foot drop, rejuvenating sweaty hikers with a cool misty spray. The blue-blazed Little Falls Trail climbs steeply away from the falls, quickly rejoining the Main Trail. Turn right, following the orange blazes once more on a mild descent along a stream.

Nearly 1.5 miles from the start, the trail outlets on paved Cherry Hill Road. Turn right and walk on the road to another Wadsworth Falls parking area on the right side of the road. (If you leave a second car here, you will avoid the return trip, cutting the total hiking distance in half. Another variation on this trip would be to park here and hike from Wadsworth Falls to Little Falls and back for a total of 1.4 miles.) Follow the path that heads out of the parking area—the children will lead the way, following the sound of the pounding water to its source. The Coginchaug River bursts over a rim of rocks 100 feet wide and plunges 25 feet, creating a miniature Niagara Falls. With fences bordering the riverbank at the top of Wadsworth Falls, older children may be able to do some exploring on their own. Enjoy the mesmerizing sights and sounds of this dramatic waterfall from above and below before heading back to your car along the familiar Main Trail.

COGINCHAUG CAVE

BEFORE YOU GO
Map USGS Durham
Current Conditions
Connecticut Forest and Park
Association (860) 346-2372
Fees None

ABOUT THE HIKE
Day hike
Easy for children
April–November
2.2 miles round-trip
Elevation gain 240 feet
High point 540 feet
Hiking time 1.5 hours
Accessibility No special
access

GETTING THERE

■ From the junction of CT 17 and CT 79 in Durham center, drive south on CT 79 for 0.8 mile.
■ Turn left (east) on Old Blue Hills Road following blue blazes on telephone poles.
■ Continue along this road for a short distance to its cul-de-sac conclusion and park on the right-hand side.

ON THE TRAIL

Kids and caves go together like cookies and milk. Coginchaug Cave, along the Mattabesett Trail, rises 30 feet high and stretches more than 50 feet along the base of a cliff. It is said to have provided shelter to Native Americans long ago. One of the children might even come across an old Native American tool here; other hikers have. Take this relatively

What do mushrooms feel like? (Photo by Cynthia Copeland and Thomas J. Lewis)

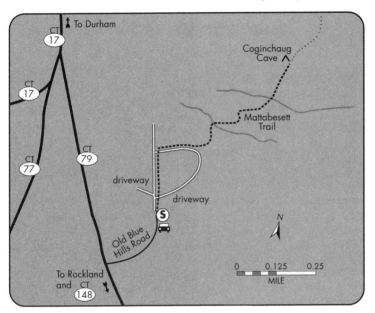

short, easy walk to the cave on an overcast day, saving sunnier days for hikes that promise long-range views.

Follow the driveway that continues beyond the cul-de-sac turn-around. The blue blazes will lead you straight into the woods at the junction of two driveways. Initially, the blazes are sparse as you follow along a jeep road bordered by utility lines. At about 0.3 mile, after a short ascent and some level walking, the trail turns right onto another jeep trail through denser woods. At 0.5 mile, bear left at a second inter-section, still on the blue blazes.

The trail winds through a thickly wooded area, past rock outcrop-pings, and then crosses a small stream. Have the children count how many stones they must step on in order to get across.

After several short climbs and descents, the blazes take you across another brook. At the 1-mile mark, a final sharp ascent brings hikers through a colony of mountain laurel. Almost immediately, a tricky de-scent sweeps left along the belly of the ridge to the cave. Give younger children a hand here. Coginchaug Cave is an impressive rock overhang that faces east; it is best to do your exploring in the morning with the sun over your shoulder. Ask the kids what it must have been like for those who used this cave as their home. What did they eat? What did they sleep on? Did the children play games on the rocks and cliffs near the cave? Return via the blue trail to your car.

18 BLUFF HEAD ON TOTOKET MOUNTAIN

BEFORE YOU GO
Map USGS Durham
Current Conditions
Connecticut Forest and Park
Association (860) 346-2372;
Guilford Land Conservation
Trust (203) 457-9253
Fees None

ABOUT THE HIKE
Day hike
Moderate for children
March–November
2.5 miles round-trip
Elevation gain 400 feet
High point 720 feet
Hiking time 2 hours
Accessibility No special
access

GETTING THERE

- From I-95 in Guilford take exit 58 and travel north on CT 77.
- At the junction of CT 77 and CT 80 in Guilford township, drive
  4.2 miles north on CT 77 to an off-road parking area on the left.

ON THE TRAIL

Don your sturdy hiking boots, pack a pair of binoculars, and head for
Totoket Mountain's Bluff Head on a bright, clear day. Much of this trail
flirts with the edge of the steep cliff, affording dizzying views but creating problems for those with curious, eager little hikers. Due to the initial
steep climb (you will gain about 200 feet within the first 500 feet of trail)
and the nature of the trail, this hike is best suited for preteens who
will appreciate the panoramas
and will exercise caution atop the
numerous outlooks.

*Returning from Bluff Head
(photo by Emily Kerr)*

The blue-blazed Mattabesett
Trail heads west from the parking
area up a very steep, wide trail.
On this initial ascent, the trail
is heavily eroded; loose soil and
shale rocks make for tough going.
Kids will need lots of encouragement. Soon this challenging
terrain gives way to more gradual
climbing on a hard-packed, heavily
wooded trail. As you travel along
the eastern edge of the Totoket
Mountain ridge, you may catch a
glimpse of the vistas across the

valley to your right. Within the first 0.5 mile, you will arrive at an overlook with a fine easterly view across farmlands and forests. Children should be reminded to stay back from the edge of this cliff, which drops straight down for 150 feet. Give your young companions the binoculars so that they can watch the distant cows grazing or farmers haying their faraway fields.

The trail plunges back into the woods, then returns to the edge of the ridge, repeating this pattern several times within the next 0.75 mile. At the second overlook, Myer Huber Pond is visible to your right (northeast). Before you arrive at the final overlook, a short descent into the woods is followed by a sharp ascent that leads to the top of Bluff Head. Near the crest, a dramatic, narrow ravine drops to the base of this cliff. Children will be able to imagine Tarzan sailing across this chasm wrapped around a jungle vine.

At a rock outcropping close to the top of Bluff Head, a footpath curls around the rock's right-hand side. Triple blue blazes indicate, however, that this is not the recommended route because the path travels uncomfortably close to the edge of the cliff. Instead, follow the trail that heads through the middle of the outcropping to the top of Bluff Head. From here, the earth appears to fall away at your feet and you are rewarded with stunning views of the seemingly miniature pond and rural countryside. Though it may seem miles away, the Myer Huber Pond is actually

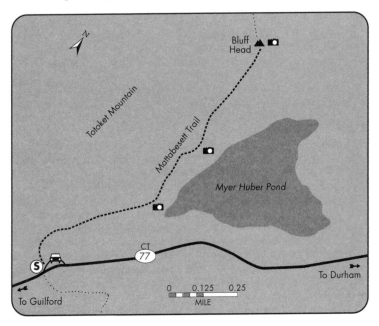

about 500 feet below you. After the kids have rested and enjoyed a snack, return the way you came, exercising caution on the final, steep descent near the parking area.

 CHATFIELD HOLLOW STATE PARK

BEFORE YOU GO
Map USGS Clinton
Current Conditions
Chatfield Hollow State Park, Connecticut Department of Environmental Protection (860) 663-2030
Fees Moderate fee; higher on weekends and holidays

ABOUT THE HIKE
Day hike
Easy for children
May–September
2.5 miles, loop trip
Elevation gain 250 feet
High point 385 feet
Hiking time 2 hours
Accessibility Accessible restrooms, parking, and picnic tables

GETTING THERE

- Take exit 63 off of I-95.
- Travel north 5.1 miles on CT 81 to a rotary that joins CT 80.
- Drive west on CT 80 in Killingworth for 1.2 miles to the Chatfield Hollow State Park entrance on the right.
- Turn here; in 0.2 mile, you will pass the well-marked head of the Look Out Trail on the right.
- Continue on the paved park road to the parking spaces near the Schreeder Pond beach.

ON THE TRAIL

On a warm summer day, the beach and swimming area at Schreeder Pond teem with activity. Parking spots are tough to come by and picnic tables are filled as quickly as they are vacated. But the 18 miles of trails that wind through the surrounding woods are yours alone. Long ago, Native Americans hunted and fished in this valley. The many Native American artifacts that have been found here indicate that the natives slept beneath the rock overhangs and held tribal meetings in the rocky hills. Kids may be lucky enough to see an arrowhead. It's unlikely, though, that they will come across any signs of the witches said to have inhabited the area. Legends tell of the two mischievous witches, "Goody Wee" and "Betty Wee," who lived in the hollow and enjoyed playing nasty tricks on their neighbors.

To begin this loop trip from the beach parking, walk along the park

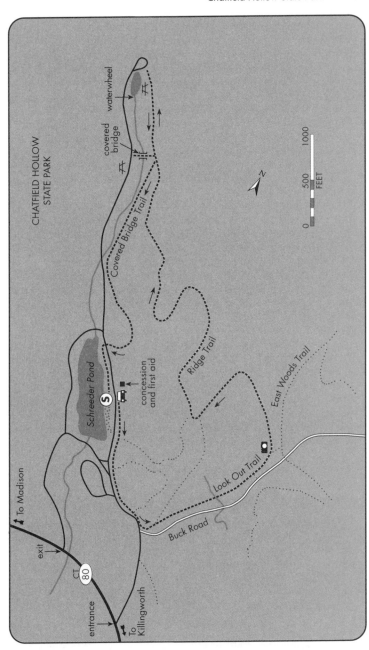

CHATFIELD HOLLOW
STATE PARK

waterwheel

covered
bridge

Covered Bridge Trail

Schreeder Pond

concession
and first aid

Ridge Trail

East Woods Trail

Look Out Trail

Buck Road

To Madison

exit

CT 80

entrance

To Killingworth

N

0   500   1000
FEET

road heading back toward the entrance. In about 0.2 mile, at the junction with Look Out Trail (white), turn left. Within the first 100 yards, the white-blazed trail splits; follow the right-hand branch. The rocky, rugged trail ascends gradually for 0.3 mile, leading hikers over a series of ups and downs; it crosses a stream and runs alongside stone walls and a huge granite outcropping on the left. The children might want to pause and touch the bark on the different kinds of trees: How does the bark on a pine tree feel different from the bark on a birch tree? As you begin to hear the sounds of a stream, a side trail branches off on the right. Ignore the side trail and continue straight to a junction with the blue-blazed East Woods Trail at 0.5 mile. Here, turn left, remaining on the white-blazed Look Out Trail that heads up to the top of a ridge with good local views. Beyond the ridge, the trail descends, curling to the right, then climbs again to the top of another unexposed ridge.

After traversing more rolling terrain and passing a distinctive rock formation on the right, you will arrive at a fork in another 0.3 mile. To the left, the white-blazed Look Out Trail wanders back to the park road. Take the right-hand path and in 50 feet, turn right onto the red-blazed Ridge Trail. This trail, rugged and rough, is similar in character to the Look Out Trail. Take turns choosing categories such as birds, tree stumps, and mushrooms and count how many of each you see along the way. Soon, you will arrive at the top of a rock ridge with 30- to 40-foot drop-offs to the left. Can the kids hear the noisy crowds on Schreeder Pond's beach? Soon they will be able to take a dip, too. The trail bends right into the woods away from the crowds over a series of easy (but tiring) ups and downs. Near the end of the Ridge Trail, be sure to stay on the path marked by red blazes. The path eventually reaches the purple-blazed Covered Bridge Trail; bear right for now and follow the Ridge Trail to its conclusion 1.8 miles from the start of the hike. Here, near a small pond with a waterwheel at its outlet, picnic tables provide a good spot for a lunch break.

Post-hike sunbathing and storytelling at Schreeder Pond (photo by Cynthia Copeland and Thomas J. Lewis)

After your snack, return on the Ridge Trail to the junction with the Covered Bridge Trail. Turn right to admire the covered bridge spanning the river (more picnic tables offer an alternative lunch spot). Return to the Covered Bridge/Ridge Trail intersection and turn right on the Covered Bridge Trail. This trail is reasonably flat, with rock ledges bordering the left side and a river on the right. The trail briefly exits onto the park road, immediately turning hard left back into the woods on an ascent. At the height of this trail, the blazes lead along some 12-foot-high cliffs. Hikers slip through a split boulder and then begin the final descent. The trail drops more steeply as it approaches the park road with well-placed rocks to assist you on your descent. At the outlet to the park road, 2.3 miles from the start of the hike, turn left and follow the road back to your car. You've earned a swim.

 WESTWOODS

BEFORE YOU GO
Map USGS Guilford
Current Conditions Westwoods Trails (State Forest, Guilford Land Conservation Trust, City of Guilford, and private ownership) (203) 457-9253
Fees None

ABOUT THE HIKE
Day hike
Challenging for children
April–November
3.2 miles round-trip
Elevation gain 450 feet
High point 150 feet
Hiking time 4 hours
Accessibility No special access

GETTING THERE

- From New Haven, drive east on I-95 north for 11 miles to exit 57.
- Turn right (southeast) onto US 1 (Boston Post Road) heading toward Guilford.
- In 0.5 mile, turn right onto Peddlers Road. (Trail maps are available at Bishops Orchards, which is on the left-hand side of US 1, just beyond Peddlers Road.)
- Drive 1 mile to a small driveway/parking lot on the left, just past Denison Drive.

ON THE TRAIL

You can't judge a trail by the trailhead. In this case, the innocent-looking path that leads from the parking area quickly becomes a trail that commands hikers to scale steep and rugged granite walls, crawl through stone passageways, and inch across sloping rock faces. The

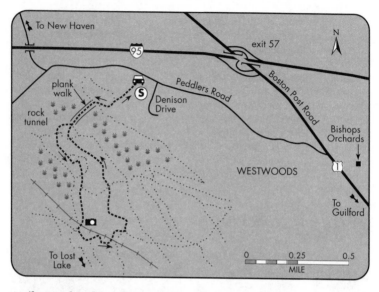

trails wander through the 1200-acre preserve for 40 miles, marked with an intricate blazing system in which shapes as well as colors differentiate the trails. Paths crisscross one another and a trail may come within yards of intersecting a previously traversed section. It's easy to get confused. Preteens who are experienced hikers will handily meet the challenges of Westwoods and brag to school chums about their day spent imitating Indiana Jones. But younger kids and even adults without much experience should opt for something a little easier.

The trail marked with white circles and occasional white rectangles begins as a continuation of the driveway on a paved path. Be sure to differentiate among the various shapes as well as colors of blazes. Soon, the circle trail splits off left while the rectangles continue straight. Follow the circle trail on a descent through a colony of mountain laurel bushes. In June, the prolific pink and white blossoms reveal why the mountain laurel was chosen as Connecticut's state flower. A green trail veers left and soon the white rectangle trail rejoins from the right; at all junctions, follow white circles. The trail crosses a swamp on a narrow, overgrown plank walk for almost 0.1 mile. Children will feel as if they are taking a brief trip through the jungle as they push back the thick vegetation on either side. At the edge of the marsh, a yellow trail veers right, an orange trail heads left, and the white trail continues straight. This time you will follow the yellow circle trail to the right. After quickly ascending a rocky ridge through more mountain laurel bushes, you will notice numerous so-called "crossover" trails splitting from the yellow circle trail. Watch carefully for the yellow circle blazes that will mark most of your route. Just beyond one of the many crossover trail intersections at the 0.6-mile mark, the trail curls to the left and plunges through a 40-foot-long rock tunnel. Near the passageway's narrow end, only crawling and squeezing will return you to daylight. (The kids may insist on a repeat of the tunnel!) Once outside the passageway, the trail turns right, following below the granite mass that houses the lengthy cave.

In the next 0.5 mile, the trail snakes over and under 30- to 50-foot rock cliffs and, again, more side trails split off to the left and right. The tremendous rock outcroppings that appear on your left at first will inch closer and closer until soon you will be climbing through a narrow ridge traversing those very rocks. After making your way across the rock face, follow the trail as it switches back right and climbs to the top of the cliff. Again the trail drops to the bottom of the cliffs and rises to

Right out of The Jungle Book— *overgrown boardwalk in Westwoods (photo by Cynthia Copeland and Thomas J. Lewis)*

another crest. Children (and their parents) will not have time to worry about blisters because this trail presents challenge after thrilling challenge from start to finish. Soon, you will pass an area where ice has exerted its force and created fissures in the rock. (A left-hand turn onto a green blazed trail at approximately 1 mile will bring you to an intersection with a white-blazed trail 0.15 mile later. Turn left again and in 0.5 mile you will be back at the swamp crossing. Continue to the parking area for a 2-mile total hike.)

If you opt to continue, you will ascend another series of ridges just beyond the intersection with the green-blazed trail. At one point, you will be forced to scoot across a sloping cliff on your bottom because a rock overhang makes standing impossible. As the trail winds through forest dominated by hemlocks, kids will get a kick out of the frequent squeezes through rock passageways. After approximately 1.3 miles, you will arrive atop a rock dome with pretty, southerly views of an adjoining ridge. Utility wires stretch across the valley below. Continue to follow the yellow circle blazes that lead hikers along the edge of the dome. Double switchbacks along a narrow path trimmed in mountain laurel lead you down the side of the dome facing the powerlines. To your left, the ridge drops precipitously. At the bottom of this ridge, the trail emerges left on an overgrown path that crosses under the utility lines. Just beyond the power lines, the yellow-blazed trail branches off to the right on a muddy path and continues to Lost Lake. At this intersection (where the blazing may be indistinct), you turn left on a blue-blazed jeep trail. The next intersection is marked with numerous blazes; bear left here, still on a jeep trail, and cross back under the powerlines. At the next intersection, stay straight on blue blazes. Within 100 feet, the blue- and white-blazed trails split. Bear left toward the white circular blazes and follow them for the remainder of the hike. After a series of additional climbs over rugged terrain (at times, children will need guidance), the trail levels off. Head straight through an intersection with the green-blazed trail. As you cross a patch of exposed granite, you will begin to hear sounds from the highway. At 2.75 miles from the start, you will cross back over the wetlands along the plank walk and soon reach the parking area and your car.

 GILLETTE CASTLE STATE PARK

BEFORE YOU GO
Map USGS Deep River
Current Conditions Gillette Castle State Park, Connecticut Department of Environmental Protection (860) 526-2336
Fees None for parking; moderate fee for castle tours

ABOUT THE HIKE
Day hike
Easy for children
May–December
1.3 miles round-trip
Elevation gain 220 feet
High point 185 feet
Hiking time 1 hour
Accessibility Accessible restrooms, parking, picnic tables, and castle first floor

GETTING THERE
- At the junction of CT 148 and CT 82 near the village of Hadlyme (in Lyme), travel west on CT 148 for 1.6 miles.
- Turn right onto River Road (unmarked, just east of the Connecticut River).
- Travel 0.7 mile on River Road to the park entrance on the left; turn left.
- Go to the end of the park road and leave your car in the parking lot.

ON THE TRAIL

If your children thrill to stories of Cinderella or Sleeping Beauty, they will be enchanted by the storybook quality of Gillette Castle and the riverside grounds. The ivy-covered castle perches atop the seventh of the Seven Sisters hills that border the Connecticut River. William Gillette, a Connecticut native and well-known stage actor at the end of the 1800s, designed every detail of his 24-room dream house. Gillette was also fascinated by trains, and he constructed a railroad that left a depot at the castle's front door and meandered through the forest to the eastern end of the property. Gillette was understandably concerned about the future of this magnificent estate and in his will he ordered his heirs to "see to it that the property did not fall into the hands of some blithering saphead" who wouldn't recognize its value. Certainly all who visit today appreciate Gillette's efforts and vision. Some folks like to come in

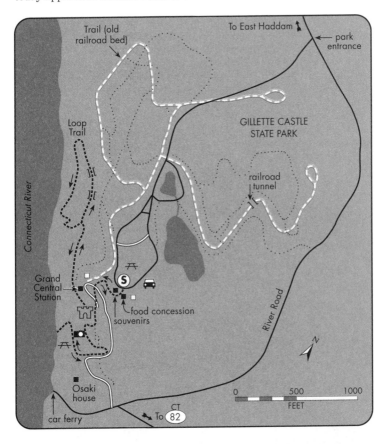

September and October, when the surrounding hills blush with autumn color. Others make it a tradition to visit during the winter holidays when the castle rooms are gaily decorated. Encourage grandparents to take the children on this hike. It's perfect for both the oldest and youngest members of the family.

To begin the hike, stroll up the paved path to the castle, passing the manicured lawns decorated with fountains and statues. From the impeccably detailed stone patio overlooking the Connecticut River, head right (northwest) to Grand Central Station, the main terminal for the now-dismantled Seventh Sister Shortline. This open-sided, stone veranda is one of the loveliest picnic spots you'll ever find. Below the station on the riverside, a sign for the Loop Trail and river vistas indicates a 0.5-mile route. Head northwesterly along this Loop Trail, counterclockwise and away from the crowded castle lawn. Magnificent footbridges and stone turrets punctuate the worn path that descends gently to a plateau near the riverbank. At the far reaches of this trail, near the water, the path switches back along a rocky ledge. Here, the bordering fence is missing, so take the children's hands. The path never dips right to the water's edge because the state's Department of Environmental Protection has decided to protect this delicate area from further erosion. Instead, the trail climbs back through an evergreen forest to the head of the loop trail and the castle.

From the castle patio (facing the river), head left down a flight of stairs and walk into the woods on a footpath. The trail wanders through the forest to a point of land on a ledge (bordered with a fence)

high above the river. Enjoy stunning water views from the overlook and then follow the trail to the left. In 0.1 mile, the path joins a gravel road; turn right. In another 0.1 mile, turn right onto a wide path that departs the road, descending along the edge of the ridge to the Connecticut River. Relax on the grass near a small beach where visitors picnic and others have set up camp. The kids can wade and watch the boats. Reverse direction to return to the castle. You may decide to explore some of the other paths

*The Gillette Castle grounds
(photo by Cynthia Copeland
and Thomas J. Lewis)*

or, for a small admission price, you can peek at the inside of the castle before returning to your car.

Notes: Park hours are daily, 8:00 AM to sunset. The castle is open Memorial Day through Columbus Day, 10:00 AM to 4:30 PM.

BUILDING THE CASTLE

It took twenty men five years just to build the main structure of the castle. It is made of steel and local fieldstone, and not one of the forty-seven doors of the castle is exactly like any other.

 DEVILS HOPYARD STATE PARK

BEFORE YOU GO
Map USGS Hamburg
Current Conditions Devils Hopyard State Park, Connecticut Department of Environmental Protection (860) 873-8566
Fees None

ABOUT THE HIKE
Day hike or overnight
Moderate for children
Year-round
2.6 miles, loop trip
Elevation gain 380 feet
High point 480 feet
Hiking time 2 hours
Accessibility Accessible parking and picnic tables

GETTING THERE
- From I-395 in Waterford township take exit 77 onto CT 85 north.
- In 7.5 miles, turn left onto CT 82 West. (A sign points the way to Devils Hopyard and Gillette Castle.)
- Drive 4.7 miles on CT 82 to Hopyard Road; turn right.
- In 3.0 miles, enter the parking area on your right.

ON THE TRAIL
Ask a dozen locals how this park got its name and you'll hear a dozen different tales. One legend claims that the numerous potholes at the base of Chapman Falls were created when the devil hopped with his hot hooves from one ledge to another, trying not to get wet. (Actually, the potholes are created as stones moving downstream become trapped in an eddy and spin around until a crater forms in the rock.) A less intriguing story claims that a farmer named Dibble grew hops in the area, and Dibble's Hopyard eventually came to be called Devils Hopyard. No

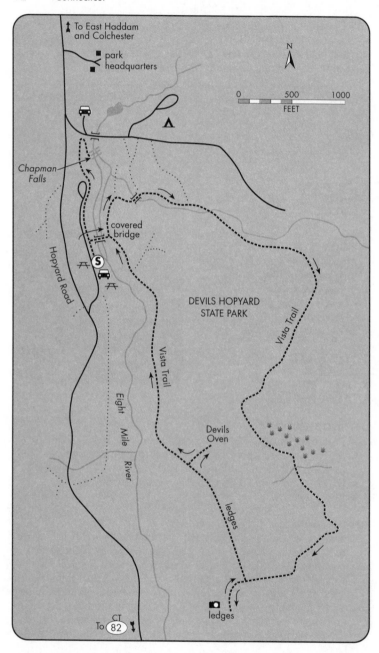

To East Haddam
and Colchester

park
headquarters

N

0   500   1000
FEET

Chapman
Falls

Hopyard Road

covered
bridge

S

DEVILS HOPYARD
STATE PARK

Vista Trail

Vista Trail

Eight Mile River

Devils
Oven

ledges

ledges

To CT 82

matter how the name originated, the 860-acre Devils Hopyard State Park draws a multitude of visitors each summer who come to enjoy the pleasant picnic areas along the bank of the Eight Mile River and the 15 miles of hiking trails. Chapman Falls, at the northern end of the park, seems to attract the most attention from visitors. Here, the Eight Mile River crashes 60 feet over the rock escarpment to the calm pool below. A camping area on an access road north of the falls provides overnighters with a choice of more than twenty open and wooded sites.

The hike begins at the covered bridge spanning Eight Mile River. Cross over the river and turn left, following the orange rectangular–blazed Vista Trail. Bear right at the first trail intersection. At triple orange blazes, after a stream crossing over a covered footbridge, turn right, following a "To Vista" sign. This rugged, root-crossed trail initially climbs along a meager tributary to Eight Mile River, going straight (east) as side trails split left. Cross the stream at 0.25 mile on a jumble of rocks (in the spring, wet feet are guaranteed). At an intersection with a white-blazed trail, continue straight, still ascending moderately along orange blazes. The path departs the stream and descends through a stand of hemlocks, entering another wet area on rolling terrain. The kids will have to pick their way across several more streams before reaching an intersection at 1.3 miles where the orange trail goes right. Follow the side trail (left), marked with an occasional orange blaze, which ends at an overlook. Here, hikers are treated to magnificent views to the south of the bucolic Eight Mile River valley.

Follow this short side trail as it drops to the exposed ledges—a great spot for a snack. Because the ledges descend in a series of tiers before

A young hiker goes along for the ride. (Photo by Emily Kerr)

the final steep drop-off, parents can relax and concentrate on the vistas with the children on the upper ledges. Return to the intersection, turning left onto the orange-blazed trail to continue the loop. The path drops moderately beside overhanging rock ledges on the right, then swings closer to the Eight Mile River. At 1.7 miles, a large yellow arrow points to the right. Follow this side trail up a short, steep ascent to a rock outcropping that harbors a small cave called the Devils Oven.

After the kids have had a chance to explore, pick your way back down the slope to the main trail and turn right as the path continues to follow the river upstream. As the trail flirts with the river's edge, it becomes more rugged with lots of stumbling potential for tired little legs. After a final brief but steep uphill climb, the trail drops along a wide gravel road. In another 0.3 mile, the blue-blazed loop trail joins from the right and in 0.1 mile you return to the covered bridge for a 2.2-mile total.

With your car in sight, it might be tempting to head toward the parking lot but instead turn right after you cross the bridge en route to Chapman Falls. (It's worth it—we promise.) Follow the paved park road past the parking spaces to a wide gravel path that soon arrives at the falls. Admire the waterfall from above and then drop to the bottom on a side trail where smooth rocks near the pool provide a great place to do some deep thinking. Best of all, the sound of the cascading water is guaranteed to drown out whining. When you're sufficiently relaxed, return to your car.

ROCKY NECK STATE PARK

BEFORE YOU GO
Map USGS Old Lyme
Current Conditions Rocky Neck State Park, Connecticut Department of Environmental Protection (860) 739-5471
Fees Moderate fee; higher on weekends and holidays

ABOUT THE HIKE
Day hike or overnight
Easy for children
Year-round
3.5 miles, loop trip
Elevation gain 100 feet
High point 50 feet
Hiking time 2.5 hours
Accessibility Accessible parking, restrooms, and picnic area

GETTING THERE
▪ From the Connecticut Turnpike (I-95) in East Lyme, take exit 72, following the signs to Rocky Neck State Park.

- Drive south for 0.5 mile to the junction with CT 156.
- Though the Rocky Neck signs indicate a left-hand turn, go right instead onto CT 156.
- In 0.6 mile, park on the right just before the bridge over the Four Mile River and the East Lyme/Old Lyme town line.

ON THE TRAIL

In the heat of a summer day, hiking the tame Four Mile River Trail to the beach can be a great way to combine hiking with swimming, wading, or sunbathing. Even in cooler weather, Rocky Neck's seashore can be enjoyed for the distinct pleasures it offers your senses. In the spring, watch at the estuary as the fresh water from Four Mile River rushes to meet the salty ocean water of Long Island Sound. Look at the cranes and herons wandering among the cattails in autumn. See the fishermen reeling in striped bass, flounder, or mackerel in the early dawn or dusk.

In winter, smell the sharp, salty breeze. But do be careful—this is the area where Lyme disease got its name. Be sure to follow the appropriate recommendations detailed in the Introduction. Campsites at Rocky Neck are within walking distance of the beach at the eastern edge of the park.

The trail, indicated by stakes painted blue, starts on the eastern side of Four Mile River. Follow the blue-blazed Four Mile River Trail along a wide, grassy path through an open field and into the woods up a small hill. When the red trail bears left, stay to the right on a path that will eventually take you to the pavilion. At 0.8 mile, bear right on a yellow side trail to an overlook called Tonys Nose. Here, rocky ledges rise 40 feet above the river and offer excellent views over the tidal flat. Return to the main trail, bearing right at all intersections, and soon merge with a paved road. Bear right beyond a small parking area. The road

Looking over the tidal flat from Tonys Nose (photo by Cynthia Copeland and Thomas J. Lewis)

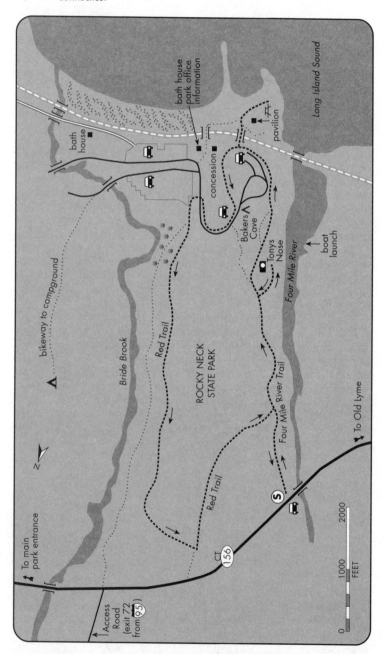

Long Island Sound

bath house
park office
information

bath house

concession

pavilion

Bakers Cave

Tonys Nose

boat launch

Four Mile River

bikeway to campground

Bride Brook

Red Trail

Red Trail

ROCKY NECK
STATE PARK

Four Mile River Trail

S

To Old Lyme

CT 156

To main
park entrance

Access Road
(exit 72
from 95)

N

0   1000   2000
FEET

travels over railroad tracks by way of an arched bridge and emerges onto the pavilion grounds 1 mile from the start. Ask kids to compare the man-made railroad bed with Mother Nature's sand dunes. What do they have in common? (Both serve to protect the inland areas from the storms and fierce winds blowing in off the ocean.) As you face the lovely ocean views, a crowded beach is to your left; to the right is a private, wooded area overlooking Rocky Neck, a perfect picnic spot. Stop here if you are not planning to relax at the public beach.

To continue your hike, head back across the bridge and bear right on a gravel road marked in blue and white. Head left through a grassy parking area and then turn right on the paved park road. The kids can try to find Bakers Cave, a rock overhang on the left-hand side of the road. The cave was named for a man who hid there during the Revolutionary War to avoid serving in the army. His family brought him food and supplies at night; he was never discovered. Follow the park road to a large parking lot where a footpath marked in red plunges back into the woods on the left, approximately 150 feet from the road. When the path divides in 0.1 mile, stay on the Red Trail that skirts a marsh frequented by nesting osprey. After another mile of pleasant woods walking, turn left (south) at a trail junction to stay on the Red Trail and in 0.4 mile turn right (north) onto the blue-blazed Four Mile River Trail. In 0.3 mile, you will arrive at your car.

  BLUFF POINT STATE PARK AND COASTAL RESERVE

BEFORE YOU GO
Map USGS New London
Current Conditions Bluff Point State Park, Connecticut Department of Environmental Protection (860) 444-7591
Fees None

ABOUT THE HIKE
Day hike
Moderate for children
Year-round
6 miles, loop trip (including sand spit)
Elevation gain 140 feet
High point 100 feet
Hiking time 4.5 hours
Accessibility Accessible parking; woods path is rough, but wide and graveled

GETTING THERE
- From I-95 in Groton, take exit 88 to turn right (south) on CT 117 ("Groton, Long Point").
- After 1 mile, turn right (west) at a T intersection with US 1 (US 1 not indicated).

- Drive 0.3 mile to the first traffic light (the Groton Town Hall is on the left).
- Turn left here onto Depot Road and drive 0.4 mile.
- Bear right under a railroad bridge where the paved road gives way to gravel.
- In another 0.3 mile, you will arrive at a parking area for visitors to Bluff Point.

ON THE TRAIL

It's hard to find a stretch of Connecticut seashore that is not overrun with condominiums, dockside boutiques, or waterfront industry. But a 780-acre tract of land known as Bluff Point offers a refuge from the crowded consequences of overdevelopment. Here, the kids can scale lofty bluffs, hike through delightful oceanside forests, and run along a sand spit that stretches half a mile into the bay. They can watch scaups, or diving ducks, plunge for crabs or barnacles as they scan the water for swans or mallards. At hike's end, weary walkers can take a dip at the small stretch of beach set aside for swimmers. For an afternoon, the kids can enjoy the ocean the way their great-grandparents did.

Walk along the gravel road, passing through the barricade for motor vehicles. For the first 0.4 mile or so, the road follows the shoreline—you might decide to wander along the sandy beach instead of sticking to the path. On the shore, you will encounter a few sunbathers and clam diggers if the weather is warm. The kids may want to pause and get an up-close look at clamming. At approximately the 0.6-mile mark, the road breaks left from the beach and travels over a wooded knoll. Ocean scents and distant sights remind everyone that this is no ordinary woods walk. At approximately 0.9 mile, on the down side of a brief grade, are rustic rest facilities. Beyond this point, the road drops and then crests another bluff where a walking path veers right and runs along a rocky ridge overlooking Long Island Sound. This is the hike's most scenic spot and the best place for a picnic or merely a rest. Kids can count sailboats while the bigger folks scan the skies for terns and tree swallows. Drop to the shore and follow it to the sand spit that reaches into the bay. (Eliminating the sand spit section of the hike will make the total mileage 3.7 miles.) Along the center of the spit, dunes sculpted by the wind and waves shelter nesting sandpipers.

After exploring this narrow strip of sand and beach grass, return to the main trail, bearing right at trail junctions to remain close to the boulder beach. At the point's easternmost tip, a massive boulder guards the beach, worn on its seaward side from the relentless pounding of the waves. The coastal path eventually leads hikers back to the main road. If you ventured to the far reaches of the sand spit, you have walked 4.5 miles to this point. You will follow this park road in a northerly direction for another 1.4 miles, traveling through a surprisingly dense forest

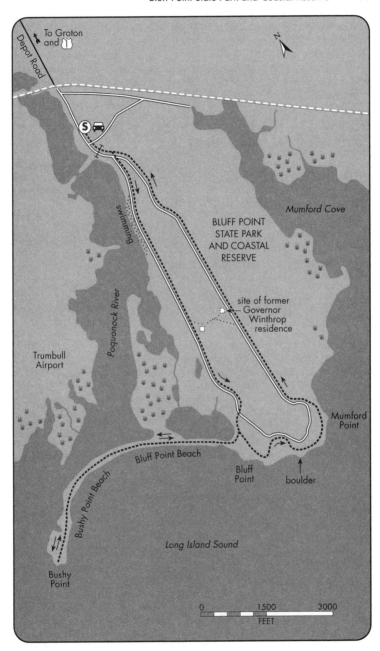

To Groton
and (1)

Depot Road

N

BLUFF POINT
STATE PARK
AND COASTAL
RESERVE

Mumford Cove

swimming

Poquonock River

site of former
Governor
Winthrop
residence

Trumbull
Airport

Mumford
Point

Bluff Point Beach

Bluff
Point

boulder

Bushy Point Beach

Long Island Sound

Bushy
Point

0   1500   3000
FEET

that is home to a large number of white-tailed deer. Challenge the kids to find evidence of these majestic animals that frequently gather at the forest's edge. Look for twigs and buds that have been chewed off and trunks that have been stripped of bark. Shortly before you arrive at the parking area, you join the original gravel road. Let the children take a plunge into the water before you begin the trip home.

THE DENISON PEQUOTSEPOS NATURE CENTER

BEFORE YOU GO
Map USGS Old Mystic
Current Conditions Denison Pequotsepos Nature Center, Avalonia Land Conservancy (860) 536-1216
Fees Nonmembers, moderate fee; members, free

ABOUT THE HIKE
Day hike
Easy for children
Year-round
2.9 miles, loop trip
Elevation gain 70 feet
High point 50 feet
Hiking time 2 hours
Accessibility Forest Loop jogging-stroller friendly

GETTING THERE
- From I-95 take exit 90 and follow signs for CT 27 north.
- Drive 0.5 mile on CT 27, to turn right onto Jerry Browne Road.
- Drive one mile and turn right on Pequotsepos Road.
- The Denison Pequotsepos Nature Center will be on your left in 0.5 mile.

ON THE TRAIL
You barely have to do more than step foot into the nature center building to make this a worthy outing. In fact, you may have a hard time convincing the kids to step foot outside once they get a look at the exciting exhibits inside. From the two-story giant red maple filled with wildlife of the Woodland Exhibit to the live crayfish, frogs, and turtles of the Wetland Exhibit and the butterflies and insects of the Meadow Exhibit, there is plenty to keep you and the kids enthralled and busy. After taking it all in, remind the kids that this is just a reflection of what they'll experience on the trails in the 250-acre sanctuary. Exit the lower level doors of the nature center by the sign directing you to the trails.

Once the kids spot the pond in front of them, they will forget all about not wanting to leave the displays. Walk—don't run if you can help it—to the well-established trail encircling the pond. As you make the roughly 0.1 mile circumference, look for ducks and geese in the water.

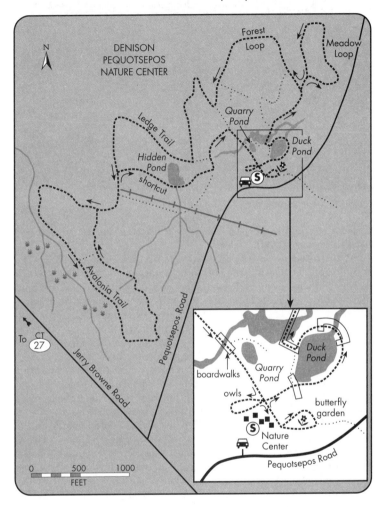

On the southeast side of the pond, you will find a boardwalk and a sign leading you onto the red-blazed Forest Loop. Head across the boardwalk to the right, following the red blazes. Past the boardwalk on your left, you will encounter large boulders, tempting for the kids to climb. In 0.1 mile, turn right onto the blue Meadow Loop. This 0.3-mile loop will take you through a meadow filled with bird boxes and an early successional forest of red cedar, highbush blueberry, and red maple. Follow the trail around back to its junction with the red Forest Loop, and turn right. The half-mile-long Forest Loop leads you past rock walls and over streams

Crossing a boardwalk (photo by Emily Kerr)

through oak and hickory in a southerly direction before turning and heading back toward the north.

At the intersection with the Ledge Trail, turn right and follow the white blazes. This rocky trail will take you along ledges, where you will be treated to overlooks of the wetland below. Look for wild turkeys wandering about on the ledges. After 0.2 mile you will come to a junction where the Ledge Trail heads in two different directions. Turn right. You will soon come to Hidden Pond, a large vernal pool, on your left. Have the kids investigate for signs of life. Continue past Hidden Pond, and head north (left) on the Ledge Trail as it takes a sharp turn.

Approximately 0.3 mile from Hidden Pond, you will reach the junction with the orange Avalonia Trail—part of the Avalonia Land Conservancy—right by the powerlines. At the loop junction in 0.1 mile, bear right, following the orange squares. The trail will take you above a seasonal brook and wetlands with a good view of the rock outcroppings on the other side before dropping you down where you can get a closer look at the plant life below. The trail heads northwest for approximately half a mile through rock walls, swampy areas, and beech groves, before turning around and heading southeast another 0.3 mile back to the loop junction, where you will bear right back to the power lines. (You can eliminate the Avalonia Trail for a shorter hike.)

For a prettier return trip, continue past the trail by the power lines to turn right on a trail marked "Shortcut." This route takes you over a boardwalk on the other (northern) side of Hidden Pond. After passing Hidden Pond, head right at a junction to turn back onto the Ledge Trail, following the sign to the nature center. At the junction with the red-blazed Forest Loop, turn right and pass Quarry Pond on your left. Are there any turtles basking in the sun? At the end of the red trail, turn right and head over to see the owls and possibly a peregrine falcon. Then head to the west side of the nature center to investigate the butterfly garden.

26 ROCK SPRING PRESERVE

BEFORE YOU GO
Map USGS Scotland
Current Conditions The Nature Conservancy (860) 344-0716
Fees None

ABOUT THE HIKE
Day hike
Easy for children
April–November
3.3 miles, loop trip
Elevation gain 310 feet
High point 500 feet
Hiking time 2.25 hours
Accessibility No special access

GETTING THERE
- From I-395 in the township of Plainfield, take exit 89.
- Drive west on CT 14 approximately 10 miles to Pudding Hill Road (CT 97), 0.7 mile past the Scotland town line.
- Travel 1.5 miles north on CT 97 to the preserve on the right-hand side of the street, marked with a 12-foot-high wooden sign (somewhat camouflaged).
- Park off the road near the trailhead.

ON THE TRAIL
Pile the kids in the car, pick up the grandparents on the way, and head to the 450-acre Rock Spring Preserve in Scotland for a hike all members of the family will enjoy. Along the smooth trail with gentle ups and downs, younger children can run ahead without parents worrying about them tripping over rocks or roots. As the trail cuts through a pine plantation, kids will be amazed at the giant trees lined up like soldiers along each side of the trail. The long stretch along river's edge offers abundant examples of busy beavers at work. And just beyond the river, a side trail takes hikers to an outlook with outstanding views of Little River Valley. Best of all—some locals don't even know about this one, so chances are you'll have the place all to yourselves!

Follow the white-blazed trail east, straight into the woods. (This trail is frequented by horseback riders; watch out for manure.) At the display board just 75 feet from the road, sign in and pick up a trail map if one is available. As you continue on the well-worn path through the woods, note the numerous flat stone walls that crisscross the property, indicating that this was once agricultural land. At 0.2 mile, double switchbacks take you to a short, rather steep descent. In the winter, the woods feel spacious and open because oak and maples abound and they have lost their leaves, letting in plenty of sunlight; there are very few evergreens here.

At 0.4 mile, signs at a trail junction offer several options; you should

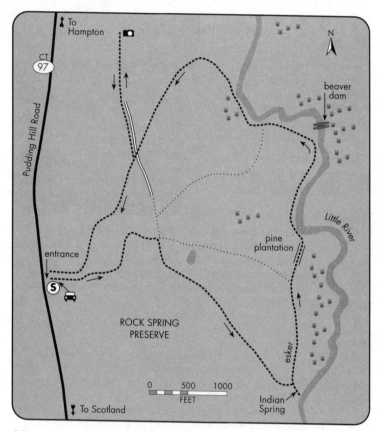

follow the sign for the spring, heading right (south). Passing some distance from a small pond and through overgrown meadows and a pine thicket, you will reach a sign for Indian Spring at about the 1-mile mark. The spring, said to have been used by Native Americans years ago as a water source, lies just 10 yards beyond the sign. Although it is hidden by a stone and cement structure built to maintain the water's purity, you may be able to see the water bubbling up from the ground just downstream. Evidence of long-ago Native American inhabitants includes an ancient burial grounds on the refuge property.

Backtrack 20 yards and veer right (north)—looking for white blazes—and head immediately up the slope of an esker, a geological feature created when the glacial ice melted. You will notice that the esker supports very little vegetation due to the poor quality of the soil. Travel the top of the esker for about 0.1 mile and turn right (northeast) at a trail junction on the downslope of the esker at 1.25 miles. (Do not follow the trail back to the entrance as indicated by the sign.) Less than 0.1 mile later, as you walk for several hundred yards between the perfect rows of towering pine trees, children will no doubt be tempted to stray off the straight path to wind among the trees. Double blazes indicate a left-hand turn as you march past the final pine soldier. While you travel along the river's edge for about 1 mile, point out to the children the tremendous examples of beaver activity. Challenge your children to find the large oak trees that have been killed by the beavers. (Beavers don't eat the oaks but they have already consumed their favorite trees and need to wear down their teeth. Suggest that the children look up to locate the

Marching through the pine plantation at Rock Spring Preserve
(photo by Cynthia Copeland and Thomas J. Lewis)

trees that are without leaves and obviously dead, then look down at the tree's base to find the girdle of teeth marks.) In some areas where the river bank is accessible and sandy, children can scamper to the water's edge and look for rainbow and brook trout in the clear water. They may even spot a snapping turtle. About 0.5 mile into the river walk, the trail skirts up a ridge with a sharp, 30-foot drop-off to the water's edge. Beyond this crest, continue to follow the white blazes, avoiding a number of side trails and crossing over tributaries and swampy areas on sturdy bridges.

The trail finally turns away from the water, heads up a moderated grade through pines, and then meanders gradually back toward the entrance through terrain similar to that on the early part of the walk. Deer tracks and droppings, evidence of the large deer population within the refuge, are abundant along the trails. A path marked in yellow and white joins the white-blazed trail at a woods road 2.3 miles from the start; turn right (north) to reach an overlook in 0.3 mile. Here, an elaborate stone bench allows hikers to rest while they take in the expansive view of Little River Valley. (Picnicking is prohibited.) Return to the white-blazed trail that turns right off the woods road and leads back to the entrance and your car in another 0.4 mile.

 ## EDWIN WAY TEALE MEMORIAL SANCTUARY AT TRAIL WOOD

BEFORE YOU GO
Map USGS Hampton
Current Conditions Connecticut Audubon Center at Trail Wood (860) 928-4948
Fees None

ABOUT THE HIKE
Day hike
Easy for children
March–October
1.4 miles, loop trip
Elevation gain 150 feet
High point 640 feet
Hiking time 1.5 hours
Accessibility No special access

GETTING THERE
- From US 44, turn south on CT 97 at Abington in Pomfret and follow this for 5.2 miles.
- Turn right onto Kenyon Road.
- In 0.5 mile look for the sign and driveway for Trail Wood on your left.

ON THE TRAIL
Nestled in Connecticut's Quiet Corner, The Edwin Way Teale Memorial Sanctuary at Trail Wood is an absolute gem. This gorgeous 168-acre sanctuary is the former home of naturalist and Pulitzer Prize–winning

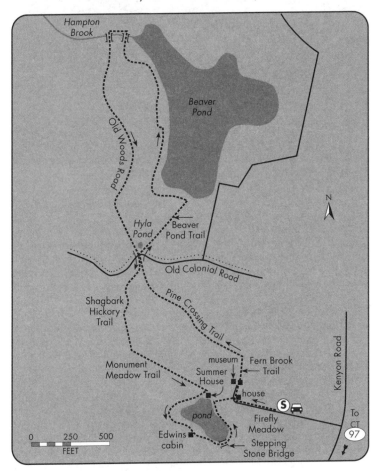

author Edwin Way Teale and his wife. The property was deeded to the Connecticut Audubon Society in 1981, following Edwin's death. Visitors to the sanctuary can see Edwin's study and writing cabin (open by appointment), as well as explore the many trails teeming with wildlife through woods and meadows and alongside ponds and streams.

From the parking area, walk up the drive and past the residence on your right. Behind the house you will find a small museum that houses information on the flora and fauna you will encounter on your hike, as well as some games for children. Here you can borrow a numbered guide to the trails. Head through the pastures and fields on the Fern Brook Trail, bearing left at your first junction onto the Pine Crossing

Searching for creatures in Beaver Pond (photo by Emily Kerr)

Trail. Follow this trail roughly 0.3 mile to a major trail junction, keeping your eyes open for Lost Spring on your left.

At the intersection, follow the signs to the Beaver Pond Trail, stopping at the large vernal pool Hyla Pond. How much water is in the pool? Can the kids spot any signs of life? After crossing through a stone wall, you will arrive on the shore of Beaver Pond where kids will definitely want to do some investigating. Can they believe that when Edwin first moved to Trail Wood in 1959, the beaver pond wasn't there? The trail continues along the perimeter of Beaver Pond and in 0.4 mile crosses over Hampton Brook. Immediately after crossing, turn left, walk a short distance, and turn left again onto Old Woods Road Trail, again crossing Hampton Brook. This is a great spot to find frogs, and the kids will have fun counting how many sets of eyes they see poking out of the water.

Old Woods Road travels through an oak and maple forest lush with ferns. Along this trail grow twenty-one of the twenty-six kinds of ferns Edwin Teale found at Trail Wood. How many different kinds can your young naturalists find? After following this trail a little over 0.3 mile, you will arrive back at the major trail intersection. Do not turn right onto Old Colonial Road, but instead bear slightly right onto the Shagbark Hickory Trail. Right past Fern Brook, the Monument Meadow Trail heads off to the left. Turn onto this trail. After paralleling a stone wall for a little less than 0.2 mile, you will arrive at the Summer House, where you can relax and take in the views of the pond below. Don't rest too long, though—there are fish to see in the pond!

When the kids tire of looking for fish, follow the trail around the pond to the right. On the opposite shore you will pass by Edwin's cabin. Beyond this, cross Stepping Stone Bridge and head toward Firefly Meadow. Do you see any of the winged creatures that give the meadow its name? You can follow the trail up through the meadow to the start of the hike or continue around the pond to a right turn on Veery Lane just short of the Summer House. Return any materials you borrowed from the museum and head back down the driveway to your car.

MASHAMOQUET BROOK STATE PARK

BEFORE YOU GO
Map USGS Danielson
Current Conditions
Mashamoquet Brook State Park, Connecticut Department of Environmental Protection (860) 928-6121
Fees None for trails; moderate fee for campsites

ABOUT THE HIKE
Day hike or overnight
Moderate for children
April–November
4 miles, loop trip
Elevation gain 290 feet
High point 520 feet
Hiking time 3 hours
Accessibility No special access

GETTING THERE
- Travel to the junction of US 44 and CT 101 in Pomfret.
- On CT 101, just 200 yards east of the junction, take Wolf Den Drive 0.7 mile.
- Turn left into the Mashamoquet overflow parking area and leave your car here.

ON THE TRAIL
This walk offers two special things for kids to look forward to: the stone Indian Chair perched on a ledge overlook and the famous Putnam Wolf Den, a cave that extends back into the rocky hillside as far as you can see. Sadly, as the story goes, the state's last wolf was shot here in the winter of 1742. After he thought that a wolf killed and injured a number of his sheep, Israel Putnam (later a Revolutionary War hero) set off in search of the wolf's lair. Several days and 35 miles later, he and a group of nearby farmers followed the wolf tracks to the now-famous den. When the first two plans—smoking the wolf out and sending in the dogs—failed, Putnam squeezed through the long, dark tunnel himself with a torch and musket. He shot the animal on his second attempt, and on his third effort, hauled the dead wolf out of the cave

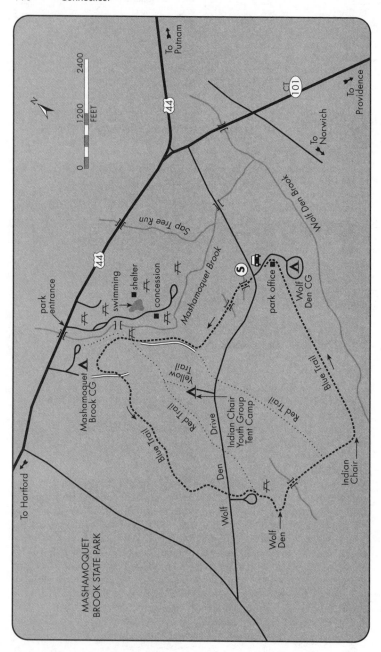

MASHAMOQUET BROOK STATE PARK

to the cheers of his astounded neighbors. Thankfully today, parks help serve the purpose of protecting native plants and animals. The park offers camping at the Wolf Den and Mashamoquet Brook Campgrounds and swimming at the bypass pool less than one-half mile from the park entrance off US 44.

To begin the hike, cross Wolf Den Drive to a well-maintained, blue-blazed trail, walking through a stone wall past a rock marked "Mashamoquet." Double blazes provide clear indications of sudden changes in trail direction. In 0.1 mile, cross a footbridge over a small stream; at 0.2 mile, cross a larger stream. (The name "Mashamoquet" is a Native American word meaning "stream of good fishing.") You will travel alongside and cut through numerous stone walls in the first 0.5 mile. At the 0.6-mile mark, turn right; the trail, a woods road, is now marked with red and blue blazes. One tenth of a mile later, the trail begins a lengthy stretch with a considerable drop-off to the right. The Red Trail turns left at 1.0 mile; you follow the blue-blazed trail that continues straight. This path meanders over streams and up a gradual hill over the next 0.4 mile. At 1.3 miles, double blazes indicate a left turn onto a wooded road; shortly thereafter turn right back onto a wooded path. Climb a gradual hill, then skirt the edge of a field at 1.5 miles.

The trail merges onto Wolf Den Drive at a little over 2 miles; head right across the road (keeping an eye on little children, there is vehicular traffic here) to the entrance marked "Wolf Den Entrance," carved in stone. Follow the parking area road 0.1 mile, still marked by blue blazes, where a sign carved in a granite boulder indicates that the trail curls back into the woods. These chiseled signs are frequent along this section of trail. The Red Trail soon joins the blue; follow a rocky descent for 0.15 mile. Timbers and stone steps make it easily negotiable for younger children. Look for the Wolf Den penetrating the hillside on the right side of the trail. How far inside the very dark and very narrow cave will the kids venture? Be sure to repeat the Wolf Den tale at the cave site so that they will fully appreciate Mr. Putnam's and the last wolf's story.

As the red- and blue-blazed trail continues on a substantial descent, turn around to see more caves dotting the rocky hill. Again, a sturdy footbridge facilitates a wide stream crossing. At 2.8 miles, the Red Trail splits off to the left; you should remain on the Blue Trail. Look for more caves and overhangs. The Indian Chair perches on the edge of a steep cliff at the 3.0-mile mark, just off the trail. Kids can climb on the chair (it makes a great photo!) but should be warned to stay well back from cliff's edge. Return to the trail and continue descending before traversing an area of rocky ups and downs. Pay close attention to blazes on this section as the trail makes some turns. At the 3.8-mile mark, you may hear sounds of campers in the campground, letting you know you are close to the end. Pass through a stone wall and onto a grassy path down to the park office to complete the hike.

RHODODENDRON SANCTUARY AND MOUNT MISERY

BEFORE YOU GO
Maps USGS Voluntown, Jewett City
Current Conditions
Pachaug State Forest, Connecticut Department of Environmental Protection (860) 376-4075
Fees None for trails; moderate fee for campsites

ABOUT THE HIKE
Day hike or overnight
Easy for children
March–October
1.9 miles round-trip
Elevation gain 190 feet
High point 441 feet
Hiking time 1 hour
Accessibility Rhododendron Trail is accessible

GETTING THERE
- Take exit 85 off I-395 in New London.
- Follow CT 138 East for 9 miles to turn left onto CT 49 north.
- In one mile, turn left into the entrance.
- At the fork at 0.7 mile bear left.
- In 0.2 mile park in the area across from the Rhododendron Sanctuary sign.

ON THE TRAIL
The 24,000-acre Pachaug State Forest—Connecticut's largest state forest—has much to offer in the way of recreational opportunities. The hike described here is especially great for young children, as they can traipse over the boardwalks of a swamp among giant rhododendrons and hike to the summit of Mount Misery, all in the same short trip. The Rhododendron Sanctuary is especially spectacular when the rhododendrons bloom, usually in early July. The Mount Misery campground is located close to the trailhead and offers sites on a first-come, first-served basis for those that want to stay the night.

The blue-blazed trail of the Rhododendron Sanctuary begins across the road from the parking area. Immediately, you will enter the woods, and in 0.1 mile you will reach a swampy area, where ferns are plentiful. By the 0.2-mile mark, you will be on a boardwalk surrounded by massive rhododendrons, native to Connecticut yet not very common in the region. If you are there at the right time, say, in early July, you are sure to be impressed by the size of the blooms. At 0.25 mile the boardwalk ends at an overlook of the White Cedar Swamp. The kids will thrill to the sounds

Kids will love following this boardwalk through the swamp.
(Photo by Emily Kerr)

of frogs jumping. If they are old enough to write or draw, have them sign the notebook located in a plastic container.

Follow the trail back to the road and turn right, following the blue blazes on the trees past the campground entrance. In 0.2 mile turn left

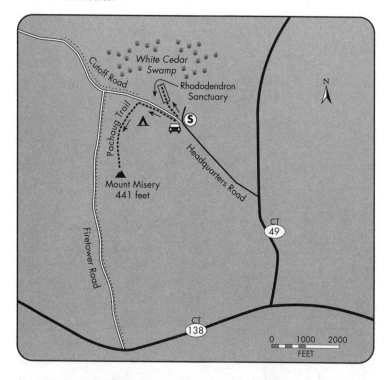

by a "Hikers Use Caution" sign as the blue blazes head into the woods. You are now on the Pachaug Trail, which starts out flat, then almost immediately begins its ascent over a series of switchbacks. If your kids seem daunted by the initial climb, reassure them that it flattens out at the top. In 0.5 mile you will reach the rocky slabs at the top of Mount Misery. This is a perfect spot to have a snack as you take in the views of the surrounding hills. Return the way you came and head back down the road to your car.

WHERE DOES THE NAME PACHAUG COME FROM?

Pachaug is a Native American word meaning "bend in the river." The river of this same name runs right through the middle of the forest. Many Native Americans of the Pequot, Mohegan, and Narragansett tribes inhabited this area at one time.

Opposite page: A toddler winds his way down from the overlook at Jacobs Hill. (Photo by Emily Kerr)

MASSACHUSETTS

BASH BISH FALLS

BEFORE YOU GO
Map USGS Ashley Falls
Current Conditions
Bash Bish Falls State Park,
Massachusetts Department of
Conservation and Recreation
(413) 528-0330
Fees None

ABOUT THE HIKE
Day hike
Moderate for children
May–November
3.7 miles round-trip
Elevation gain 840 feet
High point 1500 feet
Hiking time 3.5 hours
Accessibility No special
access

GETTING THERE
- From the junction of MA 23 and MA 41 in South Egremont, drive 0.25 mile south on MA 41.
- Turn right onto Mount Washington Road. (At 1.6 miles, a sign says "To Mount Washington State Park.")
- In 7.4 miles, turn right onto Bash Bish Road where a sign indicates that Bash Bish Falls is 4 miles away.
- In 1.6 miles, turn left at another sign that reads "Bash Bish Falls, 2 Miles."
- At 1.3 miles, pass the upper parking lot to the falls.
- Continue for another mile into New York State (where the road becomes NY 344) to a park entrance on the left.

ON THE TRAIL
This is a spectacular waterfall by anyone's standards. At its most dramatic point, a huge boulder splits the river and sends the water plunging into a deep pool in a set of twin falls. Flat, poolside rocks and worn trails climbing alongside the falls provide several points from which to watch the cascading water. Although the falls may have a number of visitors when you arrive, it's likely you'll be one of the few who hiked 3 miles to get there, because it is also accessible from Bash Bish Road by an emergency vehicle road. Though the beginning of this hike is actually in New York, the falls itself is in Massachusetts. And the trail is so dramatic and so easily accessible to folks in Massachusetts that we've included it here.

Cross the Bash Bish Brook on the park road. Instruct the kids to look for the white blazes of the South Taconic Trail bordering the right-hand side of the park road. Soon, the white-blazed trail turns right (south), your route, heading away from the brook. Pass a building with rest

Resting beside Bash Bish Falls (photo by Cynthia Copeland and Thomas J. Lewis)

facilities and head into the woods on a moderate grade, now traveling alongside a swift tributary of the Bash Bish Brook. At double blazes, the trail turns right and joins a tote road. Soon the trail curls left, leaving the stream behind. Double blazes guide you left off the tote road, farther

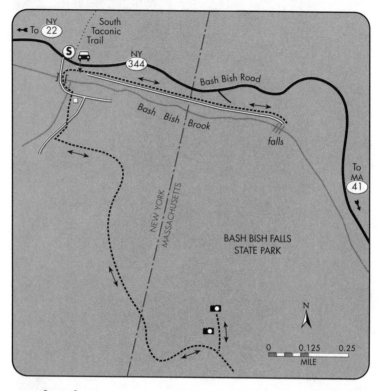

away from the stream, on a continuous, moderately steep ascent. The trail momentarily levels out and, far below, you can hear the sound of the rushing Bash Bish Brook. Ask the kids to name the colors they see in the forest—it may seem entirely green until they start examining the flora and fauna a little more closely.

Bending right (south again), the path resumes its moderate climb through mixed hardwoods and thickets of mountain laurel. Again, you will have a short reprieve from the climb before the trail winds left (east) and climbs to a small stream that trickles in from the right. After one further ascent, 1 mile from the start, you arrive at an intersection with a blue-blazed side trail leading left (northwest) to views. Follow the side trail to the rock painted with triple blue blazes. From here, enjoy the hike's only views over a bucolic setting and adjoining ridges. Because picnicking is not allowed near the falls, stop here for a snack.

Return to the parking area where you left your car and walk in an easterly direction along a woods road on the north side of Bash Bish Brook, entering Bash Bish Falls State Park in Massachusetts. (Note that no swimming or picnicking is allowed in Bash Bish Falls State

Park.) In 0.55 mile, the footpath joins an emergency vehicle road, and in another 0.15 mile, you'll arrive at the falls. Ooh and aah with the other visitors and relax on the boulders lining the falls before returning to your car.

RACE BROOK FALLS AND MOUNT EVERETT

BEFORE YOU GO
Map USGS Ashley Falls
Current Conditions Mount Everett State Reservation, Massachusetts Department of Conservation and Recreation (413) 528-0330
Fees None

ABOUT THE HIKE
Day hike or overnight
Challenging for children
April–October
5 miles round-trip
Elevation gain 1850 feet
High point 2602 feet
Hiking time 5 hours
Accessibility No special access

GETTING THERE
- From the junction of MA 41 and MA 23 in South Egremont, travel south on MA 41 for 5 miles.
- At the intersection with Salisbury Road, park on the right-hand (west) side of MA 41 in a paved turnaround.

ON THE TRAIL
On the first warm day in April, take your older children on a hike along Race Brook. You'll witness the torrent of icy water crashing down the rocky hillside in this Massachusetts wilderness and then climb to the windswept summit of Mount Everett. But be prepared—this is one of the toughest hikes in the book. It includes a walk along part of the Appalachian Trail, the path that winds over the backbone of the Appalachian Mountain range for 2050 miles from Georgia to Maine. The first section of the trail was blazed in 1922 and the final stretch in 1938; in 1968, Congress proclaimed the Appalachian Trail a national scenic trail, to be maintained as a hiking path forever. Thanks to the efforts of volunteers affiliated with the Appalachian Trail Conference, the trail is regularly maintained and reblazed.

The trail leads from the middle of the parking loop, heading initially west then immediately southwest along blue triangular blazing. This, the Race Brook Trail, cuts across a swampy area then bends to the right (west), skirting the right-hand side of a field. The path dives into

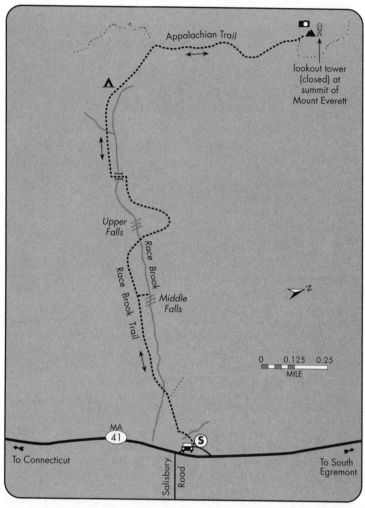

a hemlock grove on a mild ascent. At a trail junction 0.2 mile from the start, veer left, guided by the sign for the "Appalachian Trail via Falls, 2 Miles." Still following the blue blazes, you will drop down to the bank of Race Brook at 0.3 mile. On a steamy day, you will notice that the temperature plummets as you enter the ravine.

The trail follows the north bank briefly then crosses to the southern side on stepping stones, turning left up a grade then switching right to resume its westerly course. The path now climbs with conviction, leading away from the brook (the original riverside trail has been rerouted due to erosion). Soon, the river is out of sight, although the sound of running water far below is still evident. At close to 0.5 mile, a red-blazed side trail leads to the Middle Falls. Walk 200 yards along relatively level ground to this spectacular waterfall; be careful if you elect to climb down to the bottom of the falls because the path is quite steep. Kids should probably view the falls from the trail.

Return to the blue-blazed trail and turn right as the relentless ascent continues along a spongy path. At 0.8 mile, the trail cuts northwest along flatter terrain, crossing Race Brook at the bottom of the Upper Falls. Torrents of water crash down the rocky groove some 80 feet, then continue splashing along the banks of Race Brook. Pause here to let the kids catch their breath and enjoy the falls before attacking the next stiff climb.

The trail leaves the falls, heading north on a moderate, then steep ascent. In 0.2 mile, the path turns southwest on more level ground, running along a rocky ridge. As you approach the far end of this ridge, enjoy the fine views down the valley into Connecticut. The trail rejoins Race Brook on a mild ascent and soon crosses it on a log bridge. Here, the slow-moving brook beckons to hot, sticky hikers. The kids can roll up their pant legs and wade in the cool pools.

As you continue, you'll crisscross some tributaries to Race Brook, now just a trickling stream. Soon, it will disappear. On the left, on level ground, is a hidden campsite (0.25 mile before the Appalachian Trail junction). Two miles from the start, the Race Brook Trail ends rather anticlimactically at an intersection with the Appalachian Trail. Turn right and begin the steep, rocky ascent to the summit of Mount Everett. Point out to the kids the stunted trees such as scrub pitch pine and the low ground-covers of blueberry and huckleberry bushes, indications of the high altitude and fierce winds. You'll pass an occasional bald face with superb views south and east as you near the peak. With your first glimpse of the lookout tower that rises from the summit, you'll feel the burst of energy necessary to complete the first half of the hike. Although the tower is closed, the gently sloping summit offers

Race Brook's Middle Falls (photo by Cynthia Copeland and Thomas J. Lewis)

near-360-degree views, taking in Mount Greylock to the north and Bear Mountain to the south.

During a well-deserved and much-needed break, refuel with some high-energy snacks. On the return trip, witness the "birth of a brook" as Race Brook grows from a tiny ribbon of water to a forcefully flowing brook. Return to your car as you came, punctuating the descent with frequent compliments for your young, hardworking hiking companions.

 DEVILS PULPIT AND SQUAW PEAK

BEFORE YOU GO
Maps USGS Great Barrington, Stockbridge
Current Conditions The Trustees of Reservations, Western Management (Monument Mountain) (413) 298-3239
Fees None

ABOUT THE HIKE
Day hike
Moderate for children
April–November
2.8 miles, loop trip
Elevation gain 900 feet
High point 1642 feet
Hiking time 3 hours
Accessibility Accessible picnic tables

GETTING THERE

- From Stockbridge center, drive south for 3 miles on US 7 to a parking and picnic area on the right (you'll see a sign for Monument Mountain Reservation just before this area).
- If you're coming from the south and Great Barrington: from the junction of MA 23 and US 7, travel north on US 7 for 3 miles to the parking area on the left.

ON THE TRAIL

There is no question that this is the real thing—a true mountain. The climb is steady and the effort is well rewarded by breathtaking panoramas from atop the rocky summit called Squaw Peak. According to ancient folklore, a Native American maiden was hurled from the mountaintop because she fell in love with a brave from an enemy tribe. On the mountain's southern slope is a stone cairn that is supposed to have been built by sympathetic people as a monument to the maiden. Our three-year-old led the way to the top, but it may be tough going on some little legs. You might want to do as we did and carry an empty child carrier for the smaller one whose initial intentions were nobler than his or her stamina.

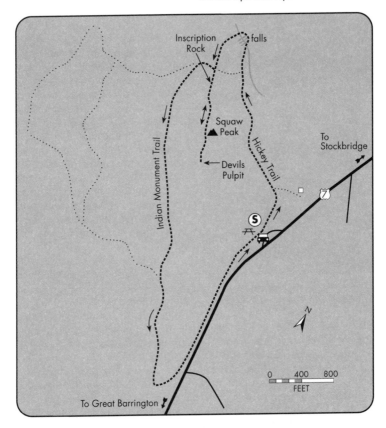

The white-blazed Hickey Trail heads north from the parking area near the trail map—a sign indicates that this is the "Steep Trail" (the other choice is the "Easy Trail"). You'll be completing the loop by returning via the Easy Trail, because most hikers agree that it is easier to ascend rather than descend a steep grade. The path heads off through a mixed hardwood forest on fairly level ground for the first 0.3 mile. Climbing can be laborious for little tykes; we play memory games to take the kids' minds off of their tiring legs. Start off by trying to name the Ten Essentials (from the Introduction) and move on to the names of the Seven Dwarves, TV characters, residents of Sesame Street, and so on. When they are reminding one another about Grumpy and Sneezy, they will be less likely to complain.

Soon, the tempo changes as the trail begins its steep ascent. The path is just rocky enough to provide good footholds. Early on, short side trails lead around muddy areas; at the first true trail intersection at 0.5

Atop Devils Pulpit (photo by Cynthia Copeland and Thomas J. Lewis)

mile where white blazes split off in two directions, continue straight, following along the stream. You will pass a waterfall on the left 0.1 mile later (the water trickles off of an overhanging boulder) and travel on level ground until a trail joins from the left. Continue straight here and go straight again in another 30 yards when a trail joins from the right. You will soon arrive at Inscription Rock, which tells of the conveyance of land to the Trustees of Reservations and the intention that this property be a "place of free enjoyment for all time."

Just beyond the rock you will begin a short, rugged climb to Squaw Peak, the highest point in the reservation. Squaw Peak is essentially a 0.3-mile-long ridge that narrows to less than 20 feet wide in some places. At this summit, 1.2 miles from the start, stand atop impressive outcroppings of granite with spectacular views of the eastern valley and the Berkshires. Look for the Housatonic, Williams, and Green Rivers winding through the lush valley. Just beyond Squaw Peak is Profile Rock, which resembles a human head when viewed from the south. Devils Pulpit is a pinnacle on the summit's eastern side. Retrace your steps past Inscription Rock to the trail intersection and turn left, beginning a gentle descent. At the next trail intersection, bear left onto Indian Monument Trail and follow this path as it gradually descends the mountain along the base of the cliffs. Always bear left, as unmarked trails split off to the right. (Remember to use the memory game to distract fussy hikers, young or old.) Soon the path becomes a woods road that eventually leaves the forest and joins US 7. Walk the remaining distance on the highway to the parking area and your car.

MOBY DICK IN MASSACHUSETTS?

In 1850, Nathaniel Hawthorne and Herman Melville hiked up Monument Mountain. They were forced to spend the night in a cave when a thunderstorm hit. The discussions that took place as they sheltered there sparked ideas for Melville's famous book, *Moby-Dick*.

LAURAS TOWER AND ICE GLEN

BEFORE YOU GO
Maps USGS Stockbridge
Current Conditions Laurel Hill Association; Town of Stockbridge Chamber of Commerce (413) 298-5200
Fees None

ABOUT THE HIKE
Day hike
Moderate for children
April–November
3.3 miles, loop trip
Elevation gain 650 feet
High point 1465 feet
Hiking time 3.5 hours
Accessibility No special access

GETTING THERE
- From the center of Stockbridge, drive south 0.2 mile on US 7.
- Turn left on Park Street and drive 0.3 mile to the road's end.
- Park in the circle.

ON THE TRAIL
Ice Glen is magnificent in the spring when the meltwaters freeze and produce natural ice sculptures that cling to the cliffs and boulders. It is also very dangerous then because hikers are forced to scramble over ice-covered rocks and crevices. The glen is an exciting place to be on Halloween, too, when Stockbridge folks make their way through this maze of boulders carrying torches. But the best time for a family to visit this dark gorge is on a day in August, because the shape and depth of the ravine ensure that even on the steamiest of summer days, it will be "air-conditioned." Before tackling the glen, stroll through the woods to Lauras Tower for a lovely view of the area surrounding historic Stockbridge.

Study the trail map at the trailhead on the south side of the parking circle. Cross the Housatonic River on a suspension footbridge and make your way over the railroad tracks. After traveling under some power

BEST HIKES WITH LEASHED DOGS IN MASSACHUSETTS

Race Brook Falls and Mount Everett, Hike 31
Bash Bish Falls, Hike 30
Devils Pulpit and Squaw Peak, Hike 32
Lauras Tower and Ice Glen, Hike 33
Tyringham Cobble, Hike 34

Upper Goose Pond, Hike 35—dogs not allowed in cabin
Pine Cobble Trail, Hike 38
Northfield Mountain, Hike 41
Jacobs Hill, Hike 42
Rock House Reservation, Hike 44
Great Blue Hill, Hike 50
Worlds End Reservation, Hike 51

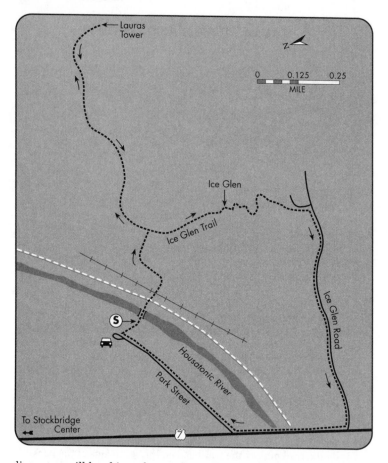

lines, you will head into the woods, climbing gradually. At a fork in the trail at 0.25 mile, bear left and follow the orange-blazed trail as it gradually ascends for about 0.7 mile and arrives at an observation tower at the summit. Do the smaller kids get bored with nothing but trees to look at on either side of the trail? Walking through the woods is more fun if you pretend to be a stalking tiger, bouncy bear cub, or wild horse.

After enjoying the pretty views of the surrounding countryside from the lookout, retrace your steps to the junction and turn left on the white-blazed Ice Glen Trail. Within 0.3 mile, the firm dirt path becomes the boulder-strewn ravine that is the Ice Glen. The blazes lead you on a twisted route through mazes of stone on the floor of the gorge that form interesting caves and tunnels. The moss-covered rocks can be slippery, especially after a rain. Some small children will need assistance

Suspension footbridge over the Housatonic River (photo by Cynthia Copeland and Thomas J. Lewis)

through the gorge while others will insist on scaling the boulders alone. If you need to motivate little children who are becoming tired climbing through the glen, look ahead and point out a good "resting rock." Urge the kids to scramble to that spot for a break and then ask them to select the next resting rock farther ahead.

After a 0.4-mile walk through the ravine, you will emerge on a wooded path and in 0.1 mile arrive at a private driveway. Continue straight down the steep drive to Ice Glen Road. Turn right here and walk 0.5 mile to US 7; turn right and follow the highway 0.3 mile to turn right onto Park Street. Along these roads bordering Stockbridge, count green cars or brown dogs or people wearing hats. Walk down Park Street to where your car is parked.

34 TYRINGHAM COBBLE

BEFORE YOU GO
Maps USGS East Lee, Otis
Current Conditions The Trustees of Reservations, Western Management (413) 298-3239
Fees None

ABOUT THE HIKE
Day hike
Moderate for children
March–October
2 miles, loop trip
Elevation gain 450 feet
High point 1350 feet
Hiking time 1.5 hours
Accessibility No special access

GETTING THERE

- Take exit 2 off the Mass. Turnpike (I-90) and head south on MA 20.
- Take an immediate right onto MA 102, followed by an immediate left onto Tyringham Road.

- In 4.5 miles, turn right onto Jerusalem Road, by the Tyringham Post Office.
- A small parking area is 0.25 mile on the right.

ON THE TRAIL

Rolling fields, idyllic countryside, tranquil forests, scenic vistas, interesting rock formations, lush meadows filled with wildflowers and berries, warbling birds, and prime picnic spots—this hike has it all. The scenery changes so often and the views are so fabulous on this relatively short loop trail that the kids will forget all about their aching legs on the steep stretches. They will even get to hike a section of the Appalachian Trail and add the word cobble—a rocky hill made of bedrock—to their vocabulary. This hike is so packed full that it will become a favorite of the entire family.

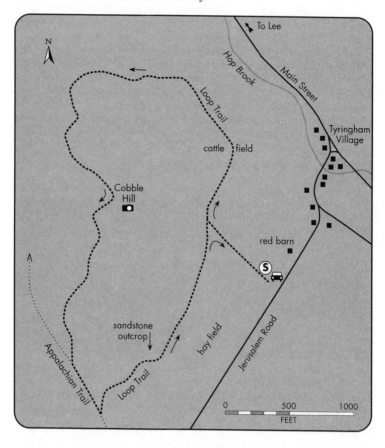

Hiking on a section of the Appalachian Trail (photo by Emily Kerr)

From the parking area, go through the narrow wooden gate marked "Trail" (there are a few of these gates on the hike; younger children will love opening and closing them) and follow the broad grassy path. At 0.1 mile, you will pass through a wide opening in the fence, and come to the beginning of the loop. Although you can go either way, it's more rewarding on the way back if you bear right here and continue to follow the wide grassy path. The trail, marked by gray wooden posts, meanders north through a cattle field with views of Tyringham Village, before it takes an immediate turn to the west and begins its ascent.

At 0.4 miles, the trail enters the woods, where you will pass through another wooden gate. Here you have a choice to go two different directions. As tempting as it might be to head downhill, the correct trail is the one to the left marked by white blazes that leads uphill. Remind your kids that what goes up must come down and distract them from the climb by having them imitate as many different bird songs as they can—there are over 200 species of birds on the reservation. This steep section curves southward through a mixed forest of pine, ash, and beech trees.

About a mile into the hike, just when the kids' legs are giving out, you will reach the top of the cobble and be rewarded with amazing views across the valley of Hop Brook and Tyringham Village, and to the forested hills on the other side. The top of the cobble has grassy areas perfect for picnics and running around, so plan on spending some time here.

When ready to tear yourself away from the scenery, continue heading southward as the trail begins its descent through a pine-hemlock forest punctuated by rocky ledges. Very quickly, the trees give way to meadows and more beautiful views of the countryside. Have your children look for butterflies and berries in season on your way toward the Appalachian Trail, 0.3 miles from the top. Upon reaching the junction with the AT, bear left and head toward Maine for 500 feet. (It's a short stretch, but might inspire the kids to hike the whole trail one day!) You will actually be going south toward Maine as the AT makes a loop through the valley, then turn left again back onto the Loop Trail. The last half mile will take you in a northeasterly direction past a large sandstone outcrop (everyone can guess what they think the shape looks like) back into hay fields and the beginning of the loop. Make a right turn through the fence opening back to the parking area.

 UPPER GOOSE POND

BEFORE YOU GO
Map USGS East Lee
Current Conditions Massachusetts AT Committee (Berkshire Chapter of the Appalachian Mountain Club); National Park Service, Appalachian National Scenic Trail (304) 535-6278; Appalachian Trail Conservancy (304) 535-6331
Fees None

ABOUT THE HIKE
Day hike or overnight
Moderate for children
April–November; cabin open Memorial Day to Labor Day
6.2 miles round-trip, 5.3 miles using two cars with a stop at the cabin
Elevation gain 1000 feet
High point 1780 feet
Hiking time 4 hours
Accessibility No special access

GETTING THERE

- From exit 2 on the Mass. Turnpike, take MA 20 east.
- In 0.8 miles, turn right on Forest Road.
- Continue on Forest Road 2.6 miles, bearing right as it becomes a dirt road.
- Follow this dirt road, now Goose Pond Road, another 0.7 mile.
- Look for the green and white triangles that indicate the AT crossing, and park in the gravel parking area on the left just past the trail.
- To leave a car at the MA 20 Appalachian Trail crossing, continue on MA 20 past Forest Road 3.7 miles. Just past the boundary between Becket and Lee, look for a pull out and parking area on the right. You may park near the center island, but please don't park in front of the house or on adjacent properties.

ON THE TRAIL

Looking for a great first overnight trip with the kids? This one is fantastic, as you can pitch your tent on one of six platforms or stay in the Upper Goose Pond Cabin if space permits. Managed by a volunteer caretaker during the season, this stop for hikers on the Appalachian Trail (AT) provides a bunk room for sixteen on the second floor. (Bring your own sleeping bag and mat.) Even though no food is provided at the

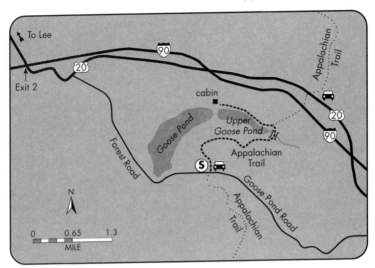

cabin, many caretakers will happily treat hungry hikers to a pancake breakfast. This can also be done as a day hike with the option of using two cars to create a shorter hike. A stop at the cabin provides a nice break for lunch, a swim, and to take in the views from the pond.

From Goose Pond Road, head north on the AT (same side as the parking lot), following the white blazes. The trail descends slightly through the woods, and at 0.5 mile crosses a long bridge over the end of an old beaver pond. Can the kids see any signs of a dam or an animal swimming in the water? The trail begins a moderate climb, and in another 0.1 mile you will reach a short rocky scramble as the trail gets steeper. Play "I spy" and see who can find various things along the way: moss, ferns, fungus, tumbled boulders.

In 1.1 miles, a sign announces that you are entering the Upper Goose Pond Natural Area. Purchased by the National Park Service to protect Upper Goose Pond from development, this area provides a corridor for the AT. (No camping or fires are permitted in the natural area except at Upper Goose Pond Cabin.) Soon after, the AT begins a descent from the ridge, with rock stairs interspersed. As you skirt the east end of the pond, stay on the stepping stones to protect the soft soil.

Approximately 2 miles from the start, you will pass a small spring, then cross a bridge over the inflow to the pond. The trail travels along the north edge of the pond, where views of the water become more frequent. After a final view in a hemlock grove, the trail turns right away from the pond and ascends slightly. In 2.6 miles, the side trail for Upper Goose Pond Cabin heads off to the left. Follow this blue-blazed trail 0.5 mile to the cabin.

The cabin at Upper Goose Pond (photo by Emily Kerr)

If you parked a second car on MA 20, continue on the white-blazed AT up over the ridge. In a little over a mile descend to the footbridge over the Mass. Turnpike, waving to the cars below. MA 20 is another 0.5 mile away.

Notes: Accommodations for the cabin are on a first-come, first-served basis, and the cabin is often full on weekends in July and August; be prepared to tent if necessary. There is a gas stove in the kitchen that may be used with the permission of the caretaker. Swimming and a canoe are available, although there is no lifeguard. The caretaker helps educate hikers and performs upkeep of the cabin. The cabin is open seven days a week from Memorial Day to Labor Day, and weekends until Columbus Day. Camping is permitted on the tent platforms all year.

36 BERRY POND

BEFORE YOU GO
Map USGS Pittsfield West
Current Conditions Pittsfield State Forest, Massachusetts Department of Conservation and Recreation (413) 442-8992
Fees None for trails; moderate fee for campsites

ABOUT THE HIKE
Day hike or overnight
Moderate for children
May–November
4.8 miles, loop trip
Elevation gain 1300 feet
High point 2313 feet
Hiking time 5 hours
Accessibility No special access

GETTING THERE
- From US 7, turn west onto West Street in the center of Pittsfield.
- Drive 2.6 miles; turn right onto Churchill Street.
- In 1.6 miles, turn left onto unmarked Cascade Street (just after a sign for Pittsfield State Forest).
- Follow this road for another 0.5 mile.

- At an intersection, turn right and you will see the entrance for Pittsfield State Forest.
- Proceed through the entrance and bear right on Berry Pond Circuit Road.
- Drive 0.6 mile to a parking lot on the left.

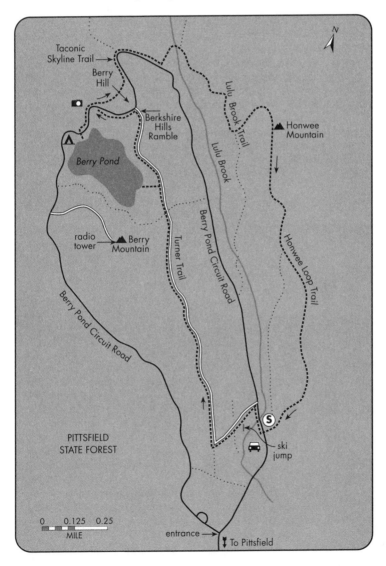

ON THE TRAIL

Although you are likely to find strawberries, blueberries, or raspberries along the trail to Berry Pond (depending, of course, on the season), the pond gets its name not from the trailside fruit but from William Berry, one of George Washington's soldiers who owned land in the Berkshires. At just over 2000 feet elevation, Berry Pond is said to be the highest natural body of water in the state. Although swimming is not allowed, kids can look for bullfrogs or fish in the clear water while the adults relax on the grassy bank.

From the parking area, look across the stream to the remnants of a ski jump that kids may want to explore before or after the hike. Head left out of the parking area, up Berry Pond Circuit Road. In about 0.1 mile, double blue triangular blazes indicate a left turn (west) off of the paved road and onto a jeep road. Shortly, an elevated platform appears on your left; it is the top of the ski jump. Ever been curious about the view a ski jumper has before launching down the chute? Have the children take a look.

Past the ski jump, you reach an intersection and continue straight, on a slight ascent. In another 0.1 mile, turn right (north) at a second intersection, now following a red-blazed jeep road. Although this, the

Turner Trail, is not heavily blazed, no side roads or intersections will confuse you. After a straight and steady climb of nearly a mile, you will see the radio tower on top of Berry Mountain through the trees. At an intersection, on fairly level ground, continue straight, still following the painted red blazes. Soon, Berry Pond comes into view and the trail sweeps right, skirting the pond. Side trails provide access to the water's edge. The main trail departs the pond and enters a field, the site of the Berkshire Hills Ramble, a self-guided nature walk. At the paved road, turn left and follow it to Berry Pond. The westward view

Binoculars are not on the "Ten Essentials" list, but they make the views from mountain summits memorable for kids. (Photo by Cynthia Copeland and Thomas J. Lewis)

of New York's Adirondacks and Catskills is spectacular and well worth a lengthy pause. At Berry Pond, enjoy your picnic lunch or set up camp. Follow the pond outlet across Berry Pond Circuit Road to watch the water cascade down this high ridge.

To continue your hike, walk back up the road the way you came for 0.1 mile, watching for the white blazes that mark the Taconic Skyline Trail. Follow the blazes into the woods on the left-hand side of the road and climb to the top of Berry Hill. The trail quickly emerges onto the road; turn left. The white-blazed Taconic Skyline Trail departs the road almost immediately, left, into the woods. Continue your steady descent along paved Berry Pond Circuit Road for another 0.2 mile, watching for the wide trailhead on the left that will take you in a northerly direction over Lulu Brook. At an intersection with the equally wide Lulu Brook Trail, turn right (southeast). In 0.5 mile, head left at a junction with the Honwee Loop Trail. (Note that any trail leading to the right will return you to Berry Pond Circuit Road and, eventually, your car.) This trail winds northeast over the blueberry-covered Honwee Mountain then heads southeast for a long steady descent, following blue blazes, to the Berry Pond Circuit Road. You will emerge from the woods across the road from the parking lot and your car.

 MARCH CATARACT FALLS

BEFORE YOU GO
Maps USGS North Adams, Cheshire
Current Conditions Mount Greylock State Reservation, Massachusetts Department of Conservation and Recreation (413) 499-4262
Fees Moderate fee for summit lot only

ABOUT THE HIKE
Day hike or overnight
Challenging for children
May–October
4.4 miles round-trip
Elevation gain 1250 feet
High point 3491 feet
Hiking time 4 hours
Accessibility Accessible restrooms

GETTING THERE
- From US 7 in Lanesborough, turn onto North Main Street, heading east, following a sign to "Mount Greylock Reservation, 10."
- In 1 mile, at the Mount Greylock Visitor Center, pick up a trail map.
- Continue on the same road (now called Rockwell Road) for another 9 miles to the summit of Mount Greylock; park here.

- From MA 2, west of North Adams, turn south on Notch Road and drive about 8 miles to the junction with Rockwell Road.
- Turn left and shortly arrive at the summit parking lot.

ON THE TRAIL

From the War Memorial tower on the summit of the state's highest mountain, kids will be able to see New Hampshire's Mount Monadnock and the Adirondacks (115 miles away) to the north. In addition to the roads, nearly a dozen trails, including the Appalachian Trail, lead to the peak of Mount Greylock in Mount Greylock State Reservation. Sneakers won't do on this hike—the climbs and descents are challenging, especially as you drop into the ravine toward the waterfall. Smaller children or those with little hiking experience may find this one too demanding.

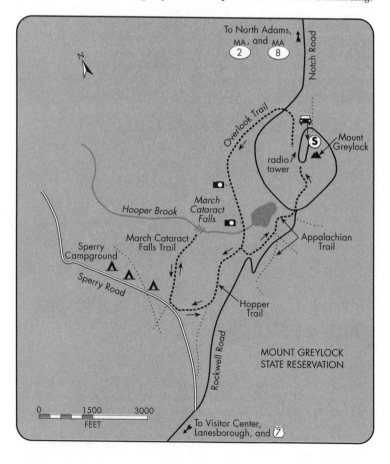

From the parking lot, head to the radio tower. To the left of the radio tower and behind the adjacent building, the blue-blazed Overlook Trail begins a modest descent. This wide path acts as a streambed during the rainy spring season (waterproof footwear is recommended then). In 0.3 mile, the trail crosses Notch Road and reenters the woods on a new section of trail that is somewhat indistinct but well blazed. After a short descent, old and new Overlook Trails merge and the path again is worn and easy to follow. The trail continues modestly downhill as it cuts a path along the rim of Greylock. Any complainers? Play "What do we hear?" It may seem quiet until the kids listen for sounds such as the wind blowing, leaves rustling, birds chirping, the drone of an airplane overhead. At 0.7 mile, the first of two side paths leads right to an overlook (thus the trail name). After each side trip, return to the main path.

At 1 mile, the trail descends to a stream crossing then ascends briefly but steeply and arrives at the intersection with the blue-blazed Hopper Trail. Turn right and drop moderately down to an intersection with Deer Hill Trail. Bear right, continuing on the Hopper Trail to an intersection with Sperry Road near the Sperry Campground at 1.6 miles. Turn right and walk along the road into the campground; soon, signs and a trail for March Cataract Falls appear on your right. The sign indicates that a mile-long, rugged trail will bring you to the falls. Actually, it is closer to a 0.6-mile journey. Although this section of trail will be tough for little guys, especially as you get closer to the falls, the trip is worth the effort. The icy cold water tumbles down the side of Greylock, generously spraying anyone who needs cooling off. Take pictures of the kids cautiously approaching the misty waterfall. The idea of getting drenched may be appealing to them now, but just wait until they start climbing back up the hillside with heavy,

War Memorial tower on the Mount Greylock summit (photo by Cynthia Copeland and Thomas J. Lewis)

water-soaked pants. (A handful of chocolate-covered raisins for the one who complains the least!)

To begin the return hike, reverse your direction and climb back up the mountainside on the Hopper Trail. At the intersection with the Overlook Trail, bear right, still on the Hopper Trail. The trail soon outlets on Rockwell Road, then immediately turns left and reenters the woods. Rejoin Rockwell Road at the end of Hopper Trail. Here, join the white-blazed Appalachian Trail. Follow the signs to the summit. You will cross Notch Road at the intersection with Rockwell Road and head northeast back into the woods. In 0.3 mile, you will arrive at your car. Before you leave, visit the tower to take in the best views Massachusetts has to offer.

 PINE COBBLE TRAIL

BEFORE YOU GO
Map USGS North Adams
Current Conditions (Above 1800 feet) Williamstown Rural Lands Foundation (413) 458-2494
Fees None

ABOUT THE HIKE
Day hike
Moderate for children
April–November
3.2 miles round-trip
Elevation gain 1000 feet
High point 1894 feet
Hiking time 3 hours
Accessibility No special access

GETTING THERE

- Take MA 2 (Main Street) in Williamstown to Cole Avenue.
- Turn north on Cole Avenue and cross the Hoosac River and railroad tracks, arriving at a T intersection with North Hoosac Road.
- Turn right at the intersection and continue on North Hoosac Road for approx 0.1 mile.
- Look for Pine Cobble Drive on the left and proceed up Pine Cobble Drive approximately 500 yards to a parking area on the left.
- The trailhead is directly across from the parking lot and is designated by a large sign.

ON THE TRAIL

This trail, a favorite among Williams College students, begins just a short distance from campus. (The Williams Outing Club also publishes a trail guide.) It is a family favorite as well because the well-worn path means that even children not yet adept at following blazes can lead the hike. The ascent is continuous and rocky at times, but with a few rest

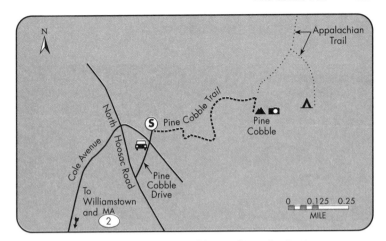

stops children should have no trouble reaching the large, open summit. There, they will delight in scaling the quartzite boulders while the adults take in the expansive view of the valley and nearby mountain ranges. The Pine Cobble Trail is also an access trail to the Appalachian Trail and Long Trail.

Marked with blue paint blazes, the trail ascends steadily with few level areas and some steep climbs. You will initially be traveling through mature third-growth forest, and later through stunted oak and beech. At the 1-mile mark, the Class of '96 Trail branches off to the left. Ascending again, cross a boulder field and then a seasonal brook before heading up a carved-out section of trail that acts as a streambed in the spring.

Soon, the trees become shorter and less dense. A final short, but steep, ascent brings you to the top of the ridgeline. To the left, the blue-blazed trail continues approximately 0.6 mile over several quartz outcrops—populated with wild blueberries in July—to a junction with the Appalachian Trail. To the right, a number of paths lead to various outlooks on the open Pine Cobble Summit. North Adams lies to the east, the Greylock Range to the south, and Williamstown and the Taconic Range to the west. Let the kids scramble around on the boulders before enjoying a picnic lunch and returning to the car.

SIGNS OF A CHANGED LANDSCAPE

Notice the level areas on the lower section of the hike? They are remnants of the shoreline of a prehistoric lake that once filled the valley to the west of Pine Cobble. Wave action at various water levels carved shelves into the cliff. White quartz sand remains in some of these areas.

GOAT PEAK LOOKOUT

BEFORE YOU GO
Map USGS Mount Tom
Current Conditions Mount
Tom State Reservation, Massachusetts Department of Environmental Management (413)
534-1186
Fees Moderate fee

ABOUT THE HIKE
Day hike
Easy for children
April–November
1.2 miles round-trip
Elevation gain 300 feet
High point 822 feet
Hiking time 1.5 hours
Accessibility Accessible
restrooms and picnic area

GETTING THERE

- Take exit 18 from I-91 in Northampton (a sign indicates Mount Tom).
- From the Holyoke–Easthampton town line, drive south on US 5 for 2.1 miles to a sign for the Mount Tom Reservation.
- Turn right into the reservation.
- Approximately 1.8 miles from US 5, reach a T intersection with Christopher Clark Road.
- There is a parking lot on the right just before the intersection.

ON THE TRAIL

Mount Tom State Reservation offers 20 miles of well-maintained and well-blazed trails. Several trails (such as that to Goat Peak) are appealing for those who prefer trees to people while hiking. This trail offers just enough of a challenge to be interesting to the older kids while remaining negotiable for the younger ones. At the summit, you will be rejuvenated by the panoramic views of the Connecticut Valley from the watchtower, one of only two on the reservation. (The annual count of the hawk migration is made from this tower.)

Before heading out, stop by the visitor center to learn about the area's wildlife and natural history. This small center houses geology, bird, insect, and small animal exhibits and is a great treat for the kids. To begin the hike, travel back down the entrance road for several hundred feet to a left-hand turn onto the Metacomet-Monadnock ("M&M") Trail. The path traverses a ridge and passes through a hemlock grove with a foliage ceiling 30 feet above you. Winding gradually uphill through the woods, the path breaks out of the hemlock forest into an area of maples. At the 0.4-mile mark, double blazes signify a right-hand turn to a much steeper section with strategically placed rocks serving as steps (though a little scrambling may be necessary). The trail turns left and continues

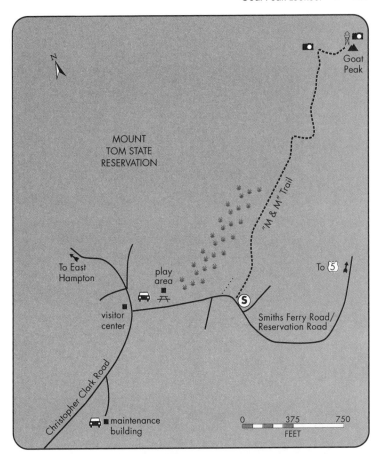

to climb steeply along a ridge with a rapid drop-off of at least 70 feet just to the left of the path.

As distant views become visible ahead, you'll realize that you are approaching the summit. Double blazes within 150 yards of the top are misleading because the trail obviously continues straight and side trails veer off to the left and right. From the summit spur at 0.6 mile (a good spot for a picnic), the tower is visible to your right, just 200 yards away. While the rocks on the spur afford excellent views of the hustle and bustle of the valley some 700 feet below, a climb up the tower rewards you with a breathtaking panorama in all directions including downtown Springfield to the south, Mount Monadnock to the north, the Berkshires to the west, and Connecticut Valley to the east. The lovely views of Mount Tom prevail as you hike the return trip to your car.

The view from Goat Peak (photo by Cynthia Copeland and Thomas J. Lewis)

ANNUAL HAWK MIGRATION

The tower is one of the best places in New England to watch for hawks. Come in the fall if you want to witness the birds as they fly past the mountain on their annual migration. Thousands of hawks and other birds are visible at this time of year.

40 MOUNT TOBY

BEFORE YOU GO
Map USGS Williamsburg
Current Conditions
University of Massachusetts Amherst, Department of Natural Resources Conservation (413) 545-2665
Fees None

ABOUT THE HIKE
Day hike
Challenging for children
April–November
2.6 miles round-trip
Elevation gain 900 feet
High point 1269 feet
Hiking time 3 hours
Accessibility No special access

GETTING THERE
- From I-91 in Deerfield, take exit 24 (MA 10/US 5).
- Follow MA 10 and US 5 north and in 0.2 mile, turn right onto MA 116 south following a sign to Sunderland and Amherst.

- In 1.8 miles, turn left (north) onto MA 47 north (Montague/ Millers Falls).
- Drive 3.8 miles and turn right onto Reservation Road (just beyond the Montague town line).
- In 0.5 mile, park on the right in a small parking lot for the Mount Toby Reservation.
- Please respect private (posted) land.

ON THE TRAIL

The strenuous hike to the summit of Mount Toby is best suited for older children who have an appreciation of geology and botany. (A trip to the library for appropriate field guides is a prerequisite for the trip.) The mountain's rugged slopes are punctuated with outcroppings of coarse conglomerate called "puddingstone." The area is also known for its wide variety of plants, most notably ferns and orchids. Local botanists claim that Mount Toby nurtures a greater diversity of plant life than any other spot in New England of equal acreage.

Maintained as a laboratory for University of Massachusetts forestry students, the 1100 acres of land that encompass the mountain are permanently protected. More than 25 miles of marked trails are open to the public, including a portion of the scenic, 36-mile-long Robert Frost Trail described here. Let the kids know that the final, steady ascent to the summit is challenging but the awe-inspiring views near the fire tower are worth the effort.

Head around the gate at the reservation entrance and begin hiking south along the jeep road. Almost immediately, turn right onto the Robert Frost Trail, blazed in bright orange. (You will follow this trail to the summit but will encounter numerous intersections with multipurpose paths [for cross-country skiing] and other hiking trails.) Immediately embark on a steady ascent. Notice the abundant goosefoot leaves, which look, as you might imagine, like a goose's foot. Can the kids guess what the leaves can be used for in an emergency? Toilet paper!

At 0.4 mile, turn right as a blue-blazed cross-country ski path continues straight. Work up a steep section followed by a sweeping descent through evergreens. At a T intersection 0.7 mile from the start, avoid the blue ski trail and turn right onto the wide orange-blazed path. Begin the first of many demanding ascents under power lines. (If you spot sarsaparilla—a common plant, not endangered—along the trail, pick a stalk or two and save them for the summit. We'll tell you why later.)

About 1 mile from the start, bear right on the wider, more traveled path—which is the combination Robert Frost and Telephone Line Trail—as a narrow trail goes straight. Over the next 0.3 mile, climb steeply and steadily under the utility lines on an eroded path with loose stones underfoot. Pause frequently to let kids catch their breath and to look back down the path for long-range views.

Just as the kids begin to insist that they cannot possibly take one more step, you'll reach the summit and fire tower. Don't be disappointed! Although the trees that rim the grassy clearing impede your view from the ground, a climb up the fire tower stairs will afford incredible views north to Mount Monadnock, east to the Quabbin Reservoir, and south to the University of Massachusetts campus. This is a worry-free summit—

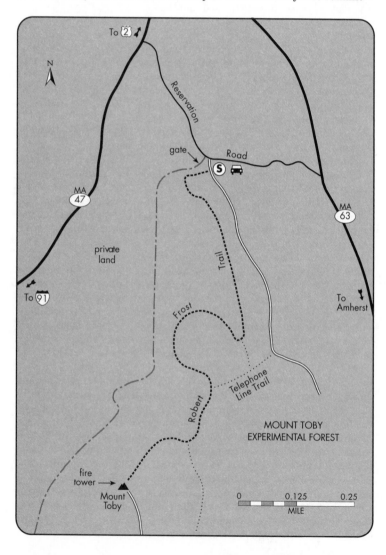

children can romp around without constant supervision because there are no sharp drop-offs. They should have adult accompaniment up the fire tower, however. (Be sure to check ahead of time to find out if access to the public is allowed. Some fire towers have become off-limits due to liability concerns.)

Remember that sarsaparilla you picked on the way up? Drop it from high up the fire tower and watch it twirl like a helicopter to the ground.

Return to your car the way you came, reminding children to exercise caution as they descend the steep trail on loose gravel.

 NORTHFIELD MOUNTAIN

BEFORE YOU GO	ABOUT THE HIKE
Map USGS Northfield	Day hike
Current Conditions Northeast Utilities System, Northfield Mountain Visitors Center (413) 659-3714 or (800) 859-2960	Moderate for children
	May–November
	5 miles round-trip
Fees None	**Elevation gain** 900 feet
	High point 1100 feet
	Hiking time 4 hours
	Accessibility No special access

GETTING THERE

- From the junction of MA 2 and MA 63 in Turners Falls, take MA 63 north for about 2 miles to the Northfield Mountain Recreation Area Visitor Center in Northfield.
- The center is clearly visible on the right-hand side of the road.
- Park in the lot near the main building.

ON THE TRAIL

Buried within Northfield Mountain is a pumped-storage generating plant that brings water from the neighboring Connecticut River to a 300-acre reservoir on top of the mountain. At periods of high electrical demand, the water is released and sent through the plant to produce electricity. Northeast Utilities created a recreation facility here for public use with more than 25 miles of well-maintained trails. For a family in relatively good physical condition, this pleasant woods walk to Upper Reservoir's overlook is an excellent first hike. There's little chance of getting lost on the moderate but continuous ascent because the route follows a carriage-width trail with clearly marked and numbered junctions. Frequent trailside maps indicate that "You are here." On the return trip, an easy-to-follow wooded path leads past impressive ledges

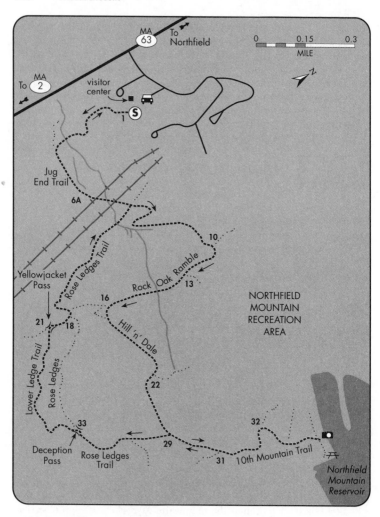

and eventually rejoins the wide path taken on the ascent. Northfield Mountain operates two nearby campgrounds: Barton Cove, situated on a peninsula jutting into the Connecticut River, and Munns Ferry, located on the river's east bank and accessible only by boat.

At the visitor center, pick up a trail map and a brochure detailing the center's family-oriented recreation and environmental programs.

From the large, painted trail map at the rear of the building, look for signs to Jug End Trail and follow the trail across a field near MA 63 and into the woods. Follow the smooth, narrow gravel road (groomed in the winter for cross-country skiing), watching for signposts with plaques describing animal tracks and wildflowers and providing nature facts interesting to children.

Continue on Jug End. At intersection 6A with 10th Mountain Trail, about 0.5 mile into the hike, Jug End heads diagonally left across the road, crosses a clearing for power lines, and dives back into the woods. Take note of the entrance for the Rose Ledges Trail on the right; you will return by this route. Follow Jug End Trail to intersection 10 with Rock Oak Ramble at 1 mile; head right. Travel 0.4 mile to intersection 16 with Hill 'n' Dale and turn left. As the kids weary of the constant uphill grade, distract them with a search for "faces" in tree trunks. After an additional 0.3 mile, Sidewinder Trail heads left (at intersection 22); bear right, still on Hill 'n' Dale. Notice the Rose Ledges Trail (intersection 29), heading right into the woods; on the return trip, you will turn off the road here. Just over 2 miles from the start, merge left at intersection 31 with 10th Mountain Trail and follow the level path. At intersection 32 go right, up a hill onto a paved road and rotary. Follow the rotary to the right, watching for the trail leading to the reservoir overlook. A large map at the overlook (2.4 miles from the start) explains which mountains are in view. A picnic table offers a pleasant lunch spot.

To return to the visitor center, retrace your steps and turn left at

Northfield Mountain's Rose Ledges (photo by Cynthia Copeland and Thomas J. Lewis)

junction 29 (at 3 miles) onto the Rose Ledges Trail following orange plastic blazes. Though the blazes are sparse at times, the trail is well worn and obvious. One-quarter mile beyond the junction, after a gradual ascent, curl right and begin to drop. Keep an eye on the kids on this section of trail because the ground falls off sharply on the left. At junction 33, head left at Deception Pass onto Lower Ledge Trail through a break in the ledges. As you travel along the base of the cliffs, kids will have a great time investigating the deep channels carved into the ledge's stone face. Who will be the first to see the portion of the cliff that has crumbled? The trail outlets at Yellowjacket Pass at junction 21, nearly 4 miles into the hike. Turn right on the gravel road, head up a steep slope, and reenter the woods on your left at an orange diamond-blazed trail, the Rose Ledges Trail. High cliffs fall from the left side of the trail and a sign warns hikers of the potential danger. Stay close to your children along this section. The Rose Ledges Trail meets the Jug End Trail at 4.4 miles. Turn left on this trail, following the earlier route back to your car.

CRUISING

If your feet are tired from all that hiking, consider taking a trip along the Connecticut River on Northfield Mountain's sixty-seat riverboat. Along the way, you may sight nesting bald eagles in Barton Cove, the site of a former dinosaur track quarry. Call ahead for schedules and reservations.

 **JACOBS HILL**

BEFORE YOU GO
Map USGS Winchendon
Current Conditions The Trustees of Reservations, Central Region (978) 840-4446
Fees None

ABOUT THE HIKE
Day hike
Easy for children
April–November
1.3 miles, loop trip
Elevation gain 180 feet
High point 1100 feet
Hiking time 1 hour
Accessibility No special access

GETTING THERE
- From the junction of NH 119 and NH 32 in Richmond, New Hampshire, travel on NH 32 south.
- In 4.5 miles, turn left onto MA 68 south following a sign to Royalston.

■ Drive 3 miles to a small sign for Jacobs Hill (keep your eyes peeled!) and parking on the right.

ON THE TRAIL

As you drive along the road that winds uphill toward the Jacobs Hill trailhead, thank your car for doing most of the climbing on this trip! Just about 0.5 mile from the start of this quick and easy hike, the woods open to reveal lovely views of hills rising over a lonely pond—an ideal picnic spot. On the return leg, you'll follow a crooked brook that empties into a deliciously swampy swamp full of croaking critters. (Have the kids bring a net in case they want to examine a frog or crayfish up close.)

Tucked away in a very rural part of the state, Jacobs Hill is a great choice for those who like to commune with nature instead of other hikers. And it's perfect for preschoolers who crave surprises around each bend (and who will be able to exercise some caution on the overlooks).

Follow the yellow blazes on an initially wide path down a slight grade; at 0.1 mile pass under powerlines to skirt the edge of a swamp. Two-tenths of a mile from the start, ascend gently through an area thick with hemlock and mountain laurel until you reach a tree with arrows pointing right and straight. Follow the path that splits right (west)—you'll be returning via the one that goes straight. Soon, the Tully Trail enters from the right. Continue going straight to a T intersection at 0.3 mile. This intersection is marked with a sign pointing left to Spirit Falls and right to a scenic vista. Turn right, keeping younger children close as the hillside drops off precipitously to the left. Can the kids find any signs that woodpeckers have been busy?

Before the 0.5-mile mark, you'll come upon a sheltered overlook with unexpected and dramatic views to the west/northwest. The Tully River winds through the valley below, swelling into Long Pond, then Tully Lake, directly beneath you. Older children (and younger ones who are able to follow instructions to stay back from the edge) can enjoy a picnic lunch on boulder chairs.

When you have finished your lunch, return to the last trail junction (the T intersection) and continue straight, following a different return route. Again, hold the hands of small children as you hike along ledges that drop steeply off to the right. Shortly, pass an overlook with views similar to those from the picnic spot. Soon the trail sweeps left (south, then east), away from the edge of the ridge, and wanders beside a noisy brook punctuated by moss-covered stones. Follow the brook to its source: a delightful bog teeming with wildlife on the right side of the trail. Pause, investigate (be sure to return creatures exactly where you found them!), then follow the path as it skirts the swamp's left edge, then departs it on an easy ascent.

At about the 1-mile mark, you'll arrive at the very first trail junction. Continue on to your car.

QUABBIN HILL

BEFORE YOU GO
Map USGS Windsor Dam
Current Conditions
Quabbin Reservoir,
Massachusetts Department of
Conservation and Recreation
(413) 323-7221
Fees None

ABOUT THE HIKE
Day hike
Moderate for children
April–November
4.8 miles, loop trip
Elevation gain 550 feet
High point 1026 feet
Hiking time 3 hours
Accessibility No special
access

GETTING THERE

- Quabbin Reservoir and the reservation are just off MA 9, west of Worcester and east of Amherst, in Belchertown.
- Off MA 9, enter the area at a sign for Quabbin Reservation and stop at the visitor center for a map.
- From the visitor center, turn left on MA 9 and head east toward Ware.
- Drive 1.5 miles and turn left at the Quabbin Park, Windsor Dam sign.
- Follow the road to the rotary at the top of the hill.
- Stay right at the rotary and follow the road to the tower.

ON THE TRAIL

The story of Quabbin Reservoir is fascinating to history buffs and naturalists alike. In the 1920s and 1930s, Quabbin was built as a water supply for metropolitan Boston, and its construction involved the "drowning" of four towns: Enfield, Dana, Prescott, and Greenwich. Today, the 3200 acres called Quabbin Park offer visitors an excellent opportunity for wildlife observation (you may even spot a bald eagle). Unlike most hiking routes, this one begins atop a summit and descends to the water's edge, finishing its loop on a steep ascent to the parking area near the summit tower. Gently rolling terrain combined with fun near the water make this a great hike for kids of most ability levels.

Walk to the tower at the opposite end of the parking area for a lovely view of the surrounding mountains and reservoir before locating the trailhead at the east side of the parking lot. At the trailhead, follow yellow blazes on a gradual descent with distant seasonal views of the reservoir to the right. (Remind the kids to conserve their energy—it will be an uphill finish.) After hiking for 1 mile, cross an open field diagonally left on a grassy road. Follow the road marked with occasional yellow blazes. At an intersection, head right on a dirt road and shortly

Visiting the Quabbin tower before the hike (photo by Cynthia Copeland and Thomas J. Lewis)

arrive at a paved road. Children should be accompanied across this road or warned to "look both ways." (A right turn onto the paved road will soon bring you to Enfield Lookout, a favorite spot for bird-watchers with scenic views across the reservoir.)

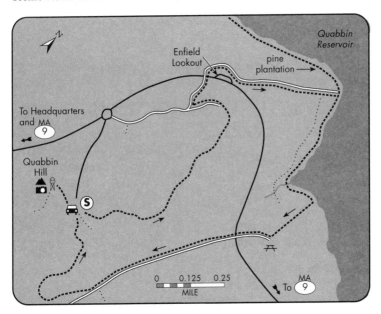

To head directly for the water's edge, cut straight across the paved road onto the continuation of the wide jeep path. After passing below Enfield Lookout, the trail swings into the woods. A long, gradual descent brings you to the edge of Quabbin Reservoir, nearly 2 miles from the start. Here, paths travel left and right. Ultimately you will head down the right-hand path to complete the loop, but a short walk to the left through the pine plantation provides some good territory for exploration.

As you continue the loop, heading southeast, children will surely prefer to walk the route along water's edge rather than staying on the trail that travels above the reservoir. (Several stream crossings virtually guarantee wet feet in either case.) The kids can get in some stone skipping practice as they stroll along the rocky beach. How far can they get stepping from rock to rock before they slip onto the sand? Soon, the rugged shore gives way to ledge and you must retreat to the trail. After picking your way across a wide, shallow brook that feeds the reservoir, you will enter an open field divided by a grassy road. Head right up the road. (This field would make a great picnic spot; tables are set closer to the paved road. Open fires, camping, swimming, and wading are prohibited.) Soon you will reach the paved road (0.3 mile from the water). Again, your services as crossing guard are required. Proceed straight across, heading into the woods on a gravel road. The cellar holes bordered by a stone wall on the left serve as a reminder of the lost towns. Follow this road to an intersection with a jeep trail entering from the left. Continue straight for a short distance to a trailhead on your right, 0.55 mile from the paved road. Follow this path on a winding ascent to the top of Quabbin Hill and your car.

 ROCK HOUSE RESERVATION

BEFORE YOU GO
Maps USGS North Brookfield, Warren
Current Conditions The Trustees of Reservations, Central Region (978) 840-4446
Fees None

ABOUT THE HIKE
Day hike
Easy for children
March–November
2.1 miles, loop trip
Elevation gain 240 feet
High point 1025 feet
Hiking time 1.5 hours
Accessibility No special access

GETTING THERE
- From the Mass. Turnpike, take exit 8.
- Follow MA 32 north, then combined MA 32/9 north for 10.2 miles.

- When MA 32 and MA 9 separate, stay on Highway 9 east for another 1.1 miles.
- Parking is on the left.

ON THE TRAIL

It's hard to tell what the highlight of this hike will be for your children—there are so many. A big draw is the large natural rock cave from which the reservation takes its name. The "Rock House," formed by glaciers and used by Native Americans as a hunting camp and shelter, is exciting for kids to explore. Other highlights include a pond, a balancing rock, a butterfly garden, and a scenic vista. To learn more about the geology and natural and cultural history of the reservation, you can order an interpretive guide from the Trustees in advance or pick one up for a small fee on site during summer weekends.

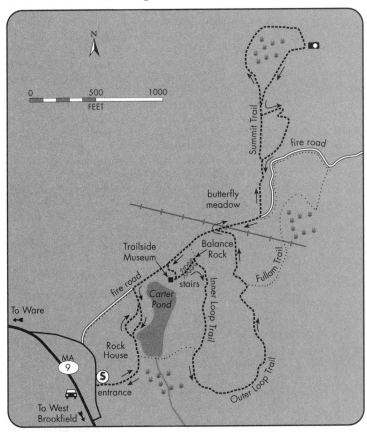

Climb the rock stairs behind the information board to begin. In 500 feet you will reach the junction of the Inner Loop Trail and arrive on the shore of man-made Carter Pond. You may hear frogs and see dragonflies and water striders flitting on the water. To follow the interpretive guide turn left on the Inner Loop Trail and look for the Rock House ahead. Can the kids tell what made this a good shelter? After exploring, follow the Inner Loop Trail as it makes it way along the western edge of Carter Pond to a junction with a fire road. Turn right on the old road and follow it a short distance to the Trailside Museum. This small cabin houses posters of wildlife and animal tracks and provides amazing views of Carter Pond off its deck. From here climb a set of rock stairs up to Balance Rock. Do the kids think this was placed here by glaciers or by giants, as some Native American stories told?

Continue on the Inner Loop Trail, now heading south along the eastern edge of the pond. At the junction with the Outer Loop Trail, about 0.5 mile from the start, turn left on the Outer Loop Trail. Follow this 0.4 mile to its intersection with the fire road. Turn right and soon come to a butterfly meadow, made to take advantage of the clearing created by the powerline. Travel another 250 feet on the fire road and make a sharp left turn onto the Summit Trail. Bear left at all the junctions, climbing moderately as the trail makes its way through the woods up to pastureland. If you peek through the trees, you may spot a cow! In 0.3 miles, the trail turns east then immediately south to bring you to a scenic vista. If your children are old enough to write, have them add their thoughts to the notebook attached to a tree at the overlook. Continue on the Summit Trail, bearing left once again at all the junctions on your way back to the fire road. Turn right on the fire road—passing the Fullam Trail on your left—then left on the Inner Loop Trail back to your car.

Scenic view of man-made Carter Pond (photo by Emily Kerr)

WACHUSETT MEADOW
WILDLIFE SANCTUARY

BEFORE YOU GO
Map USGS Sterling
Current Conditions Wachu-
sett Meadow Wildlife Sanctu-
ary, Massachusetts Audubon
Society (978) 464-2712
Fees Nonmembers, moderate
fee; members free

ABOUT THE HIKE
Day hike
Easy for children
March–October
2.5 miles, loop trip
Elevation gain 375 feet
High point 1312 feet
Hiking time 2 hours
Accessibility Accessible
parking and restrooms

GETTING THERE

- From the intersection of MA 31 and 62 in Princeton center, travel west on MA 62 for 0.75 mile.
- A Massachusetts Audubon sign indicates a right-hand turn onto Goodnow Road.
- Drive 1 mile to the sanctuary and turn left into the parking area.

ON THE TRAIL

It doesn't take long to realize what a special place Wachusett Meadow Wildlife Sanctuary is. This 1200-acre Massachusetts Audubon property, with its 12.8 miles of trails encompasses many different habitats and is a great place for exploring and learning about wildlife. And the layout is ideal for kids. The trails are well marked, have benches and good turn-around points at almost every junction, and provide many opportunities for viewing wildlife and points of interest. The hike described is a combination of five different trails, offering some highlights of the best Wachusett Meadow has to offer. But don't come here expecting everything to be exactly as described. These are active changing habitats, and what is there now may be different when you venture out. Beavers especially are hard at work building dams and changing the landscape—viewing platforms and trails sometimes have to be moved as a result. Do expect to spend time here, though—there are so many places to stop and enjoy that you won't want to rush. If you still have energy, you may also want to explore some of the other trails in the sanctuary.

From the parking area (where you will get a view of beaver wetlands and may possibly see sheep grazing nearby as habitat management), follow the sign to the information center to register, pay your admission fee, and borrow a trail map. North of the visitor center bear left on the

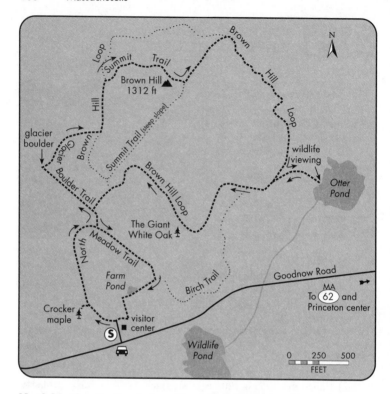

North Meadow Trail and almost immediately come to a downed Crocker maple. This enormous tree—once the largest sugar maple in Massachusetts—was blown over in an ice storm and has been left to decay naturally. Continue on the well-maintained mowed path 0.2 miles to a junction with the Glacier Boulder Trail. Turn left on this trail and enter the woods, following the blue blazes. (Blue-blazed trails lead away from the visitor center, yellow trails lead back, and white indicates trails that are considered connecting trails.) In another 0.3 mile you will reach the large chunks of a giant boulder, called an erratic, deposited by glaciers 15,000 years ago. The kids will definitely want to do some exploring before heading on.

In another 0.2 mile, reach the junction with the Brown Hill Loop and turn left, heading north. At the intersection with the Summit Trail 0.1 mile ahead, turn right and follow this short but semi-steep trail to the top of Brown Hill. At the summit, you will be treated to a 360-degree view with Mount Monadnock in the distance. Continue on the Summit Trail to a well-marked trail junction. (If you are ready to head back, you can bypass the Brown Hill Loop by turning right and heading down the short but steeper Summit Trail to its southwest intersection with the Brown Hill Loop.) At the junction, turn left and head down to the northeast intersection with the Brown Hill Loop. Turn right and hike through a forest of mixed hardwoods and ferns. In approximately 0.4 miles, head left for less than 0.2 miles on the Otter Pond Trail down to Otter Pond. How many signs of beavers, muskrats, and otters can the kids find? Can anyone see the beaver lodge?

How tall do you think this giant white oak is? (Photo by Emily Kerr)

Return up the Otter Pond Trail and turn left for the last half mile of the Brown Hill Loop. You can teach even the youngest children important environmental lessons with a game of "What if everyone did it?" What if, for instance, everyone stepped off the trail, chased the birds, dropped gum wrappers along the way, or picked flowers? About 2.2 miles from the start, pass the junctions with the Summit Trail and Glacier Boulder Trail on your right on your way back to the North Meadow Trail. A left-hand turn on the North Meadow Trail will take you by the Farm Pond. It will be hard to tear kids away from this little pond, where they will see giant bullfrogs and goldfish. This is also a great place to watch the activity in the sanctuary's nest boxes and to test your bird identification skills. Hike the last short stretch of the North Meadow Trail and turn left toward the visitor center to complete the loop.

Note: Closed Mondays except for holidays.

NORTH AMERICA'S LARGEST NATIVE RODENT

You guessed it—the beaver. Adult beavers weigh between 35 to 80 pounds. They use their flat tails to help them swim, regulate temperature, store fat, and communicate with other beavers. (They slap their tails on the water to send out an alarm.) They are probably best known for their dam-building abilities, which create wetlands that provide habitats for other wildlife, as well as being extremely valuable to people, maintaining the natural balance of our world and watersheds. Although they spend most of their time in the water, beavers don't eat fish. Their diet consists of aquatic plants and various parts of woody plants, including the bark and inner bark of trees and shrubs.

WACHUSETT MOUNTAIN

BEFORE YOU GO
Maps USGS Sterling, Fitchburg
Current Conditions
Wachusett Mountain State Park, Massachusetts Department of Conservation and Recreation (978) 464-2987
Fees None

ABOUT THE HIKE
Day hike
Moderate for children
May–November
3 miles round-trip
Elevation gain 700 feet
High point 2006 feet
Hiking time 2.5 hours
Accessibility No special access

GETTING THERE

- From MA 2 in Westminster, take exit 25 for MA 140 south.
- In approximately 2 miles a prominent sign announces Wachusett Mountain State Park.
- Turn right onto Mountain Road at a sign for Wachusett Mountain Ski Area.
- At 0.5 mile, pass the entrance to the ski area.
- Continue another 1.25 miles to the visitor center on the right-hand side and park.

ON THE TRAIL

While kids might not grasp the full impact of a view stretching 140 miles to Mount Washington, most will delight in the top-of-the-world feeling as they survey the countryside from the Wachusett summit, the highest

An energy break atop Wachusett Mountain (photo by Cynthia Copeland and Thomas J. Lewis)

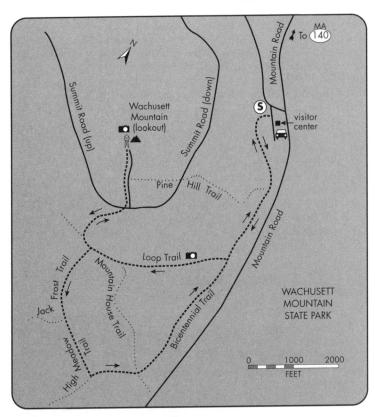

point in central Massachusetts. This is not a difficult mountain to climb by New England standards, but it is a mountain just the same, and the steady upward nature of this hike makes it a challenge for everyone. Proper footwear is a must. If you hike in early spring, you can stop for a snack on the crest while you watch the skiers arriving by chairlift to begin their "swoosh" down the slopes. A spring or fall hike (on a warm, sunny day) will most likely offer you an opportunity to watch kettles of migrating hawks soaring high over the valley.

Begin your hike at the far right corner of the parking area following the triangular blue blazes of the Bicentennial Trail. The trail heads south, traveling along the base of the mountain. At 0.2 mile, pass the Pine Hill Trail on the right; the Bicentennial Trail continues slightly left. Two-tenths of a mile later, turn right (west) onto the rock-strewn Loop Trail. At a vista about 0.5 mile from the start, southeasterly views of the surrounding farmland and distant Worcester hills begin to emerge. Climb steeply and steadily to a junction with Mountain House Trail. Turn right onto the Mountain House Trail and continue following blue triangular blazes. Stay to the right as the Jack Frost and Link Trails join the Mountain House Trail from the left. Climbing up this rugged path is much like mounting an extended flight of stairs. Children will need one or two rest stops along this stretch because the ascent is continuous. Just before the summit, cross the auto road and head back into the woods. Continue to an outlook at the mountaintop, 1.2 miles from the start. On a clear day, the Boston skyline is visible 50 miles due east. To the northwest, look for Mount Monadnock; to the north, Mount Washington, some 140 miles distant.

To complete the loop, follow the Mountain House Trail back to the junction with the Jack Frost Trail. Take the Jack Frost Trail right (south) and it quickly becomes relatively level, reaching a secondary summit in 0.2 mile. Here, join the High Meadow Trail on the left (southeast) and descend for 0.15 mile over the steepest terrain thus far. After a stretch on flatter ground, the Bicentennial Trail joins from the left. Take this even, meandering trail nearly 1 mile back to your car.

 MOUNT WATATIC

BEFORE YOU GO
Map USGS Ashburnham
Current Conditions Friends of the Wapack, *info@wapack.org*
Fees None

ABOUT THE HIKE
Day hike
Moderate for children
April–November
3 miles, loop trip
Elevation gain 650 feet
High point 1832 feet
Hiking time 2.5 hours
Accessibility No special access

GETTING THERE

- From the junction of MA 101 and MA 119 in Ashburnham, travel west for 1.4 miles on MA 119.
- Park in the area off the road on the right.

ON THE TRAIL

A not-too-tough climb to the top of Mount Watatic in Ashburnham will give kids the opportunity to do some safe summit exploring (there is no danger of them toppling off a cliff) while adults take in the four-state panoramic view. Two different return routes give kids and parents a choice between a steep descent and a more gradual one.

At the far end of the parking area, a sign for the Wapack Trail and Mount Watatic leads hikers onto a level cart road marked by yellow triangular blazes and bordered by stone walls. After passing a small pond surrounded by hemlocks, the trail climbs more steeply. At 0.25 miles, a sign pointing the way to the Wapack Trail leads to a right turn through an opening in a stone wall as the jeep trail—part of the State Line Trail—continues straight (You will be returning on the blue-blazed State Line Trail). Turn right onto the Wapack Trail and follow the yellow blazes as the route fords a stream and squeezes between two halves of an elephant-sized boulder. Soon the trail winds steeply through a hemlock grove and turns right. After a 0.3-mile ascent, the path breaks into an open area with panoramic views to the west and, to the northwest, views of Mount Monadnock.

Continuing along a high ridge, several trailside spots offer good places to stop and enjoy lunch or a snack. The trail heads through a stone wall, away from the ridge and into a hemlock forest. First gradually, then more sharply, the trail threads its way to the summit of Mount Watatic. One mile from the start, pass a wooden shelter and continue up to the pilings of an old fire tower. Turn right (southeast) to follow the trail to an exposed rocky area and the true summit of Mount Watatic at 1.2 miles, where the Boston skyline is visible to the east, the Vermont mountains to the northwest, and the Adirondacks and Mount Greylock to the west.

To return to your car, you can either retrace your steps or continue on the Wapack Trail over Nutting Hill to an intersection with the State Line Trail. To continue, pass the fire tower pilings on your left and find the sign in 0.1 miles pointing to the Wapack Trail alongside a gravel road. Follow the yellow blazes through a forest of hemlock and spruce for 0.6 mile to the top of Nutting Hill at 1.9 miles, where you will again be treated to spectacular views. Here, stone cairns guide you until the

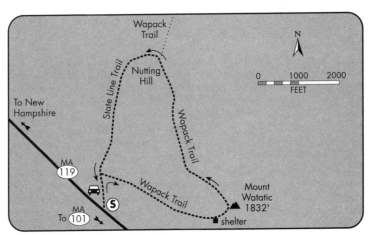

trail enters the woods and leads to a well-marked junction, 2.1 miles from the start. A large sign indicates the directions toward New Hampshire, Mount Watatic, and the Midstate and Wapack Trails. Turn left, following a small wooden sign that points the way to MA 119. Hike less than 0.1 mile to another sign pointing to the highway, and follow the blue blazes of the State Line Trail 0.8 mile back to the parking area.

 PURGATORY CHASM

BEFORE YOU GO
Maps USGS Milford, Worcester South
Current Conditions Purgatory Chasm State Reservation, Massachusetts Department of Environmental Management (508) 234-3733
Fees None

ABOUT THE HIKE
Day hike
Moderate for children
May–November
1 mile round-trip
Elevation gain 140 feet
High point 550 feet
Hiking time 2 hours
Accessibility No special access

GETTING THERE
- From the junction of US 20 and MA 146 in Millbury, take MA 146 south for 7.2 miles to Purgatory Road.
- Turn right (west) onto Purgatory Road.
- Drive 0.4 mile to the second parking area, which is on the left side of the road near the picnic pavilion.

ON THE TRAIL
If ever a geological fault was created with kids in mind, this is it. Purgatory Chasm is a lengthy gorge some 60 feet wide with sheer walls rising 70 feet high. As you wind your way through the maze of boulders lining the chasm floor, squeezing through small caves and channels with spooky names such as "Devils Coffin" and "Devils Pulpit," you may pause to watch a rock climber inching her way up the chasm wall. Families with small children may need a good deal of time and effort to get from one end of the gorge to the other, but you will enjoy every minute. You will no doubt meet a number of other folks following the same trail but somehow, on this adventure, it doesn't matter. In fact, it's fun to trade incredulous comments with other, equally awestruck people. On the return trip, you will view the gorge from perhaps a more breathtaking perspective—from above.

Navigating the boulders in Purgatory Chasm (photo by Emily Kerr)

Follow the blue blazes of the Chasm Loop Trail the length of the gorge (although you don't need to remain on the designated trail because you can't get lost and there is little vegetation to be disturbed). Remain close to younger children who will need almost constant assistance squeezing between piles of boulders and scaling others. Don't allow the inevitably slow pace to annoy you. There is so much to see and there are so many hollows and tunnels to explore that children are likely to forget that this is a hike. As you exit the chasm, continue straight on the path, ignoring the "Trail" sign by Devils Coffin that indicates a right- or left-hand turn. (You will no longer be following the blue blazes.) Soon, the route splits; head left (east) and walk approximately 0.3 mile on a wooded path to a fork, following the yellow blazes that indicate you are now on Charleys Loop Trail. Turn left (north) at a yellow arrow painted on a rock, heading back toward the chasm. The blazes will lead you along the edge of the cliffs. Side trips for better views into the gorge can be made with care. Just 1 mile from the start, you will return to the parking area.

You can alter the return trip by eliminating the woods walk and following the "Trail" sign and blue blazes to travel the entire route along the edge of the cliff. This route is not advisable for adults hiking with small children, however. They should opt for the wooded path because this section of trail does not necessitate constant supervision of the kids.

STONY BROOK WILDLIFE SANCTUARY/ BRISTOL BLAKE STATE RESERVATION

BEFORE YOU GO
Map USGS Franklin
Current Conditions Massachusetts Audubon Society;
Massachusetts Department of
Conservation and Recreation
(508) 528-3140
Fees Nonmembers, moderate
fee; members free

ABOUT THE HIKE
Day hike
Easy for children
Year-round
1 mile, loop trip
Elevation gain 30 feet
High point 140 feet
Hiking time 1 hour
Accessibility Wheelchair
accessible

GETTING THERE

- From I-495, travel north on MA 1A to its intersection with MA 115 in the township of Norfolk.
- Head north for 1.5 miles on MA 115.
- Turn left onto North Street; the entrance will be on your right.

ON THE TRAIL

Kids love water, and this hike offers plenty. The former site of a sawmill, Stony Brook Wildlife Sanctuary's wheelchair-accessible Pond Loop Trail circles Stony Brook Pond, has an extensive boardwalk between Kingfisher Pond and Teal Marsh, and ends near a waterfall. Wildlife is plentiful and children are practically guaranteed to spot something. Ducks, geese, turtles, muskrats, great blue herons, and many other types of birds and animals are common. There is even a butterfly garden at the end of the hike, where you may be able to spot different types of butterflies and caterpillars feeding on the nectar of the garden's plants. Before setting out, head to the nature center—you can check the board for the day's wildlife sightings and borrow or purchase a trail guide to the numbered stations along the trail.

The hike begins behind the nature center and heads west on a broad, flat path bordered by stone walls. Have the kids look out for the numbered posts, and stop to read the descriptions from the guide. This is a great way for children and grownups alike to learn about the different plants and animals present in the sanctuary. In a little over 0.1 mile, cross over a small spillway between Stony Brook Pond and Teal Marsh, and continue another 0.1 miles to a junction where the Pond Loop Trail takes a sharp right. Continue straight ahead and you will reach the

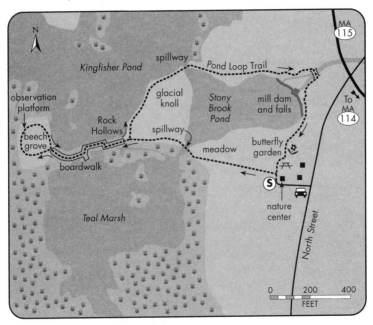

boardwalk, one of the best parts of this hike. To the south is Teal Marsh and to the north is Kingfisher Pond. Keep your eyes open for painted turtles and sunfish in the water, and birds flying overhead or nesting in the bird boxes. Having trouble luring the kids away? Let them know that they will get to cross the boardwalk again and that there is more to see ahead.

Continue on the boardwalk to a short loop around a beech grove. Partway around it you will come to an observation platform where you can look for wildlife in the marsh. Can anyone spot any ducks? What are the differences between the male and female? Which ones have green heads? Complete your circle of the beech grove, head back across the boardwalk, and turn left at the Pond Loop intersection. The trail passes the Rock Hollows and skirts the eastern edge of Kingfisher Pond before crossing over another spillway between Kingfisher Pond and Stony Brook Pond. The trail now takes you past

If you're quiet, you may see a swan in the water. (Photo by Emily Kerr)

Stony Brook Pond on your right before coming to the site of the former mill, where there is a dam and falls. If you have children in a stroller, follow the sign for the wheelchair/stroller trail that will take you around the steps and steep grade by the waterfall. At 0.9 miles, cross the bridge over the stream (whose water will eventually end up in the Charles River) and head the final 0.1 mile to the nature center. Finish your hike with a visit to the butterfly garden and a picnic in the designated area to the north of the center.

GREAT BLUE HILL

BEFORE YOU GO
Map USGS Norwood
Current Conditions The Blue Hills Reservation, Massachusetts Department of Conservation and Recreation (617) 698-1802
Fees None

ABOUT THE HIKE
Day hike
Moderate for children
April–November
2.3 miles, loop trip
Elevation gain 550 feet
High point 635 feet
Hiking time 2.5 hours
Accessibility No special access

GETTING THERE
- Off of MA 128/I-93, take exit 2B to MA 138.
- Take MA 138 north to the first traffic light.
- Turn right onto Hillside Street (not well marked).
- Continue past an intersection with a sign for Houghtons Pond.
- Nearly 1.5 miles from MA 138, turn right into a small parking area directly across from the reservation headquarters and the Brian Broderick Mounted Unit Stable.
- Use the crosswalk to carefully cross the road.

ON THE TRAIL
Climbing to the summit of Great Blue Hill has been popular since colonial days, although there are quite a few more hikers today than there were 200 years ago. Bostonians flock to the 7000-acre Blue Hills Reservation with its 125 miles of trails; it is the largest undeveloped parcel of land within 35 miles of Boston. The route described here entails a moderately challenging ascent with a rewarding view of the city from atop the summit's stone tower. Kids will thrill to the rocky scramble up and down the mountain while adults scan the tremendous vistas on the upper portion for familiar landmarks. After the hike, stop by Houghton's

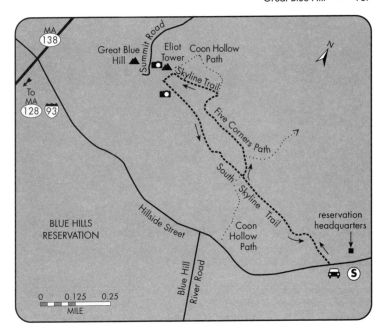

Pond (also part of the reservation) for a swim, playground jaunt, and picnic supper.

Before you begin hiking, you may want to refer to the large trail map at the headquarters building, also available for purchase. It is a good idea to pick up a copy of this park map to have with you, as it shows all the trails in the reservation and is updated with any trail renovations. To begin the hike, head back down Hillside Street following a sign to the South Skyline Trail. In about four hundred feet, you will see a granite pillar marking the beginning of the blue-blazed South Skyline Trail. Turn right and begin a rocky, rugged ascent. Don't let the kids start off at too fast a pace or they will wear out quickly. Teach them how to conserve their energy for the strenuous climb ahead. In 0.25 mile, bear left on the trail as it flattens out. Have the kids look for the blue blazes painted on the rocks. You will cross a trail junction with Houghton Path and a small stream before reaching a junction in a little over 0.5 miles with the Coon Hollow Path, marked 1123. Turn right onto Coon Hollow Path.

The Five Corners Path, marked with fluorescent green circles, soon joins your trail at intersection 1120. Head straight across this intersection to the left-hand branch of the Five Corners Path. Be sure you are following the green blazes heading west. (If you turn right, you will also be following green blazes, but you will be going north.) In another 0.3 mile you will reach intersection 1092. Here you have a choice on how to

Sandwiches taste even better after you've climbed a mountain. (Photo by Cynthia Copeland and Thomas J. Lewis)

reach the top. You can turn left and follow the blue-blazed Skyline Trail up what looks like a steep rocky staircase, or you can head straight ahead on a well-worn path, and at intersection 1082, turn left and follow the red-blazed Coon Hollow Path.

A little over a mile from the start, both trails deliver you near the top of Great Blue Hill at Eliot Tower with its commanding views of the Boston skyline and the Atlantic Ocean. What kinds of animals can the kids find in the clouds? After gazing at the city from the tower's upper floor and visiting with other hiking families, locate the blue-blazed route traversing a stone bridge. Shortly after crossing the bridge, a granite post on your left and wooden post on the right indicate your left-hand turn onto the steep, rocky, blue-blazed South Skyline Trail. The southern views as you descend via this path are tremendous, perhaps even better than those from the summit. The trail follows a gurgling stream and travels through some interesting boulder fields, with several other trails splitting off to either side along the route. Follow the South Skyline Trail all the way to Hillside Street and your starting point.

OTHER ACTIVITIES

You can also visit the Trailside Museum, managed by the Massachusetts Audubon Society. The museum is open Wednesday through Sunday and is located on MA 138, 0.5 mile north of I-93. There is a small admission fee. Or head to Houghton's Pond for a swim and a romp on the playground.

WORLDS END RESERVATION

BEFORE YOU GO
Map USGS Hull
Current Conditions The Trustees of Reservations, Southeast Region (781) 740-6665
Fees Nonmembers, moderate fee; members free

ABOUT THE HIKE
Day hike
Easy for children
Year-round
4 miles, loop trip
Elevation gain 120 feet
High point 70 feet
Hiking time 3 hours
Accessibility Limited accessibility; paths are wide and graveled, but steep in parts

GETTING THERE

- From MA 3 in Quincy, take MA 3A to East Hingham.
- At a rotary, MA 3A heads right; continue straight on a four-lane highway for 0.5 mile to Four Corners.
- Turn left here onto Martins Lane.
- Drive 0.7 mile to the reservation parking area.

ON THE TRAIL

Worlds End, a figure-eight–shaped peninsula dividing Hingham Harbor and the Weir River, is well known for its spectacular topography and landscaping. Families have enjoyed hiking its tree-lined gravel roads and admiring its dramatic glacial drumlins since the turn of the century. In the late 1800s, the property nearly became a planned community with more than 150 home sites, but instead was farmed and then turned into a private park. Three-quarters of a century later, it was again threatened by development. The public rallied and raised $450,000, enabling the Trustees of the Reservations to buy the 251-acre parcel and make it available for public enjoyment. If you look across Boston Bay toward Hull at the clusters of homes vying for ocean views and beach frontage, you will appreciate the peaceful, natural setting of Worlds End.

View from the second drumlin, looking back at the connecting sandbar (photo by Cynthia Copeland and Thomas J. Lewis)

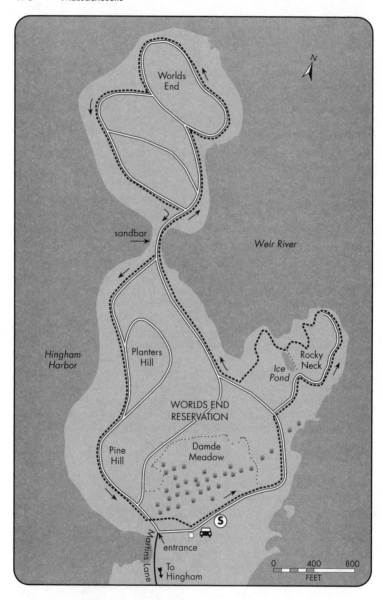

Kids will lead the way on the wide gravel and grass paths that skirt and traverse the drumlins as they delight in the constant ocean views.

The trail that begins at the corner of the parking area farthest from the road is, like the other trails here, unblazed and unnamed, but obvious. The trail here skirts Damde Meadow. At each junction, keep to the right. Soon after entering the woods, a huge rock outcrop on the left will challenge your agile little climbers. After 0.5 mile, the wide trail splits and a side trail takes you to Rocky Neck where, at the tip, the road narrows into a foot trail that leads back to the main path. With the Weir River on your right, the cart path travels along the base of open, grassy Planters Hill on your left. It may be impossible to keep kids on the trail with the neatly mown fields begging them to break into an aimless run, but warn them first about poison ivy.

Continue 0.3 mile to the sand bar connecting the two drumlins. Here, the stiff ocean breeze will be welcome on a sultry August day and not so welcome on a raw day in March. Who will be the first to see the Boston skyline? Travel the perimeter of the outer drumlin, continuing to choose the right-hand path at all trail junctures. As you walk along the eastern side of the peninsula, look beyond Hull and you will see the open Atlantic Ocean. After a 1.2-mile hike, you will return to the sandbar. Cross over to the inner parcel and stay to the right, hiking on the west foot of Planters Hill with Hingham Harbor on your right. Look for signs of foxes and rabbits and watch for quail, pheasant, and the numerous varieties of sea and shore birds that frequent the area. After an easy climb over Pine Hill, the path will bring you back to the entrance and parking area.

Notes: The reservation opens around 8:00 AM and closes promptly at sunset. Picnicking is allowed, but you must pack out your trash. Wading is prohibited.

 IPSWICH RIVER WILDLIFE SANCTUARY

BEFORE YOU GO
Map USGS Salem
Current Conditions Ipswich River Wildlife Sanctuary, Massachusetts Audubon Society (978) 887-9264
Fees Nonmembers, moderate fee; members free

ABOUT THE HIKE
Day hike (camping at sanctuary by permit only)
Easy for children
April–November
3 miles, loop trip
Elevation gain 50 feet
High point 110 feet
Hiking time 2 hours
Accessibility No special access

GETTING THERE
▪ From the junction of US 1 and MA 97 in Topsfield, drive southeast on MA 97 for 0.5 mile.

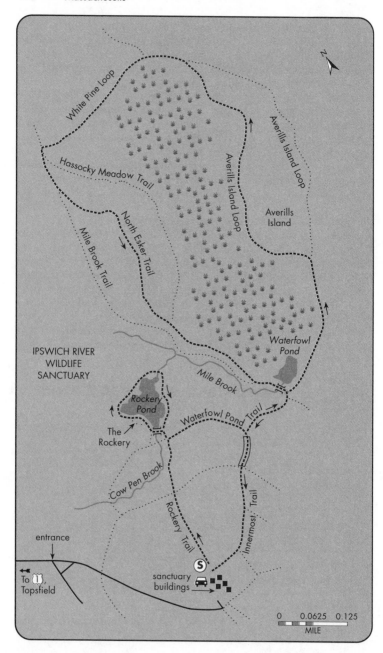

White Pine Loop

Hassocky Meadow Trail

North Esker Trail

Mile Brook Trail

Averills Island Loop

Averills Island Loop

Averills Island

Waterfowl Pond

IPSWICH RIVER
WILDLIFE
SANCTUARY

Mile Brook

Rockery Pond

The Rockery

Waterfowl Pond Trail

Cow Pen Brook

Rockery Trail

Innermost Trail

entrance

To 1,
Topsfield

S

sanctuary
buildings

0   0.0625   0.125
MILE

- Turn left on Perkins Row.
- In one mile, turn right, following signs into the Massachusetts Audubon Society property.
- The parking lot is 0.2 mile from the Perkins Row turnoff on the left.

ON THE TRAIL

The good news: the sanctuary's famed Rockery, a series of stone stairways, tunnels, and bridges built by the property's wealthy owners nearly a century ago, will make this hike unforgettable for the kids. The bad news: once they begin having fun exploring this intricate maze of precisely placed boulders, they may want to end the hike right there! But it's well worth whatever cajoling it may take to get them to continue. Within the sanctuary's 2400 acres are more than 20 miles of hiking trails with features nearly as enticing: boardwalks, rustic bridges, wildflower gardens, and unusual oriental trees and plants. You may even meet up with a snake or a turtle.

Borrow a trail map at the information center where you will also pay a moderate admission fee per person. From the parking area, head north across an open field. At the right-hand corner of the field, the trail enters the woods on a slight descent. Head straight on the Rockery Trail. Cross over the Waterfowl Pond Trail and bear left at Rockery Pond, heading for the Rockery. When you arrive at the Rockery at 0.3 mile, encourage the kids to explore all the paths and tunnels, pausing atop the stone structure for a view of Rockery Pond. Imagine hauling these rocks from

Inside the Rockery tunnels (photo by Emily Kerr)

miles away by horse and cart! Not surprisingly, it took nine years to build this rock masterpiece.

Circle the pond (with the water on your right) still on the Rockery Trail. Can you hear bullfrogs calling or make out ducks floating on the still water? Bear left onto the Waterfowl Pond Trail, heading away from the pond. At the next junction, you can turn right to cross a boardwalk and follow the Innermost Trail back to your car, or you can bear left to continue the hike. In nearly 1 mile, you will see the stone bridge that spans Mile Brook. Pause to look out over Waterfowl Pond. Bear right here, heading for Averills Island on the Averills Island Trail. Bear left 0.25 mile later, skirting the marsh on your left. In 0.5 mile, bear left again and soon after, turn left once more to join the White Pine Loop Trail. At the next intersection bear left, walking now in a southerly direction. Stay to the right (you will now be on the Mile Brook Trail for a short distance). Pass the Hassocky Meadow Trail and bear left onto the North Esker Trail. On this path, you walk along a ridge with good views of the wetlands to the east and west. This trail will bring you back to the stone bridge, where you turn right on the Waterfowl Pond Trail and then left on the Innermost Trail to return to your car.

Notes: No dogs or fires. Picnic only in designated areas. Closed Mondays.

SANDY POINT STATE RESERVATION/ PARKER RIVER NATIONAL WILDLIFE REFUGE

BEFORE YOU GO
Map USGS Ipswich
Current Conditions
Massachusetts Department of Conservation and Recreation (978) 462-4481; U.S. Fish & Wildlife Service (978) 465-5753
Fees Nonmembers, moderate fee; members, free

ABOUT THE HIKE
Day hike
Easy for children
Year-round; sometimes closed for wildlife protection
3 miles, loop trip
Elevation gain 40 feet
High point 40 feet
Hiking time 2.5 hours
Accessibility No special access

GETTING THERE
■ From I-95 take exit 57 and travel east on MA 113.
■ Continue straight onto MA 1A south to the intersection with Rolfes Lane.

- Turn left onto Rolfes Lane and travel 0.5 mile to its end.
- Turn right onto the Plum Island Turnpike.
- Take your first right onto Sunset Drive and travel 0.5 mile to the entrance of the Parker River National Wildlife Refuge.
- Sandy Point is at the end of the refuge, approximately 6 miles from the gate.

ON THE TRAIL

The 4662-acre Parker River National Wildlife Refuge, covering two-thirds of Plum Island, offers several different nature trails that traverse barren sand dunes, lush marshes, and glacial drumlins. Sandy Point State Reservation lies at the southernmost tip of the island. Plum Island is a favorite spot for birdwatchers—nearly 300 species of birds frequent the area—as well as sunbathers who have learned that by arriving early they can secure some of the few parking spaces inside the refuge. Often, on a hot summer's day, the gates are closed and the parking lot full by 8:00 AM. The benefit of this policy to the seaside hiker is relative seclusion: where else within 35 miles of Boston can the children virtually own 7 miles of unspoiled beach for the afternoon? Hiking during the warm months requires sunscreen, bathing suits, towels, pails, and shovels. (There are no lifeguards; warn children who wish to swim about strong undertows.) Be sure to make a stop at the visitor center located at the junction of Rolfes Lane and Plum Island Turnpike on the way in.

Before starting the hike, you may want to view the ocean and southern Plum Island from the observation tower adjacent to lot 7. The walk begins on a boardwalk close to the parking lot that leads to the Atlantic Ocean. (If this area is closed due to piping plover nesting season, or for a shorter hike, begin at the upper parking lot for Sandy Point, just down the road.) Turn right and continue along the sandy shore. At a row of boulders, Parker River ends and Sandy Point begins. Just beyond this marker, the rocky drumlin known as Bar Head rises above the ocean. On your walk toward Sandy Point the kids will probably be unable to resist kicking off their shoes and wading in the cool water.

At the point, turn and head north along a vast stretch of untarnished beach. If the kids have tired of wading or watching the waves come and go, have them scan the sand dunes for signs of long-destroyed summer cottages. You will arrive at a fence marking the perimeter of the refuge 1.7 miles from the start. Turn right here and in less than 30 yards turn right again onto a grassy path. This path will take you past a freshwater swamp on the outskirts of Stage Island Pool. You can catch glimpses of the water through tall cattails and other vegetation. Do the children see any butterflies? After walking along the path for 0.5 mile, you will pass through a gate and across a parking area. (This is where you can park for a shorter hike.) A trail winds for 0.2 mile through thick scrub to an observation platform atop Bar Head. After taking in the view, head back down to the parking area, turn left over a boardwalk to the beach, and retrace your footsteps to lot 7 where you parked your car.

PIPING PLOVERS

These small sandy-colored birds that run in short stops and starts became a protected species under the Endangered Species Act in 1986. Their population was and still is threatened by increased development and recreational use of beaches. Piping plovers return to their breeding grounds in spring and establish their nests on the beach close to the dunes. Beaches are often closed during this time to protect their nesting. You can help by respecting all signs and keeping your distance from piping plovers and their nests.

 LYMAN RESERVE

BEFORE YOU GO
Maps USGS Wareham, Sagamore
Current Conditions The Trustees of Reservations, South Coast Region (508) 679-2115
Fees None

ABOUT THE HIKE
Day hike
Easy for children
Year-round
2 miles, loop trip
Elevation gain 40 feet
High point 40 feet
Hiking time 1.5 hours
Accessibility No special access

GETTING THERE
■ From MA 25, take exit 2 (Buzzards Bay, Bourne).
■ Bear right off the ramp, to take an immediate right onto Head of the Bay Road.
■ Drive approximately 3 miles.
■ Parking is on the right-hand side, just past Packard Street.

ON THE TRAIL
Looking to escape the crowds of the Cape or just want a change of scenery from the beach? Try the Theodore Lyman Reserve on Buttermilk Bay. You'll still get to play on a sandy beach, but you'll also get to hike near a freshwater stream, and through freshwater wetlands and forested uplands. Red Brook, which flows through the property to Buttermilk Bay, is home to one of the last remaining native sea-run brook trout

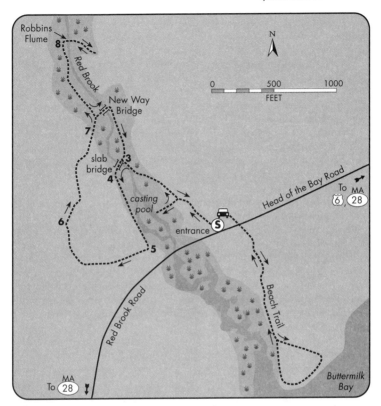

("salters") fisheries on this side of the country. Check rules and regulations before you go, but you may even want to carry along a fishing pole (or at least a stick with a string attached so the kids can "pretend" fish). The reserve was once a fishing camp and honors Theodore Lyman III, who worked hard to protect it.

To begin your hike, head out on the trail behind the sign. The trail is marked with numbers along the way so it's easy to figure out your location. Give the children the responsibility of finding each subsequent marker along the way. In less than 0.1 mile, at the sign for trailmarker 2, turn left to follow a short side path down to a casting pool. Here you will have a nice view of Red Brook and the many plants that surround it. Back on the trail, continue walking northwest for a little over 0.1 mile. Turn left at trailmarker 3 to cross a slab bridge over Red Brook. Do the kids know what makes the water look red? It's from iron in the soil near where the brook begins.

After crossing the bridge, turn left at trailmarker 4. You will now be heading southeast. Notice the changing landscape. When you reach number 5, turn right (west). You will be leaving the swampy marshy area around the brook behind and entering a restored pitch pine/scrub oak habitat. This area was restored to help endangered animal species (mainly moths) and over the years will bounce back and be maintained as a low canopy forest. The trail climbs slightly and curves north. Look at the shapes of the pines around you. Upon reaching trailmarker 6, take the first trail on the right and head back downhill. (There is a trail to the left that may look like a continuation of the main trail, but it leads to private property. Play careful attention to signs in this area.) At number 7, continue straight through a swampy area along Red Brook to number 8 and Robbins Flume, about a mile from the start. (You will want to have plenty of bugspray here.)

To return, retrace your footsteps to number 7. This time turn left to cross the New Way Bridge. Beyond this, the trail curves sharply to the right (southeast) and heads back through a swampy area to the number 3. Bear left (don't cross the bridge) and head back to the parking area.

Cross Head of the Bay Road carefully to reach the quarter-mile-long Beach Trail. Follow the path through the forest to a loop junction. You can follow the loop either way to reach the sandy beach on the shore of Buttermilk Bay. This is a great place to relax, hunt for treasures, and admire the Cape Cod Canal vertical lift railroad bridge before heading back to your car.

Finding horseshoe crabs on the beach (photo by Emily Kerr)

 **SANDY NECK**

BEFORE YOU GO
Map USGS Hyannis
Current Conditions Sandy Neck Gatehouse, Town of Barnstable Department of Marine and Environmental Affairs (508) 362-8300
Fees Beach sticker or moderate fee in season

ABOUT THE HIKE
Day hike
Challenging for children
Year-round; portions of the beach may be closed during piping plover nesting season
4.5 miles, loop trip
Elevation gain 100 feet
High point 40 feet
Hiking time 4 hours
Accessibility No special access

GETTING THERE

- From US 6 in Barnstable take exit 5 to travel north on MA 149.
- In 1 mile, at the junction with MA 6A in West Barnstable, turn left (west).
- In another 3 miles, turn right onto Sandy Neck Road.
- Continue down to the ranger station.
- After checking in, continue straight ahead to the main parking lot.

ON THE TRAIL

Sandy Neck on Cape Cod is a 6-mile-long coastal barrier beach that offers hiking trails that follow along the isolated shore, wind among sculptured sand dunes, and wander past the lush Great Marshes. Due to the loose nature of the sandy soil, walking is arduous and this is a hike for those in very good physical condition. Arrive early to take advantage of the morning coolness (or hike during the cooler seasons) and don't forget to bring water, sunscreen, and hats for everyone. A book to identify animal tracks in the sand will turn the kids' attention away from their hot, tired feet.

Head back along the entrance road—being careful of traffic—toward

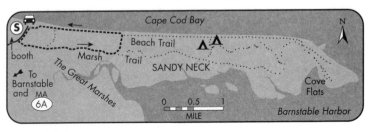

Trail through the dunes at Sandy Neck (photo by Emily Kerr)

the ranger station. You can stop here to talk with the rangers and pick up some pamphlets on the area. East of the ranger station, walk through a gate onto the Marsh Trail. Here you will see a sign indicating the distances to different numbered trails off the Marsh Trail. Because of the fragile nature of this seaside environment, it is important to locate and stick to the marked trails. The wide Marsh Trail will lead you along the edge of the Great Marshes, where you can look for swallows, red-winged blackbirds, great blue herons, osprey, and many other types of birds. In the soft, windswept sand of the trail watch for bird, deer, and skunk tracks. The Marsh Trail passes a sign for Trail 1 at 0.5 miles (where you can turn left and head toward the water for a shorter hike, turning left again at the water toward the parking area) and arrives at a sign for Trail 2 at 2 miles. Turn left (north) here between impressive dunes and arrive at Cape Cod Bay in 0.3 miles. Turn left (west) onto the Beach Trail which follows along the water. Here the kids can break into a run along the firmer beach sand, dodging the playful waves. This would be a great time to take an energy break. Lie back and relax, pointing out the shapes created by the puffy, drifting clouds overhead. (We always manage to find a galloping horse and a hippo with its mouth open.) As you walk along the beach, be alert for off-road vehicles.

Continuing the hike, after about 1.5 miles you will see the sign for Trail 1 pointing toward the dunes. Continue walking along the water for another 0.4 mile to the parking area. If it's warm enough grab your bathing suits and dive into the waves.

WHAT MADE SANDY NECK?

The rocks and sand that make up Sandy Neck are products of glaciers from around 10,000 years ago. In fact, Cape Cod is formed by a moraine left behind by a retreating continental glacier. The sand and rock you see on Sandy Neck were once part of mountains to the north and west.

FORT HILL TRAIL

BEFORE YOU GO
Map USGS Orleans
Current Conditions
National Park Service, Cape
Cod National Seashore (508)
349-3785 or (508) 255-3421
Fees Moderate fee in season
and on weekends and
holidays

ABOUT THE HIKE
Day hike
Easy for children
Year-round
1.6 miles, loop trip
Elevation gain 100 feet
High point 50 feet
Hiking time 2 hours
Accessibility No special
access

GETTING THERE

- From the junction of US 6 and MA 28 (at a rotary) on the Eastham/Orleans border, drive north on US 6 for 1.2 miles.
- Turn right onto Governor Prence Road.
- Make another right turn onto Fort Hill Road.
- Drive to the parking area on the left marked with a Fort Hill sign.

ON THE TRAIL

As you walk the Fort Hill Trail, part of the Cape Cod National Seashore, you will realize that Cape Cod is more than sand dunes, clam rolls, and lighthouses. Featuring a boardwalk through wetlands, two small hill climbs with views over Nauset Marsh, historic Indian Rock, and a stroll around the grounds of whaleship captain Edward Penniman's historic home, these trails offer a distinct vision of the Cape.

Begin on the trail that leads into the woods from the right

The unique whalebone archway in front of the Penniman House (photo by Cynthia Copeland and Thomas J. Lewis)

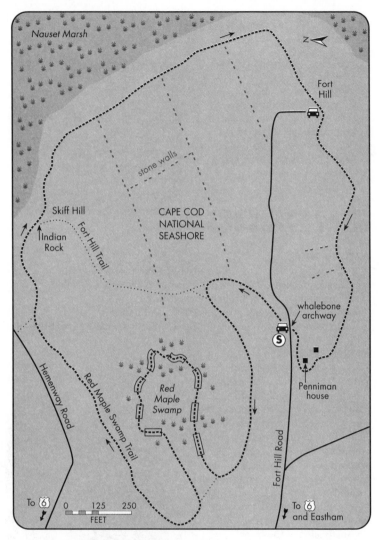

(eastern) side of the parking lot. Head uphill on rustic steps through the forest. Soon, you will leave the woods and walk along the edge of a large field that abuts Nauset Marsh. Stone walls that once marked farmers' boundaries remind hikers of the former uses of this land. Partway into the field, at 0.1 mile, take a left into the woods followed immediately by another left. Walk along the Red Maple Swamp Trail, bearing right in 0.3 mile to follow a series of boardwalks (little ones can try to keep count) through Red Maple Swamp. There's something about boardwalks that kids love—they are easy to follow and fun to run on.

At an intersection about 0.6 mile into the hike, turn right to follow the trail another 0.2 mile to a paved path. Another right turn at close to 1 mile will bring you first to an overlook of the bay and the distant Atlantic Ocean and then to a pavilion housing Indian Rock. Encourage kids to examine this boulder once used by Nauset Indians to sharpen tools and weapons and to shape fish hooks. From the back of the pavilion take the Fort Hill Trail to the left; the trail skirts the edge of Nauset Marsh. Hike for about 0.4 mile to Fort Hill and another parking area. Enjoy the views over the marsh before continuing on this trail another 0.3 mile to the Penniman House. You will travel behind the buildings, through the front yard, and under the whalebone archway at the edge of the Penniman property. Such magnificent entryways date back to the days when whaling was big business on the Cape. Your car is in the parking lot diagonally across the street to the right.

 NAUSET MARSH TRAIL

BEFORE YOU GO
Map USGS Orleans
Current Conditions
National Park Service, Cape Cod National Seashore (508) 349-3785 or (508) 255-3421
Fees Moderate fee in season and on weekends and holidays

ABOUT THE HIKE
Day hike
Easy for children
Year-round
1.25 miles, loop trip
Elevation gain 90 feet
High point 60 feet
Hiking time 2 hours
Accessibility Salt Pond Visitor Center and Buttonbush Trail portion are accessible

GETTING THERE
- Drive north on US 6 past the rotary at the Orleans/Eastham town line.
- Slow down at mile marker 94.
- At mile 94.282, turn right onto Doane Road (also called Nauset Road) into the Salt Pond Visitor Center approximately 3 miles beyond the rotary.

ON THE TRAIL
The Cape is constantly changing due to natural forces such as fierce ocean storms and the pounding surf as well as human encroachment

Crossing Nauset Marsh (photo by Cynthia Copeland and Thomas J. Lewis)

and development. Near Wellfleet, the Cape has eroded to only 1 mile wide and, in Provincetown, giant dunes threaten to overtake the highway. On the Nauset Marsh Trail, which is part of the Cape Cod National Seashore, you will witness some of the natural change affecting the Cape as the tides swell and then flush the pond and marsh areas at precise intervals. This is a super walk for young families, just over 1 mile long with a variety of water views. Watch out for poison ivy, which grows rampant on the Cape. Sneakers are fine.

The hike begins near the Salt Pond Visitor Center to the right of the outdoor amphitheater. The sandy trail, initially sprinkled with crushed white shells, quickly drops to the shore of Salt Pond and follows along the water's edge on a wide gravel path. Salt Pond was a freshwater "kettle pond" until the ocean waters spilled over from Nauset Marsh long ago and a thin channel was created linking the marsh and pond. Today, Salt Pond nurtures a wide variety of marine creatures, some swept in and out by the twice-daily tides. Can the kids spot any herons or gulls?

Head through the woods and up a low hill on a series of steps to an overlook 0.6 mile from the start. Just below the overlook lies Salt Pond Bay, with Nauset Beach to the east and Nauset Harbor beyond the marsh flats to the east-southeast. After you have enjoyed the lovely views and the sounds of the ocean birds, follow the path as it skirts the marsh and then curls to the left through airy woodlands. The eastern red cedar stands replaced the golf course that stretched along the marsh in the early 1900s. The trail crosses a bike path and then plunges into denser forest with frequent placards pointing out varieties of trees and plants. After crossing the bike path a second time, the Nauset Trail joins the Buttonbush Trail, which heads in two directions. Bear left. The Buttonbush Trail is a self-guided nature trail that has been adapted for use by handicapped and blind visitors. A short walk along this path will complete the loop and return you to the Salt Pond Visitor Center.

GREAT ISLAND TRAIL

BEFORE YOU GO
Map USGS Wellfleet
Current Conditions
National Park Service, Cape
Cod National Seashore (508)
349-3785 or (508) 255-3421
Fees Moderate fee in season
and on weekends and
holidays

ABOUT THE HIKE
Day hike
Challenging for children
Year-round
6 miles round-trip
Elevation gain 150 feet
High point 75 feet
Hiking time 5 hours
Accessibility No special
access

GETTING THERE

- On US 6 in Wellfleet (heading toward Provincetown), take the exit for Wellfleet Center and Harbor, 5 miles north of the Wellfleet town line.
- Turn left off the exit ramp and drive through Wellfleet Center.
- Turn left onto Chequesset Neck Road at 0.6 mile.
- At an intersection in 0.4 mile, turn right.
- At the Town Pier, turn right.
- Drive 2.3 miles and turn left into Great Island and a large parking area.

ON THE TRAIL

Come to Great Island, one of the Cape Cod National Seashore sites, early in the morning with sun hats, sunscreen, canteens, and rugged hiking boots. The trail circles a salt marsh, winds through pitch pine forests, climbs over towering dunes, and finishes along an extensive stretch of Cape Cod Bay beach. If you intend to extend this from a 6-mile to an 8.4-mile round-trip hike by walking out to Jeremy Point, make sure you will arrive at the connecting spit at low and receding tide. Remember that walking on loose sand takes considerable effort and young children may get frustrated at their lack of progress.

The trail of white crushed shells bordered by round logs leaves the left side of the parking lot (which is closed from midnight to 6:00 AM), winds through a wooded section, and emerges at the tidal flat near the mouth of the Herring River. The salt hay you see along the path was once a staple in the diet of grazing cattle because of its nutritional value. Turn right at water's edge and begin walking along the sandy road that encircles the tidal flat or "The Gut." Look for signs of ocean life in the

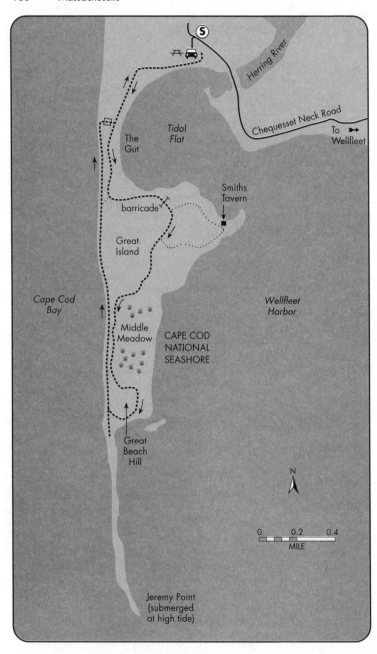

sand: gull tracks, fiddler crabs, broken shells. A short, steep boardwalk provides access to the beach on the other side of the dunes. At the end of the tidal flat, as the dunes loom before you, bear left still skirting the marsh, then head right when the trail divides just past the barricade to motor vehicles. (A short side trail on the left takes you to the site of the eighteenth-century Smith's Tavern, 1.8 miles from the start.) The narrow main trail climbs to the summit of Great Island through a cluster of pines and then drops to Middle Meadow. After skirting this marshy area, the path rolls over some dunes before climbing Great Beach Hill at 2.8 miles. Enjoy the vast views over Cape Cod Bay. From the southerly base of the hill, Jeremy Point is 1.2 miles away, accessed by a narrow spit. (Be sure that you know the tide schedule before heading to the point. Remember, this will add 2.4 miles to your hike.) You can return by walking along the beach on the Cape Cod Bay side of Great Island; or, if you prefer to make the hike 0.8 mile longer, by the way you came.

 ## CEDAR TREE NECK SANCTUARY

BEFORE YOU GO
Map USGS Vineyard Haven
Current Conditions Sheriff's
Meadow Foundation
(508) 693-5207
Fees None

ABOUT THE HIKE
Day hike
Easy for children
Year-round
2 miles, loop trip
Elevation gain 150 feet
High point 100 feet
Hiking time 2.5 hours
Accessibility No special
access

GETTING THERE

- From the junction of State Road and Edgartown Road in Vineyard Haven on Martha's Vineyard, drive southwest on State Road for about 2.5 miles to a fork.
- Bear right here, remaining on State Road.
- A hundred yards after a sign for Lamberts Cove at 3.9 miles, bear right onto paved Indian Hill Road.
- At 1.7 miles, turn right at a sign for Cedar Tree Neck onto a rough, one-lane dirt road (Obed Daggett Road).
- After 1 mile, you will arrive at the parking area for Cedar Tree Neck.

ON THE TRAIL

The island of Martha's Vineyard, just 5 miles off of the south shore of Cape Cod, attracted its first permanent white settlers in 1642 and now, nearly 350 years later, welcomes a flood of visitors each summer. You

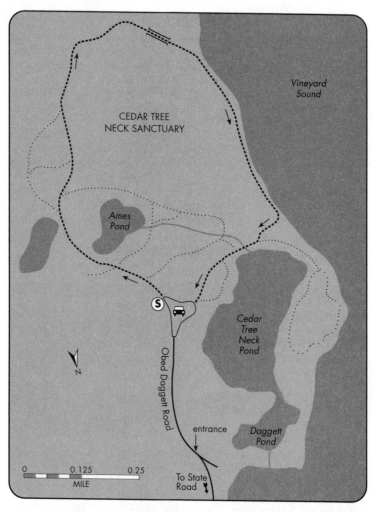

may want to plan your trip for September or October, when the days are still warm enough for outdoor fun but the crowds have returned to the mainland. (By late fall, however, many restaurants, inns, and stores have closed for the season.) The Woods Hole, Martha's Vineyard, and Nantucket Steamship Authority is the main ferry line that carries cars across to the island; the ferry leaves from Woods Hole (on the shoulder of the Cape) for Vineyard Haven or Oak Bluffs. Kids will relish the forty-five–minute ferry ride, sitting on the breezy open deck and watching the sea gulls, fishing boats, and approaching island. Call (508) 477-8600 for schedules and reservations (which should be made well in advance). The two Vineyard hikes described in this guide center around the north shore, which is more heavily wooded and better suited for hiking; the south shore is more appropriate for ocean-side recreation, such as sunning, swimming, and wading in the rolling surf.

The Cedar Tree Neck Sanctuary encompasses a freshwater pond and bog, woodlands, rocky bluffs, and open fields. The easy-to-follow nature trails wind through the forest and along the solitary beach, making it one of the island's most enjoyable walks. You are bound to find many treasures along the seashore—remember to leave them there, though!

A detailed wooden map in the parking area shows the color-coded, marked trails that wind through the Cedar Tree Neck preserve. The white trail heads out of the parking area's southeast side and ascends for the first 0.5 mile. The narrow trail squeezes through low shrubbery and mountain laurel and feels more like a trail winding through the foothills of New Hampshire's White Mountains than a path approaching the seashore.

After the initial steady climb, the trail rides up and down hilly terrain to a footbridge over a stream at 1.2 miles and a steep climb to the top of a bluff. On the down side of this hill, the ocean becomes visible. Soon the trail outlets onto one of the most beautiful stretches of beach anywhere. Mother Nature has claimed this shore for her own; white sand, rocks, and ocean birds replace portable radios and volleyball nets. Because swimming is not allowed here, encourage your young artists to draw giant pictures in the sand with sturdy sticks. Head right, strolling down the beach for approximately 0.4 mile before turning onto the red-blazed trail. (Locate this trail by looking between two great dunes for a footpath.) The red trail leaves the beach area and rises into the woods,

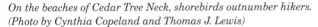

On the beaches of Cedar Tree Neck, shorebirds outnumber hikers.
(Photo by Cynthia Copeland and Thomas J. Lewis)

skirting Cedar Tree Neck Pond. Avoid side trails (blazed with white or yellow) and the red trail will eventually return you to the parking area.

Notes: The sanctuary opens at 8:30 AM and closes at 5:30 PM. No swimming, picnicking, or camping is allowed.

STAY OFF THE DUNES

If you are spending any time on the beach, it may be tempting to explore the dunes. But please stay on all marked trails to avoid damaging dune grass. The grass holds the sand in place, and without it beaches can be more easily washed away.

 FELIX NECK WILDLIFE SANCTUARY

BEFORE YOU GO
Map USGS Edgartown
Current Conditions Felix Neck Wildlife Sanctuary, Massachusetts Audubon Society (508) 627-4850
Fees Nonmembers, moderate fee; members, free

ABOUT THE HIKE
Day hike
Easy for children
Year-round
1.7 miles, loop trip
Elevation gain 75 feet
High point 50 feet
Hiking time 1.5 hours
Accessibility Wheelchair-accessible trails

GETTING THERE
- From the center of Edgartown in Martha's Vineyard, drive northwest 3 miles on Edgartown Vineyard Haven Road.
- Turn right at a blue-and-white Massachusetts Audubon Society sign.
- Travel down a one-lane road (with two-way traffic) for about 0.5 mile, heading north to the sanctuary parking area.
- From Oak Bluffs or Vineyard Haven, continue south on the Vineyard Haven–Edgartown Road 1.2 miles past the intersection with County Road.
- Turn left into the Felix Neck Wildlife Sanctuary.

ON THE TRAIL
A Massachusetts Audubon property, the Felix Neck Wildlife Sanctuary on Martha's Vineyard offers 350 acres of salt marsh, fields, forest, and beach to explore. Stop by the barn to visit the exhibit room before or after your walk.

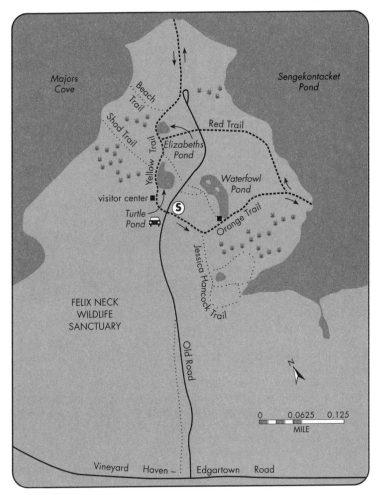

Pay the nonmember per-person admission fee at the visitor center 100 yards from the parking area. Follow the orange trail (marked by orange-tipped wooden stakes) that heads to the right (east) from the visitor center. Within the first 0.2 mile, you will come to a camera bluff just off the orange trail that overlooks Waterfowl Pond. Stop by the observation building and study the poster of various species of waterfowl. How many of these birds can the children see on the pond? Return to the orange trail and hike for 0.2 mile to the intersection with the red trail near Sengekontacket Pond. Follow the orange trail to its completion at water's edge for a pretty view over the pond.

Many hands make light (and fabulous) work at the seashore.
(Photo by Cynthia Copeland and Thomas J. Lewis)

Return to the junction of the orange and red trails and turn right, enjoying lovely water views for 0.3 mile until you head back into the woods. Soon you will cross the Old Road and, 0.9 mile from the start, reach an intersection with the yellow trail. Here, turn right and travel past Elizabeths Pond to the end of the yellow trail. After enjoying the view of Majors Cove, retrace your steps along the yellow trail, skirting Turtle Pond on the left just beyond the intersection with the red trail. There is a boardwalk over Turtle Pond where you can look for turtles and dragonflies. Continue 0.1 mile past the pond to the barn and the nearby parking lot. In the field near the parking lot, look for osprey nesting on the osprey pole or owls in the owl box. Keep in mind that the area closes at 7:00 PM.

Opposite page: Block Island, Rhode Island's Mohegan Bluffs
(photo by Cynthia Copeland and Thomas J. Lewis)

WALKABOUT TRAIL

BEFORE YOU GO
Maps USGS Chepachet, Thompson
Current Conditions George Washington Management Area, Rhode Island Division of Forest Environment (401) 568-2248 or (401) 568-2013
Fees None

ABOUT THE HIKE
Day hike or overnight
Moderate for children
July–December
6 miles, loop trip
Elevation gain 240 feet
High point 720 feet
Hiking time 3.5 hours
Accessibility No special access

GETTING THERE

- From I-395 in Connecticut, take the exit for US 44 east.
- Travel 6.9 miles on US 44 East to the George Washington Camping Area on the left.
- Turn left off the highway and drive 0.4 mile to the park office, set back from the road on the left.
- Turn and park there.

ON THE TRAIL

The Walkabout Trail (in Burrillville and Gloucester), with its 2-, 6-, and 8-mile options, is a good first family hike. The trail markers are bright and easy to follow and the route is level, though rocky and damp in places. If you hike in late summer, the trail will be less muddy, and you can end the day with a swim in Bowdish Reservoir. A plaque imbedded in a rock near the park office tells the story of the Australian sailors who blazed the trail twenty-five years ago, naming it "walkabout" in reference to the aborigines who wander the Australian countryside.

The hike begins on the nature trail where the three loops converge. Walk from the parking area back to the main camp road; on the opposite side, the trail heads northeast into the woods. Follow this path marked with frequent three-colored blazes—orange for the 8-mile hike, red for the 6-mile hike, and blue for the 2-mile loop—as it ambles through the woods. At 0.6 mile, the blue blazes depart left from the orange and red. (The blue-blazed loop is an alternative for families desiring a shorter hike: follow the blue blazes through the woods, onto a dirt road, back into the forest, and through a picnic and camping area. There it rejoins the longer loops.) The red and orange trails dip into a damp, swampy section where rustic log bridges help hikers traverse the wettest spots. After swinging onto higher ground and crossing a road at 2.2 miles, the trail begins a lengthy stretch through the forest.

At the 3.5-mile mark just after a short uphill, the orange route splits off, heading right. Remain on the red trail, crossing a stream and climbing gradually through a maze of stone walls that once marked a farmer's boundaries. Numerous fallen trees will slow you down through this section. Cross a dirt road and rejoin the orange trail at 4.5 miles. The two routes wind through soggy woodlands and then skirt the edge of Wilbur Pond for 0.5 mile. At several points of access to the pond, kids can search for frogs, salamanders, and other creatures. After leaving the pond's edge, the trail follows through wetlands with good footbridge crossings. The trail proceeds through a campground where children will enjoy a brief encounter with camping families. After a quick left turn, the path crosses a dirt road and once again merges with the blue-blazed route less than 1 mile from trail's end. The triple blazes take you directly behind some camping areas through more soggy terrain. The final stretch inches along the rocky edge of Bowdish Reservoir with frequent glimpses of the sparkling water. When you emerge from the woods your car will be in sight—and so will the beach.

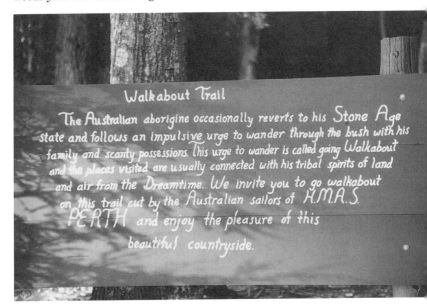

A wooden sign explains the Walkabout Trail. (Photo by Cynthia Copeland and Thomas J. Lewis)

DIAMOND HILL

BEFORE YOU GO
Map USGS Attleboro
Current Conditions Town
of Cumberland Parks and
Recreation Department
(401) 334-9996
Fees None

ABOUT THE HIKE
Day hike
Easy or challenging for
children, depending on route
March–November
**1 mile, loop trip (both
routes)**
Elevation gain 300 feet
High point 481 feet
Hiking time 1 hour
Accessibility Accessible
restrooms; call ahead for
picnic area special access

GETTING THERE

- From I-295, take exit 11 for Cumberland (note the sign for Diamond Hill State Park before the exit).
- Follow RI 114 north (also called Diamond Hill Road).
- In 3.8 miles, turn right into the parking lot for Diamond Hill.
- Park your car near the old ski lodge.

ON THE TRAIL

All hikers were not created equal—even (especially?) within the same family. Perhaps you have younger children who set a pokey pace as well as older, goal-oriented preteens who push hard for the summit and expect to encounter a few challenges along the way. Dividing and conquering may be the way to guarantee that everyone is gratified by the hike up Diamond Hill, a former ski slope in northern Rhode Island. One adult can accompany the more aggressive hikers on a challenging, rocky ascent up the former ski face. Another can meander with the little tykes along the path that winds easily over the soft shoulder of the hill to the summit. You can meet at the top (our guarantee: no one will get lost on the way up) where the kids can safely romp and explore. From there, you'll have pleasant local views that are best in early spring and fall when foliage is minimal. (You'll want to descend as a group on the easy path.)

The easy and challenging routes begin together. Sidestep the metal gate and follow the paved road that is to your left as you face Diamond Hill. Shortly, veer off the paved road onto a path that crosses a small pond on a wooden bridge, directly behind a pavilion. Here is where you may decide to divide: those up for a challenging ascent should go right toward the ski trails; those opting for a gradual climb should veer left

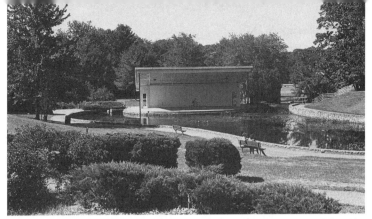

Path through Diamond Hill (photo by Cynthia Copeland and Thomas J. Lewis)

to reach the trail that leads into the woods at the edge of the open field. (The route described below is the challenging one. For the easier option, follow the directions in reverse from the summit to your car.)

Hike to the far right side of the open ski slope. Join the wide jeep path (not the narrow mountain bike, single track that is even farther to the right) on a demanding ascent, made even more difficult by loose stones rolling underfoot. Shortly, squeeze by the left side of a fence and continue the challenging climb. (Remind the kids how short the distance to the top really is—is it twice the distance to the bus stop? Half as far as the walk to school?) Three-quarters of the way to the top, crest on a plateau and take a quick rest. Follow a trail that leads right and soon sweeps left. At last, you'll encounter the last stiff climb, taking you to the Diamond Hill summit.

Circle the hill to the right, soon passing the footings for the once-busy ski lift. Just behind this, skirt a massive water storage tank. In early spring and late fall, you'll notice easterly views over Diamond Hill Reservoir beginning to emerge. Bear left at all junctions as you curl around the summit. On the western side of the hill, enjoy seasonal views of the Catamount and other hills beyond the former ski lodge.

Plan to meet the rest of your group at the footings near the water tank after you've thoroughly explored the summit. Begin the easy descent to your car on the wide, eroded jeep road. Stay to the right at all intersections. (Adventurous hikers can investigate the left-going side-trails. If you come upon a second set of footings, you will be rewarded with the best views from this hill.)

As it continues its gentle descent, the path veers close to a paved road and some private homes (on the opposite side of the road) and then narrows. Dropping easily through thick woods, the trail sweeps left, departing the road. In less than 0.1 mile, you'll reach the field where you began, facing the pavilion. If you brought a Frisbee or a ball, here's the spot for a game before piling back into the car and heading home.

POWDER MILL LEDGES WILDLIFE REFUGE

BEFORE YOU GO
Map USGS North Scituate
Current Conditions Audubon Society of Rhode Island (401) 949-5454
Fees None

ABOUT THE HIKE
Day hike
Easy for children
Year-round
1 mile, loop trip
Elevation gain 80 feet
High point 330 feet
Hiking time 1 hour
Accessibility No special access

GETTING THERE
- Take exit 7B from I-295 onto RI 44 west.
- Turn left onto RI 5 (Sanderson Road) at the fourth set of lights.
- The parking lot is the second driveway on the left.

ON THE TRAIL
If ever a hike could make you appreciate the efforts of conservation organizations, this is it. Surrounded on all sides by development, Powder Mill Ledges Wildlife Refuge offers a welcome slice of nature in the midst of chain stores and strip malls. You will definitely feel tucked away in this 120-acre refuge which houses the Audubon Society of Rhode Island's headquarters, especially as you crest the pine- and oak-covered hill that marks the site. This is a great place to teach kids about the importance of land preservation. If your children are too young to understand this concept, they will still enjoy the stream, pond, rock walls, forest, and meadow filled with birds and birdhouses.

A peaceful trail winds through the woods. (Photo by Emily Kerr)

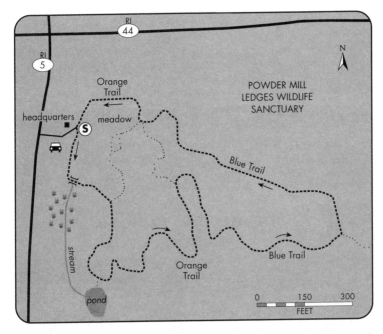

Before you begin your hike, stop in the headquarters building and register. Inside you will find a gift store and library and can pick up a trail map of the site. The trail begins near the information board outside. Here you can read about the different animals that live in the area, such as coyote, wild turkey, grey fox, white-tailed deer, and red squirrel. Head right down the mowed path that parallels the parking lot. You will be on the Orange Trail, which enters the woods in less than 0.1 mile. Immediately upon entering the trees, you will cross a wooden bridge over a stream, where the kids can look for creatures in the water. Follow the orange circles alongside a stone wall. Soon, a short side trail on the right heads down to a pond. Can the kids spot any wildlife? What kind of animals do they think live here?

Back on the trail you will cross over a boardwalk and then a wooden bridge as the route heads slightly uphill in an eastward direction before heading north. In 0.2 mile the Orange Trail intersects with the Blue Trail in the middle of a tall and peaceful stand of pines. Turn right onto the Blue Trail, heading first south, then east. Follow the Blue Trail to its intersection with the Yellow Trail under a strip of powerlines. Turn left (north) on the Blue Trail, following the powerlines a short distance, then turn left (west) again as the blue path again enters the woods. Have the kids guess how many rocks are in the walls that cross the landscape. How long do they think it took to build all those walls? After heading downhill, you will reach a junction with the Orange Trail. Continue on the Blue Trail to the second junction with the Orange Trail, where you will bear right on the Orange Trail to circle a meadow filled with bird boxes. See what birds you can find nesting before heading back to the center. Upon your return, be sure to check out the butterfly garden on the side of the building before heading home.

STONE WALLS

You will see many stone walls crisscrossing the New England landscape, such as the ones here. In the nineteenth century, when land was cleared for agricultural purposes, these stone walls kept farm animals enclosed.

 BEN UTTER TRAIL TO STEPSTONE FALLS

BEFORE YOU GO
Maps USGS Voluntown, Hope Valley
Current Conditions Arcadia Management Area, Rhode Island Division of Forest Environment (401) 539-1052 or (401) 539-2356
Fees None

ABOUT THE HIKE
Day hike or overnight (permit required)
Easy for children
April–October
3.5 miles round-trip
Elevation gain 150 feet
High point 287 feet,
Hiking time 2 hours
Accessibility No special access

GETTING THERE

- From RI 165 in Exeter, 1.8 miles east of the Connecticut–Rhode Island border and 5 miles west of the I-95 underpass, take unmarked Escoheag Hill Road.
- Travel north 0.9 mile and turn right onto the first gravel road, Austin Farm Road.
- Travel 1.8 miles east to Falls River Bridge.
- A sign posted on a pine tree on the west side of the river announces the start of the Ben Utter Trail.
- Austin Farm Road may be closed from one side during certain times of the year, so you may have to walk the 1.8 miles to the bridge from Escoheag Road or begin at the falls from Falls River Road. Another option is to take RI 165 to Frosty Hollow Road,

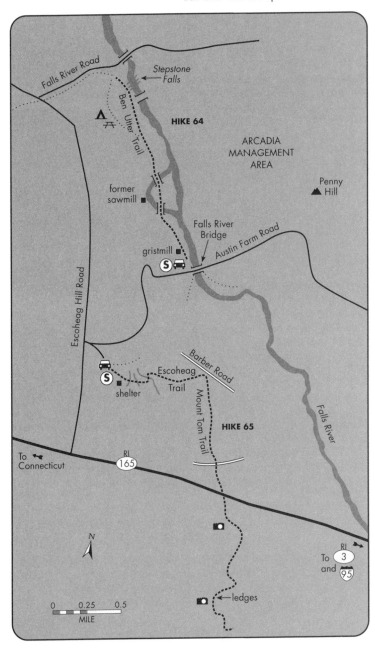

Falls River Road

Stepstone Falls ←

Ben Utter Trail

HIKE 64

ARCADIA
MANAGEMENT
AREA

Penny
▲ Hill

former
sawmill ■

Falls River
Bridge

Austin Farm Road

gristmill ■

Ⓢ 🚗

Escoheag Hill Road

Barber Road

Escoheag
Trail

Ⓢ
🚗
shelter ■

Mount Tom Trail

HIKE 65

Falls River

To ← ↤
Connecticut

RI
165

📷

To
and
95

📷 ← ledges

N

0   0.25   0.5
▬▬▬▬▬▬
MILE

RI
3

RI
95

↦

about 4 miles east of the Connecticut border, which eventually intersects with Austin Farm Road. Turn left and drive about 3 miles to the Falls River Bridge.

ON THE TRAIL

While the sight of the river tumbling and spilling down the wide, step-like rocks delights children, the ever-present sound of the cascading water soothes adult ears. The trip to Stepstone Falls via the Ben Utter Trail—lovely any time of the year, but especially appealing on a steamy day or after a rain storm—understandably rates as one of the most popular hikes in the Arcadia Management Area. While it is possible to begin the hike from the falls, it would be anticlimactic to have to walk away from this most appealing sight. A better idea is to begin at the bridge off Austin Farm Road. (Avoid hiking in Arcadia during the late fall and winter because hunting is permitted then. If you do hike then make sure to wear blaze orange for visibility.)

The yellow paint–blazed path follows the western bank of the river for the first 0.5 mile. After crossing a wooden bridge over a swampy section and passing the foundation of an old gristmill at 0.3 mile, the trail rises to a knoll overlooking the river and continues on a ridge above the water. Keep an eye on young children here. At close to 0.5 mile, the trail bears left away from the river and soon merges with a dirt road. Don't cross the road, but turn to the right and pick up the trail as it heads back into the woods. At 0.6 mile, impressive mountain laurel thickets swallow hikers for 100 yards. A bridge over a major tributary brings you to the remains of a sawmill and a small waterfall, visible across the stream on the left. The trail crosses back over the tributary toward higher ground and continues its course some distance from the river. At the 1-mile mark, the path becomes less easily traversed due to mud and fallen trees. Keep the kids moving by suggesting that they watch for the white-blazed trail back to the river's edge.

At 1.3 miles, pick up the white-blazed side trail (the yellow-blazed trail leads to a camping area with a shelter and fireplaces but no water). Though somewhat indistinct, the rocky path essentially follows along the river. Step onto the bridge at 1.6 miles for a good view of the rushing water and the cascades. The kids can play "Poohsticks" (from one of the classic A. A. Milne Winnie the Pooh tales) by tossing sticks off one side of the bridge and quickly running to the other side to see whose stick

BEST HIKES WITH LEASHED DOGS IN RHODE ISLAND

Walkabout Trail, Hike 61
Diamond Hill, Hike 62
Ben Utter Trail to Stepstone Falls,
   Hike 64

Escoheag and Mount Tom Trails,
   Hike 65
Pachaug Trail around Beach
   Pond, Hike 66

will appear first. At 1.7 miles, you will reach Stepstone Falls and Falls River Road. Stop for a picnic lunch before retracing your route back to the parking area on Austin Farm Road and your car.

 ESCOHEAG AND MOUNT TOM TRAILS

BEFORE YOU GO
Maps USGS Voluntown, Hope Valley
Current Conditions Arcadia Management Area, Rhode Island Division of Forest Environment (401) 539-1052 or (401) 539-2356
Fees None

ABOUT THE HIKE
Day hike
Moderate for children
April–early November
5.2 miles round-trip
Elevation gain 420 feet
High point 435 feet
Hiking time 3 hours
Accessibility No special access

GETTING THERE

- From RI 165 in Exeter, 1.8 miles east of the Connecticut–Rhode Island border and 5 miles west of the I-95 underpass, take unmarked Escoheag Hill Road.
- Travel north 0.9 mile and turn right onto the first gravel road, Austin Farm Road.
- After 100 feet, take another right onto a road that leads to a circular parking area in 0.1 mile.
- Look for the white-blazed trail at the southern end of the parking area.

ON THE TRAIL

The Escoheag Trail to the Mount Tom Trail offers kids who love to scramble up and down rocky hills a number of places to climb, especially within the first mile. Children under five will need assistance with several rocky stream crossings in the initial leg of the trip. Younger ones will feel safe running ahead on the second mile of trail crossing Mount Tom ridge; it is well worn, extremely level, and straight. On the approach to the final cliffs offering fine views, the people-sized boulders, perched precariously on either side of the trail, will inspire kids to invent all sorts of trailside games. The Arcadia Management Area operates several campgrounds, the closest being the one off Escoheag Hill Road. Check online to find campground locations and rates if planning an overnight in the area.

Head at once down a rocky slope with conveniently placed log steps. Watch for a side trail at 0.1 mile (marked with a blue-and-red ribbon) that leads to an impressive stone shelter atop a massive outcropping. The views may be somewhat obstructed by foliage, but stopping at such an appealing point so early in the walk will interest children in what lies ahead. Back on the main trail, at 0.3 mile, a smooth rock plateau offers a potential picnic spot on the return trip. Several stream crossings test the kids' ability to select appropriate stepping-stones. After crossing the largest of the brooks at 0.5 mile, the trail takes a sharp right turn. Soon, cliffs will appear on the left side of the trail.

Just short of 1 mile, Escoheag Trail meets a dirt road (Barber Road). Do not cross the road, but take a sharp right-hand turn back into the woods onto Mount Tom Trail (look for the trail and "No Snowmobile" signs). For 1 mile as the trail travels the ridge, the path is very level (and somewhat soggy at first). Kids will enjoy the tunnel effect of the abundant mountain laurel bushes.

The path meets a dirt road 0.8 mile from the beginning of the Mount Tom Trail. Diagonally across the road on the right the trail continues in a southerly direction. At 1.1 miles, Mount Tom Trail crosses RI 165. Here, the kids should wait for you so that you can cross this highway together. Walk in an easterly direction across the highway to rejoin the trail (watch for the sign). Two-tenths of a mile from the highway are cliffs with pretty western and southern views. While the adults enjoy the panoramas, the kids can try their hand at "rock climbing" on the trailside boulders. Continue for another 0.6 mile to the ledges of Mount Tom, which offer lovely views to the south and west. The drop-offs are steep, so keep an eye on the kids. Relax with a snack and then return to your car the way you came.

Stone shelter along the Escoheag Trail (photo by Cynthia Copeland and Thomas J. Lewis)

PACHAUG TRAIL AROUND BEACH POND

BEFORE YOU GO
Map USGS Voluntown
Current Conditions Arcadia Management Area, Rhode Island Division of Forest Environment (401) 539-1052 or (401) 539-2356
Fees None

ABOUT THE HIKE
Day hike
Challenging for children
April–November
6.4 miles round-trip
Elevation gain 340 feet
High point 440 feet
Hiking time 5 hours
Accessibility No special access

GETTING THERE
- From Voluntown, Connecticut, drive east on RI 165 across the causeway that divides Beach Pond (just over the Connecticut border).
- The parking area is on the left.

ON THE TRAIL
The blue-blazed Pachaug Trail, a woods trail that wanders for about 30 miles through southwestern Rhode Island into southeastern Connecticut, offers a combination of enticing features: water, views, rock formations, and forest. The portion of the trail that skirts Beach Pond is one of Rhode Island's most rewarding inland hikes, though also one of the most strenuous. While younger children will have difficulty navigating the rugged terrain, the older ones who are more experienced hikers will delight in the challenging scrambles as the trail winds around the lake. Near hike's end, they will find renewed energy in their search for the "Lemon Squeezer."

Join the Pachaug Trail (traveling the same route in the beginning as the yellow-blazed Tippecansett Trail) on the eastern end of the parking area as it skirts the beach and bath house. Follow the prolific blue-and-yellow blazes up an immediate ascent to a high bluff overlooking the pond. Within the first 0.1 mile, the trail swings toward the pond though it remains about 30 feet above the water; side trails afford good pond views. Soon the trail veers back into the woods, challenging hikers with the first steep climbs and descents. At 0.4 mile, the path bears diagonally left across a dirt road; 0.1 mile later, the Pachaug Trail leaves the Tippecansett Trail and heads northwest (left) on rolling terrain. The next 0.5 mile takes hikers to the water's edge at regular intervals via side trails. Kids will enjoy climbing the numerous large, flat rocks that border the path and jut out over the water. A swampy area and stream

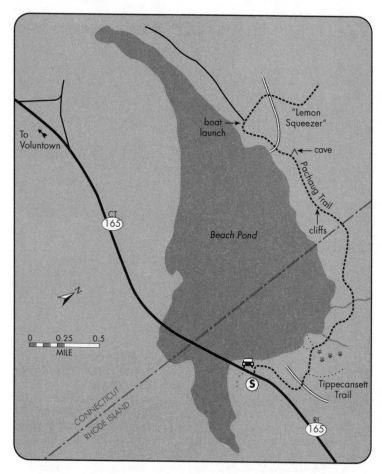

crossings at 0.8 mile present a soggy challenge but soon the trail resumes its rolling, rocky character. Kids can look for fox or raccoon tracks in the mud—or otters in the water—in the area near the stream.

After a stream crossing at 1.3 miles, the trail turns away from the pond and does not offer water views for more than 1 mile. The trail crosses several active streams and follows under cool stands of hemlocks. Along this section of the trail, children can watch for indications (marked trees) that they have entered Connecticut. At 1.7 miles, younger hikers will need assistance traversing a steep cliff. For the next 0.3 mile, the numerous ups and downs with rock obstacles make for tough going. The trail follows one narrow ridge that is cut into a rock face 30 feet high. A bluff at 1.8 miles might make a pleasant spot for an energy break. Just before the 2-mile mark, the trail passes an Indian cave with a precarious rock overhang that will tempt children to enter; the ceiling seems close to collapse, however, so kids should admire the cave from several feet away. After a pleasant stretch in the woods, the trail crosses a dirt road at 2.2 miles. Soon after, the pond becomes visible again as the trail continues about 10 feet above the water.

You will reach the boat launch area after a strenuous 2.5-mile hike. (A second car can be left here if you don't wish to hike the return route. Follow the boat launch signs from CT 165.) The trail picks up at the far end of the parking lot, close to the road, and continues north. After traveling along cliff's edge for 30 yards, the trail heads into the woods and crosses a woods road at 2.7 miles. At 2.8 miles, a steep drop into a gorge followed by a rocky ascent demands careful climbing and scrambling. Small children with a short stride will have to be carried in some places. The interesting rock formations and small caves will bring out the adventurous spirit in everyone. A double blue blaze at 2.9 miles indicates a right-hand turn. The trail clings to the base of cliffs towering 60 or 70 feet high. The first child to see the Lemon Squeezer (a tight passage between the side of a cliff and a long rock slab) wins. (**Hint:** it is along the cliff just to the right of the blue-blazed trail about 0.5 mile from the boat launch area.) It is important that children follow the path at stream's edge rather than try to maneuver along the cliff to the Lemon Squeezer. Continue to a set of smaller cliffs at 3.2 miles or turn around at the Lemon Squeezer and head back to your car the way you came.

ARCADIA TRAIL

BEFORE YOU GO
Map USGS Hope Valley
Current Conditions
Arcadia Management Area, Rhode Island Division of Forest Environment (401) 539-1052 or (401) 539-2356
Fees None

ABOUT THE HIKE
Day hike
Easy for children
April–November
3 miles round-trip
Elevation gain 320 feet
High point 466 feet
Hiking time 2 hours
Accessibility No special access

GETTING THERE
■ From the junction of RI 165 and RI 3 in Exeter, take RI 3 south for 1.5 miles to a large log structure on the right. (If you pass the sign that says "Entering Richmond," you've gone too far.)

■ Park here and begin your hike at the southwest corner of the
building.

ON THE TRAIL

Arcadia Trail in the Arcadia Management Area is maintained by the
Rhode Island chapter of the Appalachian Mountain Club and is popular in the summer months with local folks as well as out-of-towners
due to the easy and interesting jaunt to the public beach and picnic
area. (Even in the fall, though, you are bound to encounter fellow hikers.) Brook crossings, small ponds, and forest strolls will keep children

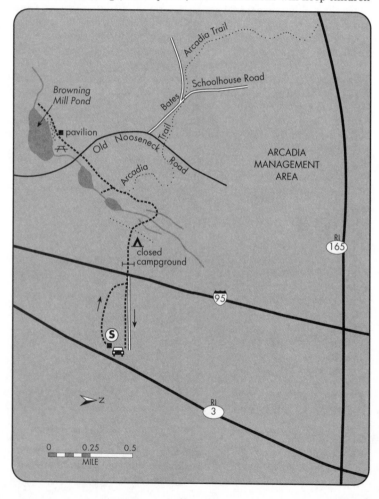

enthused until it is time to dive into Browning Mill Pond. Camping is available within the Arcadia Management Area off Escoheag Hill and Frosty Hollow Roads. Camping is primitive and a permit is required. There is a modest fee for camping. For more information about over-nighting in the area, check online before you set out.

The white-blazed trail is narrow but readily identifiable. It sweeps quickly west along noisy I-95, then merges with a wide dirt road before slipping under the overpass for I-95, and meets a gate. Go through the gate into a camping area (now closed) and continue straight through the campground heading west on the road to a T intersection. Walk straight across the intersection and join the Arcadia Trail indicated by double yellow blazes. In the next 0.5 mile, several brook crossings demand careful stepping; the bridge traversing one swampy and rocky area (at about 0.8 mile) is in poor condition.

Just after you notice a small lily pond on the left at about 1 mile, a double yellow blaze indicates a right-hand turn. Instead of continuing on the Arcadia Trail, follow the white-blazed trail straight ahead. The trail turns right in 50 feet. At the right turn, a side trail accesses a small pond and affords good views of the water and a small cascade. Back on the trail, you will pass another small pond on your left. Soon you will reach part of the nature trail created in the mid-1970s by the Youth Conservation Corps. Signs identify common and not-so-common plants and trees. At 1.3 miles you reach paved Old Nooseneck Road. Straight across the road is Browning Mill Pond with picnic tables, pavilions, and a beach for swimming.

After the children have enjoyed a refreshing swim and picnic lunch, you can take the path to the western end of the pond and then reverse the directions to reach your car.

Note: On the way back, if your group feels particularly energetic, you can extend the hike by bearing left at the intersection with the yellow-blazed Arcadia Trail, where a right turn leads back to your car. This trail meanders through the woods for over 0.5 mile, crossing Old Nooseneck Road and at first paralleling Bates Schoolhouse Road—a dirt road—before turn-ing right on this road in about 0.1 mile. The trail heads left through a road barricade onto a grassy, un-used road as Bates Schoolhouse Road heads right, and soon turns

Hold it gently, admire it, then set it free. (Photo by Cynthia Copeland and Thomas J. Lewis)

right at double blazes into the woods. The path continues on rolling terrain through the woods for 1 mile before ending at RI 165. By reversing the directions and returning to your car, you will have completed a 6.5-mile hike.

 FISHERVILLE BROOK WILDLIFE REFUGE

BEFORE YOU GO
Map USGS Slocum
Current Conditions Fisherville Brook Wildlife Refuge, Audubon Society of Rhode Island (401) 949-5454
Fees None

ABOUT THE HIKE
Day hike
Easy for children
March–November
2.4 miles, loop trip
Elevation gain 90 feet
High point 300 feet
Hiking time 1.5 hours
Accessibility No special access

GETTING THERE
- Take I-95 to RI 4 and then RI 102 north.
- Follow RI 102 north 4.2 miles to turn right on Widow Sweets Road.
- In 0.4 mile take your second right onto Pardon Joslin Road.
- The parking lot will be on your right in 0.7 mile.

ON THE TRAIL
A visit to Fisherville Brook makes for an extremely pleasant and peaceful outing. The five miles of trail on this 937-acre property travel through diverse habitats, including a favorite of kids—a pond, at the end of which is a waterfall. There are many bridges to cross and even a historic cemetery, set against a spectacular backdrop of fields abundant with wildflowers.

South of the parking area, turn right on the Blue Pond Trail, where you will immediately be greeted by the fragrant scent of white pines. Walk on a soft bed of needles along the blue trail 0.2 mile to its junction with the Yellow Cedar Swamp Loop Trail. Turn right here to follow this 0.3 mile trail until it meets up again with the blue trail. Along the way, see who can identify the white cedar trees that give the trail its name.

Head right onto the Blue Trail and descend slightly to a bridge across Fisherville Brook on the northern side of Upper Pond. The trail then travels through fields with bluebird boxes and plentiful wildflowers—can you spot any colorful birds or butterflies? Soon a side trail will lead to a small graveyard dating back to the 1700s. Have the kids try to imagine what the lives of the people now lying in the cemetery were

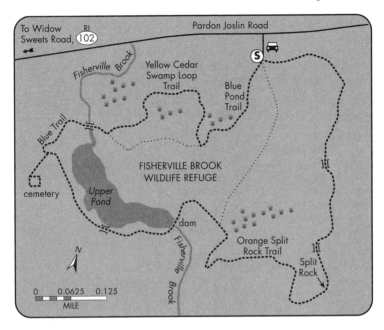

like back then. What kind of clothes did they wear when they were out walking? (Definitely not Gore-Tex and fancy hiking boots!) How might the landscape have been different back then? Or the same?

Return to the Blue Trail and turn right, following it as it skirts Upper Pond. In a little over a mile you will again cross Fisherville Brook, this time on the southeast side over a dam. When the kids are through watching the water spilling out below the dam, continue  following the Blue Trail through dense ferns to a junction with the Orange Split Rock Trail. If you are ready to call it quits, turn left on the Blue Trail and follow an old road back to the parking area for a total hike of 1.5 miles.

To follow the Orange Split Rock Trail turn right and immediately cross a small stream. As the trail meanders through the beech and

Black-eyed susans are just one type of wildflower you'll see in the meadow. (Photo by Emily Kerr)

oak forest, have your kids keep their eyes peeled for Split Rock and large glacial erratics. Any fallen logs? See what kind of life they can find in that ecosystem. As you travel east, then north, on the Orange Split Rock Trail you will cross over two footbridges. Approximately 0.2 mile from the end, the trail curves west and you arrive back at the parking area.

IF A TREE FALLS IN A FOREST...

...Who moves in? Rotting logs provide the perfect moist home for many creatures. Centipedes, millipedes, spiders, and sow-bugs are just a few of the creatures that take up residence in fallen logs. Some types of salamanders make their homes underneath. These creatures, along with different types of fungi, help turn the logs into nutrient-rich soil. In fact, because so many creatures make their home or living in a dead tree, scientists often say that a dead tree can be more alive than a live tree.

 LONG POND WOODS

BEFORE YOU GO
Map USGS Voluntown
Current Conditions
Audubon Society of Rhode Island (401) 949-5454; also Department of Environmental Management, The Nature Conservancy
Fees None

ABOUT THE HIKE
Day hike
Moderate for children
April–November
2.4 miles round-trip
Elevation gain 300 feet
High point 405 feet
Hiking time 2.5 hours
Accessibility No special access

GETTING THERE
- Take Rockville exit (RI 138 west) off I-95.
- Take Canonchet Road south from RI 138 in Rockville.
- At the fork with North Road, bear left (still on Canonchet Road).
- Drive 0.6 mile to a parking area on the right.

ON THE TRAIL
This section of the Narragansett Trail, which travels through western Rhode Island and part of Connecticut, winds through the 340-acre Long and Ell Ponds Natural Area and rates as one of the most enticing inland walks. Children and adults alike will marvel at Long Pond's distinctive

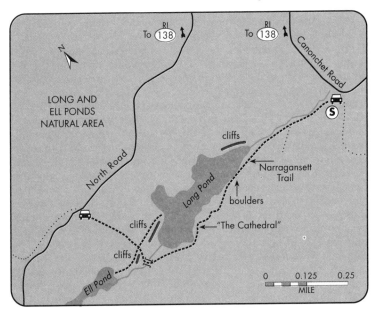

grove of hemlock trees referred to as "The Cathedral," its granite cliffs towering 70 feet above the water, and its colony of giant rhododendrons. (If you visit in July, the rhododendron plants will be in bloom.) A deep ravine joins Long Pond to Ell Pond, a smaller lake surrounded by swamp and a quaking bog. Don't be misled by this hike's relatively short distance—rocky ascents and steep drops will have even the fittest children huffing and puffing. Kids should be encouraged to wear proper hiking boots, not slippery sneakers.

This trail, which will take you along the edge of the ridge rising from Long Pond, begins at the western corner of the parking lot. After a short woods walk, the path divides; take the yellow-blazed right-hand trail. The trail wanders through an area covered with mountain laurel along a shallow, sloping ledge, then winds through a maze of boulders and trees rising over Long Pond. At about 0.4 mile, you will come upon two huge glacial boulders left here by receding glaciers long ago. The larger one may remind kids of a ship's hull cutting through the water.

Frequently, as you travel on the trail about 35 feet above the water, you will see the cliffs or bluffs to your right across the narrow neck of Long Pond and also down at the eastern head of the pond. At 0.5 mile, the trail begins one of numerous descents through a hemlock grove and then climbs back up to the height of the ridge. The yellow-blazed path follows along the ridge and descends through another shaded forest area strewn with rocks. This area, known as The Cathedral, boasts hemlocks that are among the oldest in the state—some approach 200 years old. If you can find a tree stump, have children count the rings.

The trail continues its rugged ascents and descents, heading west, and at 0.8 mile tumbles down into the damp channel that joins the two ponds. Here, you will see the distinctive giant rhododendrons towering up to 16 feet. Crossing the sometimes swollen ravine on the log footbridge requires careful stepping and assistance for younger hikers. Although the trail out of the ravine is steep, strategically placed stones make ascending the 60 vertical feet to the top quite negotiable for children. A dramatic cliff wall dominates the left side of the trail. After scrambling out of the gorge, you'll come to a four-way trail intersection. Straight ahead, a northbound trail leads to a parking area on North Road. First, take the eastern and western side trails that lead to high cliffs with impressive views of Long and Ell Ponds. Back at the trail intersection, continue to follow the footpath north to the reservation exit. On the way, you will descend another huge granite slab, pass under a second area of mighty rhododendrons, and walk along the edge of a 15-foot-high cliff before reaching the road. (Hold the hands of younger children along this stretch.) You can retrace your steps 1.2 miles or, if the kids have had enough scrambling for one day, turn right onto North Road, walk 1 mile, and turn right onto Canonchet Road. Stroll 0.6 mile to your car parked on the right.

Notes: Camping and fires are prohibited. The area is open year-round, sunrise to sunset.

Looking over Long Pond (photo by Cynthia Copeland and Thomas J. Lewis)

FRANCIS C. CARTER MEMORIAL PRESERVE

BEFORE YOU GO
Map USGS Carolina
Current Conditions
The Nature Conservancy,
Rhode Island Chapter Office
(401) 331-7110
Fees None

ABOUT THE HIKE
Day hike
Loop route moderate for children; one-way easy for children
March–October; closed
November and December
4.9 miles complete loop, 1.3 miles one-way on Yellow Trail with two cars
Elevation gain 140 feet
High point 200 feet
Hiking time 4 hours
Accessibility No special
access

GETTING THERE
- From I-95 take exit 3A onto RI 138 east.
- Follow RI 138 east two miles to the intersection with RI 112.
- Follow RI 112 south through Richmond.
- In 4.5 miles, past the intersection with RI 91, turn right on Old Mill Road.
- Follow Old Mill Road 0.7 mile until it curves sharply to the left.
- Here, bear right onto the dirt road, which is the Narragansett Trail.
- Follow this straight to the parking area.
- If you want to do the shorter, one-way hike on the Yellow Trail, leave a second car at the parking area on RI 112, just before Old Mill Road.

ON THE TRAIL
If you are looking for a tranquil hike, this is it. You will feel like you are walking, surrounded in bird song, in a sea of green amongst the low-lying shrubs and ferns in the pine and oak forest. Depending on what time of year that you visit, you may find vernal pools with frogs and salamanders, flowering shrubs in bloom, or ripe blueberries and huckleberries. In the grasslands you will be treated to colorful wildflowers and sightings of several different types of grassland birds. The many loop trails in this 841-acre preserve—the largest nature preserve of the Rhode Island Chapter of The Nature Conservancy—make it easy for you to pick a long or a short hike and provide many good turnaround points, as well as the option to do a one-way hike by leaving a car at

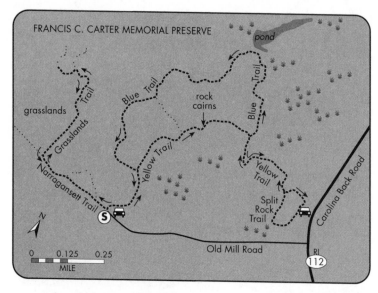

a second parking area. You will definitely want to bring along a plant identification guide and pick up a self-guided hike brochure and a bird checklist provided by The Nature Conservancy at the information board near the parking area.

To begin, head through the gate straight onto the Narragansett Trail. In a few feet, turn right onto the Yellow Trail, marked in yellow rectangular blazes. Immediately cross through a stone wall and into the woods. The trail meanders through dense shrubs in an oak forest. Is there any laurel in bloom? In 0.25 mile you will reach the junction with the Blue Trail on which you will be returning. Cross through another set of stone walls, and in 0.5 mile pass another junction with the Blue Trail, continuing straight on the yellow. For children bored with the apparently same scenery, have them look for different colors and shapes on the forest floor. Do they see any orange fungus? Dark green moss? On closer inspection, everything doesn't look the same after all.

A little over 0.5 mile from the start look for the yellow number 7, which corresponds to the self-guided hiking map, and the rock cairns on the side of the trail. It is not known who built these or why—have fun seeing who can come up with the most creative guess. Right past station 6, the trail descends slightly, passes rock outcroppings on the left, and meets up once more with the Blue Trail. Turn right onto the Yellow Trail as it climbs slightly and twists and turns through more rock outcroppings and boulders. Stay on the Yellow Trail past the numbered stations and the junctions with the Split Rock Trail and Red Trail all the way to the vernal pool at station 1, 1.3 miles from the start. This is your ending point if you're opting for the shorter route and you've left your second car at this RI 112 parking area.

To return, head back on the Yellow Trail and immediately turn left on the white-blazed Split Rock Trail. See who can find the rock that gives this 0.3-mile-long trail its name. When the Split Rock Trail rejoins the Yellow Trail, turn left and follow the Yellow Trail back to its intersection with the Blue Trail. If you're tired, you can follow the Yellow Trail back to the car. But for a longer hike, turn right here onto the Blue Trail. In 0.5 mile, search for glimpses of a pond through the trees. In another 0.5 mile, you will have an option to turn left and leave the Blue Trail, or to continue straight on the Blue Trail. Stay straight all the way back, about 0.3 mile, to the junction with the Yellow Trail. Turn right to follow the Yellow Trail back to the Narragansett Trail. The parking area is to the left.

To reach the grasslands, turn right on the Narragansett Trail and follow the dirt road 0.3 mile to the Grassland Trail. Take a moment to read about the various plants and animals of the grasslands on the colorful information board before exploring the trails on the east and south perimeters of the grasslands. This field is home to many types of swallows and sparrows, including the regionally rare grasshopper sparrow. On other parts of the trail, you will see examples of succession—where pine and shrubs are taking over what was once a field—and pitch pine and scrub oak barrens. To return to your car, head back up the Narragansett Trail to the parking area.

Fungus growing on a log (photo by Emily Kerr)

EAST BEACH, NINIGRET CONSERVATION AREA

BEFORE YOU GO
Map USGS Quonochontaug
Current Conditions Rhode Island Department of Environmental Management, Division of Parks and Recreation (401) 322-0450 or (401) 322-8910
Fees Moderate fee in-season; higher on weekends and holidays

ABOUT THE HIKE
Day hike or overnight
Moderate for children
Year-round
5 miles round-trip
Elevation gain 10 feet
High point 10 feet
Hiking time 3.5 hours
Accessibility No special access

GETTING THERE

- Take East Beach Road off US 1 in Charlestown, just east of the RI 216 intersection.
- This road leads to the parking area for this beach sandwiched between Ninigret Pond and the Atlantic Ocean.

ON THE TRAIL

In the spring bring a kite, in the summer carry a bathing suit and towel, and in the fall take along a book to identify seashells, especially if you opt to camp here and anticipate having some time on your hands. This 2-mile-long beach lies between the Atlantic Ocean and Ninigret Pond, a popular spot for clamming, in the Ninigret Conservation Area. As with most ocean walks, there are no paths to follow, just the water's edge, so children can lead the hike just as well as the parents. Although it may seem that without trail intersections, stream crossings, or rocky scrambles, a hike such as this might get monotonous, the ocean never ceases to fascinate younger folks. They thrill to the sheer expanse of water and to the roaring, rolling waves that continuously deposit tiny treasures in the sand for collecting or tossing back into the foamy water. In the summertime, the parking lot (which accommodates fewer than 100 vehicles, for a fee, in-season) often fills quickly; so arrive early or hike in the off-season.

Head south from the parking area along a sandy strip to the ocean's edge. Gaze eastward up the beach to the distant boulders guarding the Charlestown Breachway, your destination. With little but windswept sand between you and these rock soldiers, they seem much closer than

Beach walkers enjoying East Beach (photo by Emily Kerr)

2.5 miles away. Hugging the water's edge for easier walking, hike down the beach, pausing often for the kids to poke in the sand for seashells and stones buffed and polished by the relentless waves. At 0.5 mile and again at 1.5 miles, you will pass camping areas on the left. Once you have walked beyond these populated spots, the crowds thin and you share the beach with seagulls rather than sunbathers. At the Breachway, approximately 2.5 miles from the start, spread out the picnic lunch while the kids scramble up and down the large rocks. Explore the edge of Ninigret Pond on the return trip if you wish, equipped with binoculars for bird-watching, and eventually return as you came along the beach.

 TRUSTOM POND NATIONAL WILDLIFE REFUGE

BEFORE YOU GO
Map USGS Kingston
Current Conditions Trustom Pond National Wildlife Refuge, U.S. Fish & Wildlife Service (401) 364-9124
Fees None

ABOUT THE HIKE
Day hike
Easy for children
Year-round
3 miles loop trip
Elevation gain 40 feet
High point 40 feet
Hiking time 1.5 hours
Accessibility In planning stages

GETTING THERE
- From I-95 south, exit onto RI 4 south, which will merge into RI 1 south.
- Continue for 23.5 miles from I-95 on RI 1.
- One mile west of Perryville take the Moonstone Beach Road exit (left exit).

- In another mile turn right onto Matunuck Schoolhouse Road at the four-way stop.
- Drive west 0.7 mile to the refuge entrance on your left.

ON THE TRAIL

This is by far one of Rhode Island's most valuable places. Once a farm, the 787-acre Trustom Pond National Wildlife Refuge now encompasses various wildlife habitats, including Rhode Island's only undeveloped coastal salt pond. It is virtually impossible to leave here without seeing some type of wildlife in the fields, shrublands, woodlands, beaches, and ponds that make up the refuge. The friendly volunteers at the visitor center are extremely knowledgeable and can alert you to recent sightings before you set out. A camera is a must on this hike, and if your kids have their own, they will be snapping away the entire time.

Head south on the wide, graveled path behind the parking area. Soon you will reach the Farm Field Loop Trail which borders a habitat restoration area. Here, native warm-season grasses that remain upright year-round are being restored to provide better cover for wildlife. Turn left (east) on the Farm Field Loop and follow the trail as it curves south to two viewing platforms of the Farm Pond on the left. If you're lucky, you may get to see a snapping turtle swimming in the pond—don't get too close!

Continue heading south. At the junction of the Red Maple Swamp and Otter Point Trails in 0.2 mile, bear left on the Otter Point Trail and follow the old road through trees and shrubs. Glimpse the water of Trustom Pond to your right and then your left before reaching Otter Point in 0.7 mile. How many swans can you count? This is a great place to take some photos.

Tear yourself away from the view—it's even better at Osprey Point—and head back to the junction with the Red Maple Swamp Trail. Turn left onto this trail, cross a boardwalk over a small stream and in 0.2 mile look for an old windmill on your left, a remnant from the site's former days. Continue on the Red Maple Swamp Trail, pass a giant maple, and reach the Osprey Point Trail approximately two miles from your start.

A swan swims with its young. (Photo by Emily Kerr)

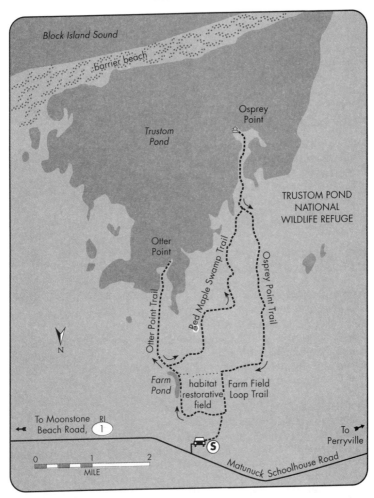

Turn left and walk on a peninsula to an elevated observation platform. The vantage point here is amazing and the swans too numerous to count. Search for cormorants on the rocks as you look south toward a barrier beach and Block Island Sound. This undeveloped beach is an important nesting site for the piping plover and least tern. To finish your hike, head north on the Osprey Point Trail, bearing left at its junction with the Red Maple Swamp Trail. Follow the Osprey Point Trail north, then east, to its intersection with the Farm Field Loop Trail. Turn left and skirt the western edge of the field to make another left turn onto the trail leading to the parking area.

U.S. FISH AND WILDLIFE VISITOR CENTER

Be sure to visit the Kettle Pond Visitor Center in nearby Charlestown. There are interesting things for all ages as well as trails on the property.

 FORT BARTON/SIN AND FLESH BROOK

BEFORE YOU GO
Map USGS Fall River
Current Conditions Town of Tiverton (401) 625-6710
Fees None

ABOUT THE HIKE
Day hike
Easy for children
Year-round
2.8 miles round-trip
Elevation gain 80 feet
High point 100 feet
Hiking time 2 hours
Accessibility No special access

GETTING THERE

- From RI 24 in Tiverton, take RI 77 south to Lawton Avenue, following a sign for Fort Barton.
- Travel on this street 0.3 mile to an intersection with Highland Road.
- On the right side of Lawton Avenue is the Tiverton Town Hall and across the intersection is a cliff with a large sign for Fort Barton.
- Parking is off Highland Road in a marked area.

ON THE TRAIL

From atop the observation tower at the site of Fort Barton on the Smith Rock Trail, kids will not have a hard time imagining themselves as Revolutionary War soldiers scanning the harbor for British ships. Although nothing resembling a fort remains at this site, the park is dotted with boulders and mounds for climbing. (The earthworks that have survived are intentionally unrestored.) The trail from the fort site winds back and forth across the brook like one strand in a braid; some of these frequent crossings have rather rickety bridges, though one Tiverton resident assured us that the bridges will be replaced soon. Children will need the help of an adult to manage these river crossings as they currently are.

You reach the fort by walking across Highland Road from the parking area to a paved road with a chain across it. This road climbs quickly, winding around to an observation tower that provides remarkable views of the narrow strait where patriots once feared the logical crossing of British soldiers trying to capture more American territory. Give the kids a little history lesson to enhance their appreciation of this historic spot.

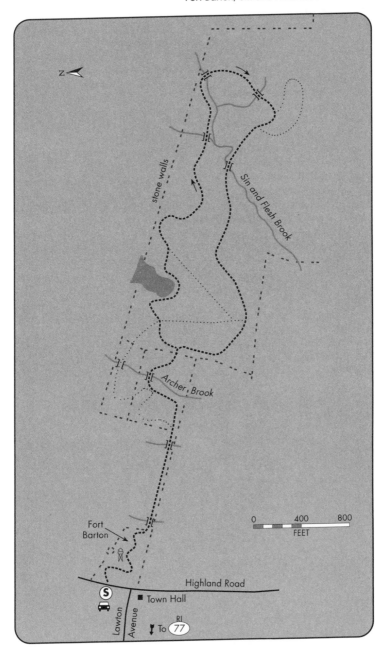

N

stone walls

Sin and Flesh Brook

Archer Brook

Fort Barton

0   400   800
FEET

Highland Road

Ⓢ
🚗
Lawton Avenue

■ Town Hall

To 🛈 77
RI

The main trail through Fort Barton Woods, which begins behind the fort site on a gravel path, is marked with red arrows. (The blue trails are secondary paths leading to points of natural interest such as unusual patches of mushrooms or wildflowers.) Heading southeast, the trail descends quickly by way of a steep and rugged set of stairs through a nature area where various species of plants and trees are noted with wooden tags. With a fence on the left and a stone wall on the right, continue straight ahead, on the red-blazed trail, crossing two bridges. (Appoint one of the kids to keep track of the bridges; the total count by trail's end should be seven.) Cross Archer Brook on the third bridge and follow the red trail through a stone wall. Just beyond that point, the red trail splits, indicated by signs on a towering red oak. This hike, primarily heading east and west, is a terrific opportunity for a young hiker to practice compass-reading skills. Ask him or her to keep track of your direction and give frequent updates.

Follow the left-hand path, initially traveling north. (You will loop around and emerge from the right-hand side.) Heading generally east, skirt the edge of a pond and cross Sin and Flesh Brook over a fourth bridge about 1.2 miles from the start. Then cross the brook three more times within the next 0.5 mile. The kids will have a delightful time exploring the streambank. The brook and path wind around one another, making for an interesting walk, though somewhat treacherous stream crossings. (Instruct kids who run ahead to wait for adult help crossing the bridges.) Return to the fort site by following the red arrows west to the initial split in the red trail at the oak tree. Here, bear left to retrace the first 0.4 mile of the hike and return to your car.

 EMILIE RUECKER WILDLIFE REFUGE

BEFORE YOU GO
Map USGS Westport
Current Conditions
Audubon Society of Rhode Island (401) 949-5454
Fees None

ABOUT THE HIKE
Day hike
Easy for children
Year-round
1.5 miles, loop trip
Elevation gain 40 feet
High point 40 feet
Hiking time 2 hours
Accessibility No special access

GETTING THERE
■ From I-195 east in Massachusetts, take State Route 24 south to the RI 77 south exit.

- Follow RI 77 south 4 miles to a right turn on Seapowet (spelled Sapowet on some maps) Avenue.
- Parking is 0.2 mile on the right.

ON THE TRAIL

Grab your insect repellent and prepare to see glorious views of a salt marsh. Two of the three main trails at this refuge skirt the edge of the marsh, where you will be treated to beautiful panoramas and sightings of the wildlife that abounds throughout. A third trail takes you through a forest, where birds are plentiful. A large portion of this 50-acre refuge was the site of a former farm donated in 1965 to the Audubon Society of Rhode Island by the artist Emilie Ruecker. You will easily see why the landscape was an inspiration for her paintings. The farm is now left in its natural state for all to enjoy, but careful observers will see signs of its earlier days.

After checking out the information board, find the Red Trail in the northeast corner of the parking area. Have the kids be on the lookout for what the locals call "puddingstone" in a rocky outcrop shortly into your hike. Larger rocks are formed by many small pebbles stuck together. Listen for different birdsongs as you pass through the woods into a more open area where grapevines grow amongst the trees.

In less than 0.5 mile, you will come to the Yellow Trail. Turn right and follow the Yellow Trail as it begins its loop around a peninsula in the marsh. You will find benches along the way where you can sit and enjoy the views of the salt marsh and the Sakonnet River. Can the children see mussel shells on the beach? On the western edge of the peninsula

Examining a shell by the marsh (photo by Emily Kerr)

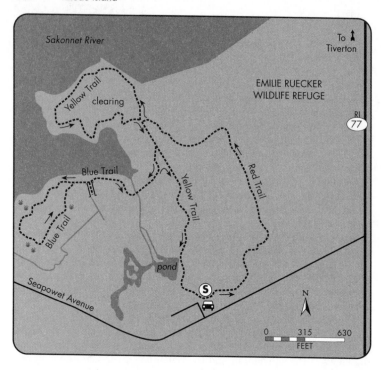

look for a sign and a path leading to the clearing in the middle of the yellow loop. Return to the Yellow Trail and follow it east then southeast to where it joins the Blue Trail in 0.7 mile.

Turn right on the Blue Trail; pass through a stand of black cherry trees, and cross a small wooden bridge. You will soon come to a sign that says Blue Loop. Bear right to circle another peninsula through the marsh. Immediately to your left is a large painted sign indicating the various birds you may see in the water or on the mud flats. Who can find a great blue heron or a double-crested cormorant? How about a glossy ibis or snowy egret? When you're done with bird identification, point out that if you look across the water, you can see where you were on the Yellow Trail on the other side. There's nothing like seeing how far they've come to give your kids a sense of accomplishment.

Continue on the Blue Trail, bearing right at the beginning of the blue loop and following the trail to its junction with the Yellow Trail a little over a mile from the start of your hike. Turn right on the Yellow Trail. This final stretch takes you through spruce and pine and past a small pond. Here the kids can look for frogs, toads, and salamanders before returning to the parking area.

WILDERNESS ETHICS

As tempting as it may be to go off exploring, remember to stick to the trails. A few careless footsteps can do extreme damage to fragile plants and disturb wildlife. Do not collect plants and animals—even the smallest ones play an important role in maintaining the balance of the natural environment.

 CLIFF WALK

BEFORE YOU GO
Map USGS Newport
Current Conditions
Newport County Convention and Visitors Bureau (401) 845-9123, (800) 976-5122; Friends of the Waterfront (401) 847-1355
Fees Parking fee in summer

ABOUT THE HIKE
Day hike
Moderate for children
Year-round
6 miles round-trip
Elevation gain 40 feet
High point 40 feet
Hiking time 3 hours
Accessibility No special access, but partially stroller-friendly

GETTING THERE
- From the east or west, drive into Newport via RI 138.
- Turn south on RI 138A and drive 2 miles to Memorial Boulevard.
- Turn right and you will soon come upon Easton Beach (also called First Beach) on the left, where there is parking for "Cliff Walkers." During the summer there is a fee for parking here.
- A drive down Bellevue Avenue followed by a left down any number of side streets will bring you farther into the hike with less crowded parking conditions. Narragansett Avenue is the best place to park.

ON THE TRAIL
While the adults are gazing at the mansions—the sixty- or seventy-room "summer cottages"—that line one side of this path, the kids will no doubt be looking in the other direction at the sea crashing against the rocky shoreline, the surfers skimming precariously atop the waves, or the boats bobbing far from shore.

Much of this route, especially during the early part of the hike, is easy to navigate with a stroller. On most occasions when the path rises high above the sea, sturdy fences will prevent accidents, but there are

Midway along the famed Cliff Walk with the Mansion Rough Point in the distance (photo by Cynthia Copeland and Thomas J. Lewis)

spots where the path skirts precipitous cliffs and younger children will need to be watched. Don't come to Newport expecting a solitary hike; this is one of the state's most popular attractions, especially during the summer months.

The hike begins behind a hotel named the Chanler at Cliff Walk on what is essentially a sidewalk. In less than one mile, you will reach Forty Steps, a stairway leading to the rocks at water's edge. On the right, just past the steps, you will have your first unobstructed views of the mansions, some of which are part of the Salve Regina University complex. Here, late nineteenth-century architecture contrasts with modern dormitories and other contemporary buildings. Just beyond the college is The Breakers, summer home of Cornelius Vanderbilt. This mansion, as well as Rosecliff, Marble House, and others, is open to the public for a fee. At 1.7 miles, Rosecliff, where *The Great Gatsby* was filmed, is shielded from view behind a massive wall.

If the kids are getting bored with the ocean scenery, play hiking bingo: see who will be the first to spot a sailboat, a surfer, a fisherman, a seagull. Count dogs, people wearing hats, babies in strollers, or people sporting sunglasses. Or take turns verbally designing your own dream oceanfront mansions. (Notice the vast difference in descriptions between the preschooler and the preteen, or the preteen and the parent!) After traveling through two tunnels and passing Marble House, the trail becomes rockier and heads for the southern tip of the peninsula called Lands End. Here the cliffs plunge 25 feet to the water. Kids will need assistance on some tricky ascents as you pass more palatial estates. This may be a good turnaround point for younger children, as it can be somewhat treacherous.

After a 3-mile walk, you will round a tip of land, where you will have magnificent views of Rhode Island Sound. The trail ends on Ocean Avenue. Hike back along the shore to the parking area.

Note: Guided tours are available in the summer.

NORMAN BIRD SANCTUARY

BEFORE YOU GO
Maps USGS Prudence Island, Newport
Current Conditions
Norman Bird Sanctuary
(401) 846-2577
Fees Nonmembers, moderate fee; members, free

ABOUT THE HIKE
Day hike
Moderate for children
Year-round
2.5 miles round-trip
Elevation gain 120 feet
High point 70 feet
Hiking time 2.25 hours
Accessibility Accessible welcome center and one universally accessible trail

GETTING THERE

- From RI 138A in Middletown, turn east onto Green End Avenue.
- At the corner of Green End Avenue and Third Beach Road (a four-way intersection), take a right onto Third Beach Road. (A sign on a telephone pole indicates the way to Norman Bird Sanctuary.)
- Drive 0.7 mile to the sanctuary and park near the sanctuary buildings.

ON THE TRAIL

Although many folks come to this 300-acre property with binoculars and bird-watching guidebooks, others come—several thousand each year—to visit Hanging Rock. Whether its name derives from the unusual configuration of this hunk of puddingstone or the legend that criminals were once hung there is not known. You can be sure, however, that your children will not soon forget scaling the steep, bumpy cliff wall and traveling along the ridge to Hanging Rock with spectacular views over the ocean, marshes, and Gardiner Pond. By the very nature of the sanctuary's diverse terrain, the hike divides itself into two parts: the initial route takes you over wide, grassy paths through rather tame territory; the second half of the walk traverses narrow, rugged wooded trails to Hanging Rock, adding spice to what would have been a rather sedate outing by kid standards. As you travel all of the sanctuary paths, you'll wish you had brought a tape recorder rather than your camera to record the visit. Despite the number of birds you see, you will hear even more. And for some reason, once you've left it's harder to remember the lovely sounds of this place than the sights.

Begin your walk on the universally accessible trail on the northwest side of the welcome center. Follow the boardwalk south as it leads you

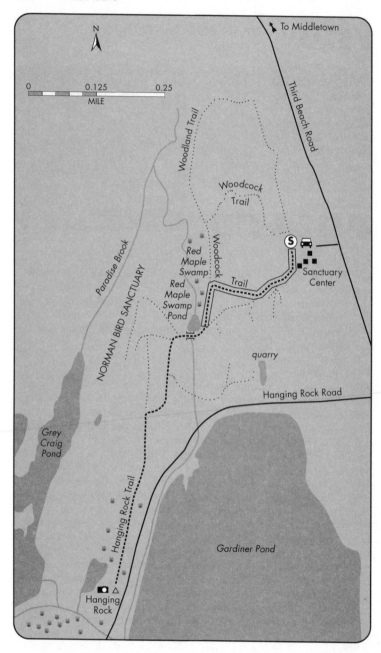

N

0   0.125   0.25
MILE

To Middletown

Third Beach Road

Woodland Trail

Woodcock Trail

S

Sanctuary Center

Paradise Brook

NORMAN BIRD SANCTUARY

Red Maple Swamp

Woodcock Trail

Red Maple Swamp Pond

quarry

Hanging Rock Road

Grey Craig Pond

Hanging Rock Trail

Gardiner Pond

Hanging Rock

Dramatic ocean views from Hanging Rock (photo by Cynthia Copeland and Thomas J. Lewis)

along the edge of a field formally used as a community garden. Be sure to stop and read the educational signs describing each habitat along the way. The boardwalk takes a right turn into the forest and then turns right again onto the Woodcock Trail. At the next T intersection, take a left turn and follow the boardwalk along the east side of Red Maple Swamp. When the boardwalk ends at the south end of Red Maple Swamp, walk approximately 300 feet, passing over a small bridge, to reach Hanging Rock Trail.

Follow this trail (which runs along Hanging Rock Road) to reach the pudding rock cliff that is your destination. Climb up, letting the kids go first so that you can follow closely behind. They'll love the feeling of being genuine rock climbers as they choose solid footholds and inch up the rock face. Follow the rock ledges to the left for magnificent ocean views from Hanging Rock. To either side, the rock drops away to valleys far below. Rest here before returning the way you came.

If you visit in March, you may witness woodcocks engaged in their strange and noisy mating ritual; the first woodcock courtship of each year is celebrated with guided walks for families as a sign that spring has arrived. Before you leave, take time to visit the education animals on display in the barn next to the welcome center.

Notes: A trail map is available at the headquarters. Picnic in the designated area near the barn. The sanctuary is open year-round, seven days a week, from 9:00 AM to 5:00 PM. Gate closes at 5:00 PM.

RODMANS HOLLOW

BEFORE YOU GO
Map USGS Block Island
Current Conditions The Nature Conservancy (401) 466-2129; also the Rhode Island Department of Environmental Management, Block Island Conservancy, Town of New Shoreham
Fees None

ABOUT THE HIKE
Day hike
Moderate for children
Year-round
3.7 miles, loop trip
Elevation gain 100 feet
High point 70 feet
Hiking time 3 hours
Accessibility No special access

GETTING THERE

- From New Shoreham center on Block Island, drive south on Pilot Hill Road to a right turn onto Mohegan Trail.
- Drive about 1 mile and bear right onto Lakeside Drive.
- In another mile, turn left onto Cooneymus Road (called Cherry Hill Road on some maps).
- Drive 0.7 mile and park on the right side of the road across from the Rodmans Hollow sign.

ON THE TRAIL

Sitting just 12 miles off the Rhode Island coast, Block Island has been popular as a summer retreat for 120 years. The island is accessible year-round by ferry, and for kids this is sure to be one of the trip's most memorable events. The ferry ride from Point Judith takes about an hour. Currently, cars cost more than $70 round trip and there is a charge of $15.65 (same-day round trip) for each person twelve or older and $7.60 for each kid, ages five through eleven. (You can rent mopeds and bicycles on the island if you prefer to leave your car on the mainland—in the summer a great idea!) You should make a reservation by calling (866) 783-7340 or online at *www.blockislandferry.com* (months in advance if you plan to take your car across during the summer). Because camping on the island is forbidden, you may want to arrive early in the day and leave on the evening ferry or stay overnight in one of the hotels or guesthouses. Rodmans Hollow, one of several popular hiking areas, is a 128-acre wildlife refuge with several different trails that offer visitors a good look at the variety of plant and animal life on the island.

Begin on the rutted jeep trail (Black Rock Road) near the "Rodmans

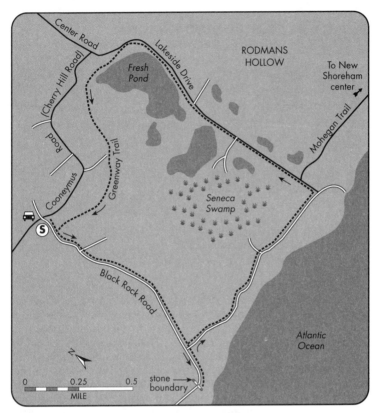

Hollow" sign. At 0.3 mile, a greenway trail splits off to the left; continue straight on the main trail. In another 0.5 mile, a dirt road bears left while you continue straight on a less traveled road. At 1 mile from the start, the road ends, marked by a stone boundary to prevent vehicle access. From here, watch the patterns created by the ocean's incessant attacks and retreats. (Unofficial trails lead to the bluffs, which are dangerous and contain poison ivy; use caution in this area.) For a shorter hike, return the way you came. To continue, turn left at the rock barricade and right within 0.1 mile, bearing right at all subsequent forks to stay close to the ocean. You will arrive at an intersection with Mohegan Trail 1 mile from the bluffs. Turn left onto this road and immediately join Lakeside Drive. Follow Lakeside Drive for 1 mile past Seneca Swamp and a series of small ponds to a left-hand turn onto a greenway trail. Follow the greenway trail 0.7 miles to its junction with Black Rock Road. Turn right along Black Rock Road and follow it a short distance to the parking area on Cooneymus Road.

BLOCK ISLAND NATIONAL WILDLIFE REFUGE

BEFORE YOU GO
Map USGS Block Island
Current Conditions
U.S. Fish & Wildlife Service
(401) 364-9124
Fees None

ABOUT THE HIKE
Day hike
Easy for children
Year-round
1.5 miles round-trip
Elevation gain 10 feet
High point 5 feet
Hiking time 2 hours
Accessibility No special
access

GETTING THERE

- From New Shoreham center on Block Island, drive north on Corn Neck Road to its conclusion (about 4 miles).
- Park in the Settlers Rock parking area at road's end.

ON THE TRAIL

A sandy beach road stretching along the dunes of Block Island's northernmost tip is the major trail within and adjacent to the 127-acre Block Island National Wildlife Refuge. In addition to the always fascinating sights and sounds of the ocean, this hike includes two points of historical interest: Settlers Rock, where the island's original inhabitants landed with their cattle in April 1661, and North Lighthouse, the fourth lighthouse on this point, built in 1867. Kids will be amazed at the number of birds here: this is an important stopover point for many migratory birds and home to many others, including a number of rare and endangered species.

North Lighthouse through the mist (photo by Cynthia Copeland and Thomas J. Lewis)

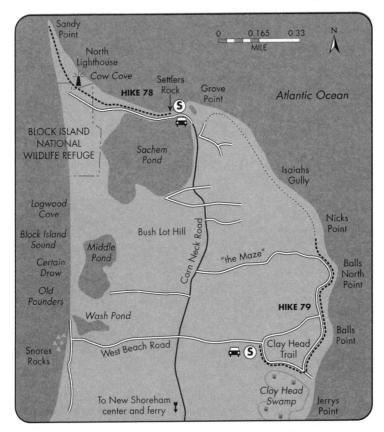

The monument erected near Settlers Rock marks the beginning of the hike along the beach road. As you walk past Sachem Pond, skirting the sand dunes, children should be reminded to stay on the road to avoid disturbing bird nesting areas. Have the kids look for fluffy, grayish brown gulls blending in the beach sand.

Continue walking along the edge of Cow Cove, scanning the sand for pieces of driftwood, stiffened seaweed, or bits of shells. After about 0.5 mile, you will reach North Lighthouse, which has started to be renovated and is a maritime museum. Sandy Point, which extends further north into Block Island Sound, is a sand spit that continues to expand (several feet each year) as the sediments from the eroding cliffs of Clay Head and Mohegan Bluff are continuously washed ashore here. Take time to explore, then return to Settlers Rock the way you came.

Note: No swimming is allowed in this area; there are dangerous riptides.

RARE SPECIES

Block Island is home to fifteen rare or endangered species. The rarest species found here is not a bird, but rather the American burying beetle. The American burying beetle is black with orange-red markings. In 1989 it was federally listed as endangered. This nocturnal beetle lives for only one year and usually reproduces just once. The refuge supports the only known population of this species east of the Mississippi River.

 CLAY HEAD TRAIL

BEFORE YOU GO
Map USGS Block Island
Current Conditions The Nature Conservancy (401) 466-2129; also Rhode Island Department of Environmental Management, the Lapham family
Fees None

ABOUT THE HIKE
Day hike
Easy for children
Year-round
2 miles round-trip
Elevation gain 180 feet
High point 100 feet
Hiking time 2 hours
Accessibility No special access

GETTING THERE

- From New Shoreham center on Block Island, drive north on Corn Neck Road 3.3 miles.
- Turn right (east) onto a dirt road (unmarked but with a wooden post that says "Clay Head Trail").
- Drive to a small parking area off the road 0.3 mile from Corn Neck Road at a second sign.

ON THE TRAIL

Hiking the trails at Clay Head will appeal to anyone who appreciates ocean bluffs, beachcombing, and bird-watching. The cliffs known as Clay Head tower 50 to 100 feet over the pounding surf and stretch 2 miles along the northeastern side of the island. If you visit in the fall (especially late September or early October), you will witness flocks of birds stopping here during the peak of migration. More than 100 different species may be present at any time, giving even bird-watching novices a chance to spot a rare variety. Look for barn owls, black-throated warblers, and peregrine falcons.

The trail at the head of the parking area, well marked with arrows on wooden stakes, winds through a salt marsh (Clay Head Swamp) and travels over a short boardwalk. On the right, you will notice an interesting contrast as a peaceful, hilly pasture separates you from the formidable ocean. In about 0.3 mile, you will reach the beach. Admire the cliffs of Clay Head to your left, composed of sand and the multicolored clay for which this area is noted. These cliffs are your destination.

This rocky beach is a good place for kids to search for sea treasures as well as a good spot to stop for a snack on the return trip. Avoid a multitude of side trails heading left (west); stay to the right on the Blue Stone Trail. The path leads over a grassy area to the top of the bluffs where the view of the surging waves is just as impressive. Follow the Clay Head Trail as it travels south-to-north along the upper edge of the bluffs and eventually tapers off and ends, 1.5 miles from the start. Here, you reverse direction and head back to your car. Clay Head's 12-mile-long trail system with numerous, unmarked side trails crisscrossing the rolling expanse of low vegetation is sometimes referred to as "the Maze." Keep landmarks well in mind if you leave the north–south trail on the bluff's edge.

 MOHEGAN BLUFFS

BEFORE YOU GO
Map USGS Block Island
Current Conditions Block Island Chamber of Commerce (800) 383-2472
Fees None

ABOUT THE HIKE
Day hike
Moderate for children
Year-round
4 miles round-trip
Elevation gain 400 feet
High point 200 feet
Hiking time 2 hours
Accessibility Partially accessible

GETTING THERE
■ No driving is necessary; exit the ferry landing near New Shoreham center on Block Island. (See Hike 77 for ferry details.)

ON THE TRAIL
The breathtaking cliffs that constitute Mohegan Bluffs rise 200 feet above the ocean, distinctly marking nearly five miles of Block Island's coastline. It is hard to imagine the child who wouldn't stand in awe of the mighty cliffs, strong and steadfast against the battering of relentless waves and the mighty winds rolling in off the ocean. Visitors might be surprised to find out that, according to geologists, the bluffs are eroding

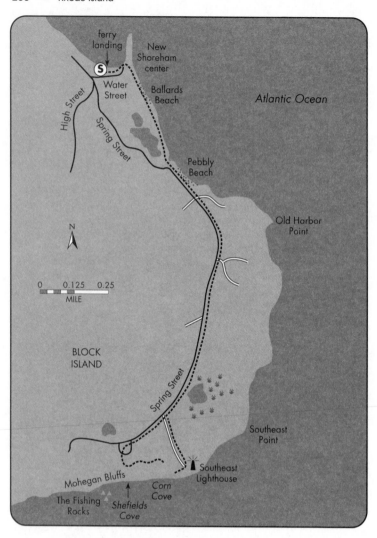

at a rate of about five feet each year. If you opt to descend the cliff wall to the shore, children will need a hand. Another highlight within the 42-acre overlook is the Southeast Lighthouse, built in 1874. This historic building can be seen by ships 35 miles away.

The hike begins near the ferry landing. Walk east down Water Street to Ballards Beach and then 0.4 mile more along the shore (in a southerly direction) to Pebbly Beach. Soon, Spring Street swings close to the water's edge. Take this road left (south) as it gradually ascends for the next mile until you reach the entrance to Mohegan Bluffs and the Southeast Lighthouse on the left, 1.5 miles from the start. Head to the lighthouse and then follow the stairs to the base of the cliffs. Children will need assistance on this stretch. Here, explore the beach to the left and right. As you wander, the kids can look for driftwood and shells, pretty rocks, and interesting tracks in the sand.

Eventually retrace your steps and climb back to the top of the cliffs at the lighthouse. Return to Spring Street and turn left. Walk just over 200 yards to an automobile turnaround on the left side of the road. Here, a hiking trail leaves the turnaround southward and travels along the top of the bluffs heading east. As you hike along the edge of these awesome cliffs, look out over Corn Cove, Sheffields Cove, and the Fishing Rocks. Can the kids understand why folks long ago thought the world was flat? (And how might they have known that it is in fact round? One sees the masts first, followed by the whole hull, as tall ships approach on the rounded horizon.) When the trail ends, return to the ferry the way you came.

USEFUL CONTACTS

GENERAL

The Appalachian Mountain Club
5 Joy Street
Boston, MA 02108
(617) 523-0636
www.outdoors.org
Publishes hiking-related material and books

Appalachian Trail Conservancy
799 Washington Street
P.O. Box 807
Harpers Ferry, WV 25425-0807
(304) 535-6331
www.appalachiantrail.org

National Park Service
Appalachian National Scenic Trail
Park Office
Harpers Ferry Center, P.O. Box 50
Harpers Ferry, WV 25425
(304) 535-6278
www.nps.gov/appa

The National Audubon Society
700 Broadway
New York, NY 10003
(212) 979-3000
www.audubon.org

The Nature Conservancy
4245 North Fairfax Drive, Suite 100
Arlington, VA 22203-1606
(703) 841-4850
www.nature.org

New England Orienteering Club
9 Cannon Road
Woburn, MA 01801
www.newenglandorienteering.org
Publishes detailed New England maps

New England Trail Conference
33 Knollwood Drive
Longmeadow, MA 01028
www.wapack.org / netrails

U.S. Geological Survey
Distribution Branch
Box 25286
Federal Center, Building 810
Denver, CO 80225
www.usgs.gov
Distributes USGS maps

CONNECTICUT

The Audubon Center in Greenwich/Audubon Connecticut
613 Riversville Road
Greenwich, CT 06831
(203) 869-5272
www.greenwich.center.audubon.org

Connecticut Audubon Society
2325 Burr Street
Fairfield, CT 06824
(203) 259-6305
www.ctaudubon.org

Connecticut Audubon Society at Hartford
118 Oak Street
Hartford, CT 06106-1514
(860) 527-6750
www.ctaudubon.org

Connecticut Department of Environmental Protection
Bureau of Outdoor Recreation, State Parks and Forests Division
79 Elm Street
Hartford, CT 06106-5127
(860) 424-3200; (866) 287-2757 toll free in Connecticut
http:/ /dep.state.ct.us /stateparks /
Upon request provides information on state parks and forests,
including information on camping and backpacking

Connecticut Forest and Parks Association
16 Meriden Road
Rockfall, CT 06481-2961
(860) 346-2372
www.ctwoodlands.org

The oldest private nonprofit conservation organization in Connecticut, the CFPA established and maintains the 700 miles of the Blue-Blazed Hiking Trail System in the state. Publishes the *Connecticut Walk Book*, a guide to these major hiking trails in Connecticut.

The Denison Pequotsepos Nature Center
109 Pequotsepos Road, P.O. Box 122
Mystic, CT 06355
(860) 536-1216
www.dpnc.org

Guilford Land Conservation Trust
Box 200
Guilford, CT 06437
(203) 457-9253
www.guilfordlandtrust.org

Nonprofit organization dedicated to preserving open space in Guilford, with approximately 2500 acres in holdings

The Nature Conservancy
Connecticut Chapter
55 High Street
Middletown, CT 06457-3788
(860) 344-0716
http://nature.org/wherewework/northamerica/states/connecticut/

Owns and manages over 8000 acres in Connecticut

The New Canaan Nature Center/The Nature Education Initiative at Devils Den
PO Box 1055
Weston, CT 06883-1055
(203) 966-9577
www.newcanaannature.org

Manages public education programs at Devils Den Preserve in Weston, Connecticut

Sharon Audubon Center
325 Cornwall Bridge Road
Sharon, CT 06069
(860) 364-0520
www.audubon.org / local / sanctuary / sharon / index.htm

State of Connecticut Commission on Culture and Tourism
One Financial Plaza
755 Main Street
Hartford, CT 06103
(860) 256-2800
www.tourism.state.ct.us

Westwoods Trails
(203) 457-9253
www.westwoodstrails.org
Largest recreational trail system in Guilford

The White Memorial Foundation and Conservation Center
80 Whitehall Road
Litchfield, CT 06759
(860) 567-0857
info@whitememorial.org
www.whitememorialcc.org

MASSACHUSETTS

Appalachian Mountain Club
Berkshire Chapter
www.amcberkshire.org

Friends of Quabbin, Inc.
Quabbin Visitor Center
485 Ware Road
Belchertown, MA 01007
(413) 323-7221

Friends of the Wapack
P.O. Box 115
West Peterborough, NH 03468
info@wapack.org
www.wapack.org
Dedicated to preserving the 21 miles of interstate Wapack Trail

The Laurel Hill Association
P.O. Box 24
Stockbridge, MA 01262
Maintains trails around Stockbridge

The Massachusetts Audubon Society (Mass Audubon)
208 South Great Road
Lincoln, MA 01773
(781) 259-9500
www.massaudubon.org
Protects more than 30,000 acres of land in New England and
maintains over 40 wildlife sanctuaries open to the public

Massachusetts Department of Conservation and Recreation
251 Causeway Street
Boston, MA 02114
(617) 626-1250
www.mass.gov/dcr/forparks.htm
Upon request will send detailed brochure of Massachusetts forests
and parks, including related camping information

Massachusetts Office of Travel and Tourism
10 Park Plaza, Suite 4510
Boston, MA 02116
(617) 973-8500
www.mass-vacation.com

National Park Service
Cape Cod National Seashore
99 Marconi Station, Site Road
Wellfleet, MA 02667
(508) 349-3785
(508) 255-3421 Salt Pond Visitor Center
(508) 487-1256 Province Lands Visitor Information
www.nps.gov/caco/

New England Cartographics
P.O. Box 9369
North Amherst, MA 01059
(413) 549-4124
www.necartographics.com
Publishes color maps and books of New England

Northfield Mountain
99 Millers Falls Road (Route 63)
Northfield, MA 01360
(413) 659-3714 or (800) 859-2960
www.nu.com / northfield
A four-season recreation facility owned by Northeast Utilities

Parker River National Wildlife Refuge
6 Plum Island Turnpike
Newburyport, MA 01950
(978) 465-5753
www.fws.gov / northeast / parkerriver /

Sandy Neck, Town of Barnstable
Department of Marine and Environmental Affairs
1189 Phinney's Lane
Centerville, MA 02632
(508) 362-8300
www.town.barnstable.ma.us / SandyNeck /

Sheriffs Meadow Foundation
Wakeman Conservation Center
RR1, Box 319X
Vineyard Haven, MA 02568
(508) 693-5207
www.sheriffsmeadow.org
Conserves and manages over 2200 acres of land on Martha's
Vineyard

The Trustees of Reservations
572 Essex Street
Beverly, MA 01915-1530
(978) 921-1944
www.thetrustees.org
Custodians of approximately 100 properties across Massachusetts

University of Massachusetts Amherst
College of Natural Resources and the Environment
Amherst, MA 01003
(413) 545-2665
www.umass.edu / nrc / index.html
Owns and manages Mount Toby and Cadwell Memorial Forests

Williamstown Rural Land Foundation
671 Cold Spring Road
P.O. Box 221
Williamstown, MA 01267
(413) 458-2494
www.wrlf.org
Maintains several trails in the Williamstown area

Williams Outing Club
SUB Box
Williams College
Williamstown, MA 01267
http://wso.williams.edu/orgs/woc
Publishes hiking guide with maps covering the Williamstown area
and Greylock Reservation

RHODE ISLAND

Arcadia Management Area
Rhode Island Division of Forest Environment
260 Arcadia Road
Richmond, RI 02832
(401) 539-1052 or (401) 539-2356
www.riparks.com

Audubon Society of Rhode Island
Powder Mill Ledges Wildlife Refuge
12 Sanderson Road
Smithfield, RI 02917
(401) 949-5454
www.asri.org

Block Island Chamber of Commerce
Block Island, RI 02807
(800) 383-2474
www.blockislandchamber.com

Friends of the Cliffwalk
19 Catherine Street
Newport, RI 02840
(401) 847-1355
www.cliffwalk.com

George Washington Management Area
Rhode Island Division of Forest Environment
2185 Putnam Pike
Chepachet, RI 02814
(401) 568-2248 or (401) 568-2013
www.riparks.com

The Nature Conservancy
Block Island Program/Nature Center
352 High Street
Block Island, RI 02807
(401) 466-2129
*www.nature.org / wherewework / northamerica / states / rhodeisland /
preserves*

The Nature Conservancy
Rhode Island Chapter Office
159 Waterman Street
Providence, RI 02906
(401) 331-7110
*www.nature.org / wherewework / northamerica / states / rhodeisland /
contact*

Newport County Convention and Visitor's Bureau
Visitor Information Center
23 America's Cup Avenue
Newport, RI 02840
(401) 845-9123 or (800) 976-5122
www.gonewport.com

Norman Bird Sanctuary
583 Third Beach Road
Middletown, RI 02842
(401) 846-2577
www.normanbirdsanctuary.org

Rhode Island Department of Environmental Management
Division of Parks and Recreation
2321 Hartford Avenue
Johnston, RI 02919-1719
(401) 222-2632
www.riparks.com

East Beach, Ninigret Conservation Area
c/o Burlingame State Park
1 Burlingame Road
Charlestown, RI 02813
(401) 322-0450, seasonal
(401) 322-8910, year-round
www.riparks.com / eastbeach.htm

Rhode Island Division of Forest Environment
1037 Hartford Pike
North Scituate, RI 02857
(401) 647-4389 or (401) 647-3367
www.dem.ri.gov / programs / bnatres / forest /

Rhode Island National Wildlife Refuge Complex
U.S. Fish & Wildlife Service
Kettle Pond Visitor Center
50 Bend Road
Charlestown, RI 02813
(401) 364-9124
www.fws.gov / northeast / ri.htm
Visitor center for the refuges and for the trails on the properties

Rhode Island Tourism Division
One West Exchange Street
Providence, RI 02903
(800) 556-2484
www.visitrhodeisland.com
Will send on request a camping guide describing state, municipal,
and privately owned campgrounds

Town of Tiverton
343 Highland Road
Tiverton, RI 02878-4499
(401) 625-6710
www.tiverton.ri.gov

INDEX

accessories, 21–24
American burying beetle, 236
American Legion State Forest, 63
amphibians, 35
Appalachian Trail, 119, 121, 128, 129, 130, 131, 136, 138, 139
Arcadia Management Area, 200–210
Arcadia Trail, 207–210
Atlantic Ocean, 171, 218
Audubon Center in Greenwich, 32–35
Audubon Society of Rhode Island, 198, 225
Averills Island, 174
Avalonia Land Conservancy, 102

Bakers Cave, 97
Ballards Beach, 239
Bantam Lake, 53
Bar Head, 175–6
Barrack Mountain, 47–49
Barton Cove Campground, 147
Bash Bish Brook, 116–118
Bash Bish Falls State Park, 116–119
Beach Pond, 205
beachwalking, 17
beaver, 157
Beaver Pond, 108
Ben Utter Trail, 200–203
Berkshires, 52, 124, 134
Berry Pond, 132–135
birdwatching, 25
black fly season, 21
blazes, trail, 16
Block Island National Wildlife Refuge, 234–235
Block Island Sound, 221, 235
Block Island, 232–239
Blue Hills Reservation, 166–168
blueberries, 134, 139, 215
Bluff Head, 80–82

Bluff Point State Park and Coastal Reserve, 97–100
Bog Meadow Pond, 46
Bowdish Reservoir, 194, 195
Bristol Blake State Reservation/ Stony Brook Wildlife Sanctuary, 164–166
Browning Mill Pond, 209
Burr Pond State Park, 60–63
butterfly garden, 102, 153, 154, 164, 166, 200
Buttermilk Bay, 176, 178
Byram River, 34

camping: permitted, 24, 29, 41, 53, 60, 63, 93, 95, 111, 112, 121, 130, 132, 135, 137, 147, 194, 195, 202, 203, 209, 218; prohibited, 152, 190, 214, 232
Cape Cod, 176–187
Cape Cod National Seashore, 181–187
Carter Pond, 154
Castle Craig, 69–72
Cathedral, The, 213–214
Catskill Mountains, 38, 43, 52
caves/tunnels, 21, 40, 49, 58–59, 60, 78–79, 87, 94, 97, 109, 153– 154, 163, 173, 207
Cedar Tree Neck Sanctuary, 187–190
Chapman Falls, 91, 93, 94
charcoal manufacturing display, 38
Charlestown Breachway, 219
Chatfield Hollow State Park, 82–85
Chaugham Lookout, 65
Chauncey Peak, 72–75
Clay Head Trail, 236–237
Cliff Walk, 227–228
clothing, 20, 22
Cobble Mountain, 43

Coginchaug Cave, 78–79
Coginchaug River, 77
Corn Cove, 239
compass, 20
Connecticut Audubon Society, 107, 108
Connecticut River, 66, 90, 145, 148
Cow Cove, 235
Crane Lookout, 59
Crescent Lake, 73, 74

Dean Ravine, 47–49
Denison Pequotsepos Nature Center, 100–102
Devils Coffin, 163
Devils Den Preserve, 37–40
Devils Hopyard State Park, 91–94
Devils Oven, 94
Devils Pulpit, 122–124
Devils Pulpit (Purgatory Chasm), 162
Diamond Hill, 196–197
dogs, 19, 29–30, 43, 125, 202

East Beach, 218–219
Edwin Way Teale Memorial Sanctuary at Trail Wood, 106–108
Eight Mile River, 93, 94
Eliot Tower, 168
Elizabeths Pond, 192
Emergency shelter, 20
Emilie Ruecker Wildlife Refuge, 224–226
encounters with wildlife, 19
Enfield Lookout, 151
environmental concerns, 14–16
equipment, 21–24
Escoheag Trail, 203–204
ethics, wilderness, 14–16, 227

Felix Neck Wildlife Sanctuary, 190–192
fire, starting, 20
fire towers, 19
first-aid kit, 20

Fisherville Brook Wildlife Refuge, 210–212
flashlight, 20
food, 14, 24–25
footgear, 21
Ford Pond, 45, 46, 47
Fort Barton, 222–224
Fort Hill Trail, 181–183
Forty Steps, 228
Francis C. Carter Memorial Preserve, 215–217

Gardiner Pond, 229
Gillette Castle State Park, 88–91
Goat Peak Lookout, 140–142
Godfrey Pond, 40
Great Beach Hill, 187
Great Blue Hill, 166–168
Great Island Trail, 185–187
Great Marshes, 179–180
Gut, the, 185

Hanging Rock, 229, 231
hawks, 142
Herring River, 185
Hidden Pond, 102
hiking etiquette, 14–16, 227
hiking tips, 13–14
Hingham Harbor, 169, 171
Houghtons Pond, 167, 168
Housatonic River, 41, 125

Ice Glen, 125–127
Indian Chair, 109, 111
Indian Rock, 181, 183
Indian Spring, 104
Indian Spring Pond, 32, 35
Inscription Rock, 124
Ipswich River Wildlife Sanctuary, 171–174

Jacobs Hill, 148–149
Jeremy Point, 185, 187
Jessie Gerard Trail, 63–65

Kettle Pond Visitor Center, 222

Kimberlin Nature Education Center, 32

lakes, investigating, 18
Lamentation Mountain, 72–75
Lauras Tower, 125–127
Leatherman Cave, 58–60
Little River Valley, 106
Long and Ell Ponds Natural Area, 212–214
Long Island Sound, 37, 40, 68, 71, 95, 98
Long Pond Woods (RI), 212–214
lost, getting, 16
Lucius Pond Ordway/Devils Den Preserve, 37–40
Lulu Brook, 135
Lyman Reserve, 176–178
Lyme disease, 17–18, 95

Macedonia Brook State Park, 41–44
March Cataract Falls, 135–138
Martha's Vineyard, 187–192
Mashamoquet Brook Campground, 111
Mashamoquet Brook State Park, 109–111
Massachusetts Audubon Society, 155, 168, 190
Mattabesett Trail, 73, 74, 75, 78–79, 80–81
Mattatuck Trail, 52, 59
Metacomet and Monadnock Trail (MA), 140
Metacomet Trail (CT), 69–71
Midstate Trail, 162
Mohawk Mountain, 49–52
Mohawk Trail, 47, 51, 52
Mohegan Bluffs, 237–239
Mott–Van Winkle Classroom, 55
Mount Greylock, 136
Mount Greylock State Reservation, 135–138
Mount Misery, 112–114
Mount Misery campground, 112
Mount Toby, 142–145

Mount Tom (RI), 203–204
Mount Tom Pond (CT), 56
Mount Tom State Park (CT), 55–57
Mount Tom State Reservation (MA), 140–142
Mount Tom Tower (CT), 55–57
Mount Watatic, 160–162
mountain laurel, 86
Munns Ferry campground, 147
Myer Huber Pond, 81

Narragansett Trail, 212, 216, 217
National Audubon Society, 32
national wildlife refuges, 174–5, 219, 234
nature centers/visitor centers, 19, 32, 41, 45, 53, 100, 140, 147, 164, 168, 184, 222, 231
Nature Conservancy, 37, 215, 216
Nauset Harbor, 184
Nauset Marsh, 181–184
Nauset Marsh Trail, 183–184
navigation, 20
New Canaan Nature Center, 41
Ninigret Conservation Area, 218–219
Ninigret Pond, 218, 219
Norman Bird Sanctuary, 229–231
North Lighthouse, 234, 235
Northfield Mountain, 145–148

ocean views, 16

Pachaug, 114
Pachaug State Forest, 112–114
Pachaug Trail, 114, 205–207
packs, 22
Parker River National Wildlife Refuge, 174–176
Penniman House, 181, 183
Peoples State Forest, 63
Pine Cobble Trail, 138–139
Piping Plover, 176
Pittsfield State Forest, 132–135
Planters Hill, 171
Plum Island, 175

Point Folly, 53
poison ivy, 18
ponds, investigating, 18
Powder Mill Ledges Wildlife
  Refuge, 198–200
Profile Rock, 124
puddingstone, 143, 225, 229
Purgatory Chasm, 162–163

Quabbin Hill, 150–152
Quabbin Reservoir, 150

Race Brook, 119–122
Race Brook Falls, 119–122
repair kit, 20
reptiles, 35
Rhode Island Sound, 228
rhododendrons, 112, 214
Rhododendron Sanctuary,
  112–114
Robert Frost Trail, 143
Rock House, 153, 154
Rock House Reservation, 152–154
Rock Spring Preserve, 103–106
Rockery Pond, 173
Rockery, the, 173
Rocky Neck, 95, 97
Rocky Neck State Park, 94–97
Rodmans Hollow, 232–233
Rose Ledges Trail, 147–148
Ruecker, Emilie, 225

Sachem Pond, 235
safety, 16–21, 30
Sakonnet River, 225
Salt Pond, 184
Salt Pond Visitors Center, 184
Sandy Neck, 179–180
Sandy Point, 235
Sandy Point State Reservation,
  174–175
sarsaparilla, 143, 145
Schreeder Pond, 82–84
selecting a hike, 26–28
Sengekontacket Pond, 191
Settlers Rock, 234, 235
Sharon Audubon Center, 44–47

Sheffield's Cove, 239
Sherwood Island, 35–37
Sherwood Island State Park,
  35–37
Sin and Flesh Brook, 222–224
Sleeping Giant, 66–69
Sleeping Giant Park Association,
  66–67
Sleeping Giant State Park,
  66–69
South Taconic Trail, 116
Southeast Lighthouse, 238, 239
Split Rock, 212, 217
Squaw Peak, 122–124
Stage Island Pool, 175
State Line Trail, 161–162
Stepstone Falls, 200–203
Stone Stairs, the, 64
Stony Brook Wildlife Sanctuary,
  164–166
sun protection, 20
swamp, 21
swimming (permitted), 29, 62, 82,
  85, 95, 98, 111, 131, 132, 167,
  168, 175, 194, 209

Taconic Skyline Trail, 135
Taylor Brook campground, 60
Teale, Edwin, 106–108
Ten Essentials, the, 16, 20
Ten Mile River, 41
ticks, 17–18
Tonys Nose, 95
Totoket Mountain, 80–82
towers, 51, 57, 68, 71, 121, 138,
  141, 144, 145, 168
Trail Wood, 106–108
Trailside Museum, 168
Trustees of Reservations, 124,
  127, 153, 169
Trustom Pond National Wildlife
  Refuge, 219–222
Tully River, 149
Tyringham Cobble, 127–130

University of Massachusetts, 143
Upper Goose Pond, 130–132

Veeder Boulders, 65
visitor centers/nature centers, 19, 32, 41, 45, 53, 100, 140, 147, 164, 168, 184, 222, 231

Wachusett Meadow Wildlife Sanctuary, 155–157
Wachusett Mountain State Park, 158–160
Wadsworth Falls State Park, 75–77
Walkabout Trail, 194–195
Wapack Trail, 160–162
water, safe, 17

waterfall/cascades, 14, 48, 75, 91, 116, 121, 124, 137, 164, 202, 210
Waterfowl Pond, 174, 191
weather, 17
Weir River, 169, 171
West Peak, 69–72
Westwoods, 85–88
White Cedar Swamp, 112
White Memorial Foundation and Conservation Center, 53–55
wildlife encounters, 19
Wolf Den, 109, 111
Worlds End Reservation, 169–171

ABOUT THE AUTHOR

Emily Kerr grew up hiking, camping, canoeing, and cross-country skiing with her family. She now shares her love of the outdoors with her husband, two sons, and her dog—her favorite and most reliable hiking buddies. A full-time mom and freelance writer, she lives with her family in Exeter, New Hampshire.

Author Emily Kerr with her sons, Carter and Davis
(photo by Thomas Nelson)

THE MOUNTAINEERS, founded in 1906, is a nonprofit outdoor activity and conservation organization, whose mission is "to explore, study, preserve, and enjoy the natural beauty of the outdoors...." Based in Seattle, Washington, it is now one of the largest such organizations in the United States, with seven branches throughout Washington State.

The Mountaineers sponsors both classes and year-round outdoor activities in the Pacific Northwest, which include hiking, mountain climbing, ski-touring, snowshoeing, bicycling, camping, kayaking and canoeing, nature study, sailing, and adventure travel. The club's conservation division supports environmental causes through educational activities, sponsoring legislation, and presenting informational programs. All club activities are led by skilled, experienced volunteers, who are dedicated to promoting safe and responsible enjoyment and preservation of the outdoors.

If you would like to participate in these organized outdoor activities or programs, consider a membership in The Mountaineers. For information and an application, write or call The Mountaineers Program Center, 7700 Sand Point Way NE, Seattle, WA 98115; (206) 521-6000.

The Mountaineers Books, an active, nonprofit publishing program of the club, produces guidebooks, instructional texts, historical works, natural history guides, and works on environmental conservation. All books produced by The Mountaineers fulfill the club's mission.

The Mountaineers Books
1001 SW Klickitat Way, Suite 201
Seattle, WA 98134
800-553-4453
mbooks@mountaineersbooks.org
www.mountaineersbooks.org

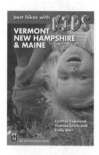